PRAISE FOR *FROM CRIME SCENE TO COURTROOM*

"Taking readers deep into the world of a forensic pathologist, these cases are sometimes unsettling, but always engrossing. The depth of Wecht's medicolegal acumen is on great display, as is Kaufmann's inquisitive nature. Together they illuminate the hows and whys of modern death investigations and their aftermath."

—Michael Welner, MD, forensic psychiatrist, chairman of The Forensic Panel, and forensic consultant for ABC News.

"Cyril Wecht, beyond any and all doubt, is the most Promethean intellect in the medicolegal field. His extraordinary insights and diversity of expertise, along with Dawna Kaufmann's writing and research, present the reader with an incredibly well-documented and riveting page-turner."

—Robert K. Tanenbaum, JD, former New York homicide prosecutor and author of *Outrage*, his twenty-fifth book.

"Finding the devil relies on science and our ability to discern the details. Wecht and Kaufmann have admirably done that in this informative book. Prepare your friends for the stimulating conversations you will have with them about these spell-binding cases."

—Glenn S. Lipson, PhD, ABPP Diplomate in forensic psychology; program director, California School of Forensic Studies, Alliant International University, San Diego.

FROM CRIME SCENE TO COURTROOM

CYRIL H. WECHT, MD, JD
AND DAWNA KAUFMANN

FROM CRIME SCENE TO COURTROOM

EXAMINING THE MYSTERIES
BEHIND FAMOUS CASES

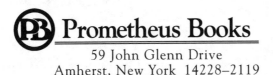 **Prometheus Books**

59 John Glenn Drive
Amherst, New York 14228–2119

Published 2011 by Prometheus Books

Cover image © 2011 Media Bakery, Inc.
Jacket design by Grace M. Conti-Zilsberger.

Inquiries should be addressed to
Prometheus Books
59 John Glenn Drive
Amherst, New York 14228–2119
VOICE: 716–691–0133
FAX: 716–691–0137
WWW.PROMETHEUSBOOKS.COM

15 14 13 12 11   5 4 3 2 1

Library of Congress Cataloging-in-Publication Data

Wecht, Cyril H., 1931–
    From crime scene to courtroom : examining the mysteries behind famous cases / by Cyril H. Wecht and Dawna Kaufmann.
        p. cm.
    Includes bibliographical references and index.
    ISBN 978–1–61614–447–0 (cloth : alk. paper)
    ISBN 978–1–61614–448–7 (ebook)
    1. Criminal investigation—Case studies. 2. Death—Causes—Case studies. 3. Forensic pathology—Case studies. I. Kaufmann, Dawna, 1971–. II. Title.

HV8073.W383 2011
364.152092′273—dc23

                                                                                    2011023754

Printed in the United States of America on acid-free paper

CONTENTS

FOREWORD
by Geraldo Rivera

There was a time not long ago when crime mysteries were cracked only by confessions, sometimes coerced; and by eyewitness testimony, often unreliable. Police lineups and identity parades created a "bring in the usual suspects" mentality that has probably led to as many false-positive identifications as accurate ones. Around the beginning of the twentieth century, fingerprints added a scientific aspect to criminal investigation. When British colonial official Sir Edward Richard Henry convinced Scotland Yard that each individual's prints had unique characteristics, cops around the globe soon had an objective tool to catch a thief or murderer.

It would be over eighty years before Professor Alec Jeffreys of the University of Leicester in England discovered a more powerful kind of fingerprint, the incredibly precise DNA genetic profiling, which made so much of routine police procedures and prejudices irrelevant.

Now, the cop with an attitude, the suspect trying to squirm free, or the eyewitness with the faulty memory faces the power of scientific certainty.

Unbiased and unafraid, justice now has a colossal ally, and, in case after case, the name of justice renewed is Dr. Cyril H. Wecht.

Often introduced on television by me and others as "the famed forensic pathologist," Dr. Wecht soars beyond even that lofty description. He is a modern-day Sherlock Holmes. But unlike Arthur Conan Doyle's intuitive but fictional "consulting detective," Wecht is a real genius who has brilliantly employed the latest technologies to crack some of our most enduring mysteries.

The renowned scientist helped me investigate the facts and circumstances surrounding the assassination of President John F. Kennedy; Elvis Presley's drug overdose; O. J. Simpson's slashing double homicides in Brentwood in 1994; and the child murder that obsessed America in the years before Caylee Anthony went missing, Boulder, Colorado's, little princess, JonBenét Ramsey.

It is for good reason that the building in which Dr. Wecht worked for his nineteen years as the elected coroner of Allegheny County, Pennsylvania, is now named for him.

In this, his latest book, Dr. Wecht and ace investigative journalist Dawna Kaufmann take us inside seven riveting cases, including two of the most notorious ones I've ever covered. If you think you know all there is to know about how Michael Jackson died or if Casey Anthony killed her beloved Caylee, fasten your seat belts. The man who moves easily between a morgue and a courtroom is about to break some news.

Geraldo Rivera is an author, attorney, and Peabody award–winning journalist and war correspondent who, since 1970, has been at the forefront in covering every significant news and political story affecting America. Currently he hosts the biweekly program, Geraldo at Large, *on the Fox News network.*

PREFACE

Every day in America nearly seven thousand people die. That's about two and a half million deaths per year. When a death is unexpected, medically unattended, or suspicious—which occurs in about one-quarter to one-third of the cases—it becomes necessary to determine whether the demise was due to foul play. A specially trained physician, known as a medical examiner or forensic pathologist, is asked to perform an autopsy to inspect the body, externally and internally, and to issue a report that can close the case, or open it to the legal system for criminal prosecution. Despite the many death cases to probe, fewer than five hundred forensic pathologists are licensed to practice today.

The word *autopsy* comes from the Greek term *autopsia*, meaning "see for yourself." It's a surgical procedure performed on a dead body to learn the cause and manner of death. The cause could be from trauma, such as a gunshot, knife wound, vehicle accident, beating, drowning, or poisoning; or from a medical affliction, such as heart disease, diabetes, stroke, cancer, or the like. A scalpel is used to make a "Y-incision" across the decedent's chest, from shoulder to shoulder, and down to the pubic area, so that the internal organs can be removed, weighed, and sliced for microscopic inspection. A vibrating saw is used to open the skull so the scalp can be pulled down to expose, remove, and preserve the brain. At each point in the process, morgue assistants photograph the work, and the medical examiner dictates his or her findings into a handheld microcassette recorder; the transcribed notes will later become part of the autopsy report. Tissue samples are reviewed microscopically, and blood and urine samples are sent to a toxicology laboratory to discover whether the deceased had alcohol and/or drugs—licit or illicit—in his or her bloodstream at death. It's possible that numerous physical conditions might have led to the death, so once all the results are in, the forensic pathologist will list all factors for cause of death on the eventual report. Once the procedure is finished, the decedent is stitched up, washed, and released to a mortuary for embalming, burial, or cremation; a body can usually rest in an open casket without any visible signs of an autopsy having been performed. A death certificate is issued at this time.

Family members may also request that an autopsy be performed, either by the medical examiner or via an independent forensic pathologist who will provide the family with a second opinion on the case. Autopsies can occur after embalming has been done, and even after a body has been buried. Exhumations may be ordered by the courts if new evidence surfaces in a matter, or if the family wants a fresh review of the case.

Assessing the manner of death is the next step for the forensic pathologist, who may list it as one of five choices: homicide, suicide, accident, natural, or undetermined. This declaration is prominently displayed on the autopsy report and becomes part of the official record that family members, and often the media, have access to.

While it may take a few weeks for all of the test results to come in, the autopsy doctor may share preliminary information with law enforcement, even though the office of the medical examiner is wholly independent from police and prosecutors. Letting authorities know that someone died at the hands of another person ensures public safety by allowing a criminal investigation to be started swiftly. If someone is arrested for murder, prosecutors and defense attorneys will receive the completed autopsy information prior to the defendant's trial, and the forensic pathologist will be a critical witness in the courtroom.

As a board-certified forensic pathologist for the past fifty-four years, I have personally performed approximately seventeen thousand autopsies and consulted on an additional thirty-seven thousand other post-mortem protocols. I'm also a lawyer in my home state of Pennsylvania. I served as the Allegheny County Coroner, an elective post, from 1970 to 1980, and from 1996 to 2006, performing autopsies for the Pittsburgh area and surrounding counties. Recently I received the great honor of having the Allegheny County Medical Examiner facility dedicated as the Cyril H. Wecht Institute of Forensic Science and, separate from that, the Cyril H. Wecht Institute of Forensic Science and Law was established at Pittsburgh's Duquesne University, where I am the board chairman and hold three professorial appointments. As a private consultant, I continue to perform autopsies—domestically and internationally—and testify at trials. Sometimes I'm retained by prosecutors, and other times by defense counsel, but I don't color my findings to favor one side or the other. The scientific facts are the scientific facts.

Despite the breadth of my experience, I remain fascinated by the always new twists and often incredible scenarios that play out in death investigations. That is why, with due respect to all my colleagues practicing other medical specialties, there is simply no field of endeavor as challenging and intellectually stimulating as forensic pathology. The ramifications and impact of the work we do in examining bodies to determine the mechanisms of death are far ranging. The civil and criminal justice systems, law enforcement, public health and safety, healthcare personnel and facilities, industrial and environmental hazards—all these areas of daily life—rely on competent, diligent medicolegal investigations to function effectively. A civilized society is greatly enhanced by the professional endeavors of forensic pathologists functioning in coroner's and medical examiner's offices and as private consultants.

For more than a decade, I have known and admired my co-author, Dawna Kaufmann, a true crime journalist of national and worldwide renown. As a print reporter and radio talk show host, she zeroes in on the highest-profile criminal cases of our time, combining her astounding memory for the background details of each character and event with an unparalleled skill for research. So savvy is Dawna in getting her interview subjects to talk that she convinced Mark W. Felt Sr. to finally confess to the public that he was Watergate's "Deep Throat," thereby solving one of the greatest pop culture puzzlers of the twentieth century.

While Dawna initially called me for scientific and medicolegal opinions on numerous cases—including the deaths of JonBenét Ramsey, Laci Peterson, Nicole Brown Simpson, Princess Diana, President John F. Kennedy, Senator Robert Kennedy, Marilyn Monroe, and hundreds of others—I found I was learning a great deal from her, as well. In 2008, we wrote *A Question of Murder* (Prometheus Books) about the death investigations of Anna Nicole Smith and her son Daniel; Stephanie Crowe and Danielle van Dam, two child homicides in San Diego with vastly different trials and outcomes; and the "involuntary euthanasia" of viable patients at New Orleans' Memorial Medical Center in the aftermath of Hurricane Katrina—this work was used by the *New York Times* to win the Pulitzer Prize for Investigative Journalism. Moreover, Dawna and I have also lectured together, fashioning entertaining PowerPoint presentations of our most provocative cases.

Now we have collaborated on this book, *From Crime Scene to Courtroom: Examining the Mysteries behind Famous Cases*, and once again, we have merged my autopsy and scientific acumen with Dawna's flair for talking with people and fleshing out their stories. We have chosen seven cases that will no doubt encourage readers to consider the impact of forensic science on finding resolution for these tragic deaths.

Cyril H. Wecht, MD, JD

I admit it: I'm nosy. I have a need to know, anything and everything. For that I blame my parents who taught me my first phrase, "Who says so?" Those early days of skepticism and demand for sources led me to all sorts of destructive behavior, such as pulling apart toys, clocks, and electronics to figure out how they worked. Delight ensued when I learned how to put the items back together. For years I worked as a Hollywood comedy writer, using those skills to crack the code of professional joke and sketch crafting on television series including *Mad TV* and *Saturday Night Live*. My faux news segments of "Weekend Update" and gags for late-night monologues were a subversive pleasure when I considered that that was where a large segment of America got its news . . . until I began to realize that that *was indeed* where a large segment of America got its news, and suddenly that wasn't so funny to me anymore. So, in the mid-1990s, I decided to focus on events of greater importance. I became a freelance investigative journalist for the *National Enquirer, Star,* and *Globe* tabloids, just as the O. J. Simpson double murder case hit the press, and I was part of the team that many consider the most aggressive and impressive reporters among the media, from Simpson's arrest through his two trials. When that case ended, I was swept into the JonBenét Ramsey investigation, breaking important stories about the search for the killer of the six-year-old Colorado beauty queen, a case that is still ongoing. Since then, I've written about thousands of other high-profile homicides, kidnappings, celebrity deaths, and sex crimes for other newspapers and magazines, including the *Los Angeles Times* and *Cosmopolitan* and for the auspicious textbook *Criminalistics: An Introduction to Forensic Science* by Richard Saferstein, PhD. I have also hosted and been a guest on various radio shows dealing with the dual subjects of crime and comedy.

When I first called Dr. Cyril Wecht about medicolegal issues for my writing, I didn't know much about the world of scientific crime fighting, but he graciously explained concepts in plain English that brought clarity and depth to my articles. I came to understand that an autopsy procedure is the Rosetta Stone, or the key, to any practical death investigation. The satisfaction I once felt in tearing apart objects for answers he was achieving with his elegantly wielded scalpel on a deceased body in order to solve a real-life mystery. What could be more riveting than that? Dr. Wecht is also one of the smartest and kindest men I've had the privilege of knowing.

Around this same time, I began wondering about the human psyche; in particular, that of the individuals who perpetrated the crimes I wrote about. At what point in their development did they first show violent inclinations, and why? And how did their actions affect people they knew and the relatives and friends of their victims? I was fortunate to be mentored by Robert K. Ressler, retired supervisory special agent of the FBI, who brought the notion of profiling criminal behavior to the organization and interviewed most of the prominent serial killers and sexual deviants of modern time. Ressler and Wecht encouraged me to attend the annual conferences of the American Academy of Forensic Sciences—of which Cyril is a past president—and I knew then I had found my life's calling. There I was exposed to some of the greatest experts in the business; I became familiar with all the forensic disciplines used by law enforcement today, and I got a feeling for where things will be headed tomorrow.

In the pages ahead, you will read about seven cases that Cyril and I have handpicked to illustrate both medical and psychological complexity. The causes and manners of death, and the alleged perpetrators and victims, couldn't be more diverse. In some instances, Dr. Wecht performed the original autopsy, and in others he conducted a secondary procedure or consulted on the matter. I have reported on three of the cases—those involving Casey Anthony, Drew Peterson, and Michael Jackson—and I expect to write more about the latter two as they continue through the legal system. The material in the other chapters is equally heartrending and thought provoking. All the sources cited at the end of the book should be searchable through the keywords or links provided.

As you read these chapters, you will ask yourself: Was a young mother wrongly accused, or did she duct-tape and chloroform her baby daughter, leaving her to die slowly in a car trunk? Did an American military hero torture himself and commit suicide, or was he murdered? Why did the founder of the Rolling Stones drown in his swimming pool, and should the case be reopened? Did a decorated former policeman beat his wife to death, or did she slip and fall in her bathtub? Did police arrest the correct person in the rape-murder of a little girl, or is there a predator still on the loose? How could a respectable mother of three die in police custody, and could her death have been prevented? Was the world's greatest entertainer slain by his doctor, and will there be additional arrests?

We have provided you with the facts. You will weigh the evidence and act as the thirteenth juror.

Dawna Kaufmann

ACKNOWLEDGMENTS

There are numerous people we would like to thank for helping to make this book come to fruition, beginning with the loved ones of the subjects of each chapter. We recognize that your loss will never go away, but we hope that, in writing about the individual's death, we have portrayed what made each of them so memorable in life. It's an honor to be able to share with readers what we have learned, and perhaps to also provide you with some measure of comfort.

Deep praise goes to our executive editor, Linda Greenspan Regan, for her excellent suggestions and skill; our tireless copyeditor, Julia DeGraf; and to the rest of the fine team at Prometheus Books, who are both professional and considerate.

We give a fond salute to Dr. Wecht's office staff for unfailing support and good cheer, from Florence Johnson and Darlene Brewer, to Sigrid Wecht, Esq., whose legal and administrative acumen are always top-notch.

Special mention for research and encouragement goes to Brett Bush and Mark Nardone, Caseen Gaines, Debra Storch, Treva Silverman, and Zia Shields. And for particular assistance on the chapters that concern them: José Baez, Esq.; Tracy Shue, Jason M. Davis, Esq., George Brown, and Roger Anderson; Geoffrey Giuliano, and Jeff James of Dick Clark Productions; Joel A. Brodsky, Esq.; Chris, Mimi, and Corey Bechen, Jennifer Martin, Greene County (Pennsylvania) district attorney Marjorie Fox, first assistant district attorney Linda Chambers, and witness coordinator Cherie Rumskey; Noah, Ella, Nathaniel, and Tobias Gotbaum, and Michael C. Manning, Esq., Leslie O'Hara, Esq., and Anne L. Slawson of Stinson Morrison Hecker LLP; Brian Oxman, Esq.; and Kevin O'Sullivan of AP Images.

Finally, much gratitude is extended to our family members and friends, whose excitement in reading our work is eclipsed by the inspiration they have provided to us.

CHAPTER ONE

CASEY ANTHONY
Big Trouble Comes in Small Packages

For years to come, law enforcement students will study this case because it spans a number of forensic disciplines, from pathology, anthropology, entomology, and laboratory work to police investigation, behavioral science, and legal strategies. At its center, the case against Casey Marie Anthony should be about a wrongful death. But the road to justice has proven most circuitous, with the jury's verdict as controversial as the crime itself.

On June 15, 2008, in Orlando, Florida, it was said that a bitter showdown took place between Casey and her fifty-year-old mother, Cynthia, a nurse better known as "Cindy." Cindy and her husband—Casey's father, George, fifty-seven, a retired Ohio detective working as a security guard—lived with their daughter and granddaughter, Caylee Marie, who was almost three. Cindy was criticizing Casey's parenting skills, and Casey was arguing back loudly. At one point, Cindy said she would fight for custody of the baby and allegedly put her hands around Casey's throat. Out of deference to George, who reminded the women that it was Father's Day, they ended the fracas, but the next day, Casey was still furious. While Cindy was out of the house, Casey told her father goodbye and said she was going to work. As she left, she was holding little

Caylee. It would be the last time George would see his precious grand-daughter alive.[1]

Over the next few weeks, Casey called her parents but didn't see them. When Cindy would ask to speak to Caylee, Casey would say the child was with her nanny, either traveling or at an amusement park. Casey said she was busy working at a local theme park, which pleased her parents. Casey also spoke with her older brother, Lee, who never detected anything amiss.[2] On July 3, a frustrated Cindy posted on her MySpace® account a heartfelt message she hoped her daughter would see. It read, in part, "This precious little angel from above gave me strength and unconditional love. . . . Jealousy has taken her away. Jealousy from the one person who should be thankful for all of the love and support given to her." If she hoped the posting would make Casey relent and bring Caylee to her, she was wrong. On July 7, Casey wrote a post on her own MySpace account. It was titled "Diary of Days" and read, in part, "What is given can be taken away. Everyone lies. Everyone dies. Life will never be easy. . . ." Reportedly, Casey's post was written while she was watching the film *American Psycho*.[3]

On June 30, Casey's white 1998 Pontiac Sunfire—which was registered to her parents—had been found abandoned in front of a local Amscot, The Money Superstore™, and towed to Johnson's Wrecker Service, an impound yard. On July 15, George Anthony received a certified letter from Johnson's and went with Cindy to pick up the car. Crossing the lot with the facility manager, Simon Birch, George noticed a terrible odor as they approached the car—a smell he recognized from his detective days. He drove the vehicle home with all its windows open and the air conditioning blasting, and parked it in the garage. When Cindy and Lee passed by the car, they also noted the obvious odor, which led Cindy to ask, "What died?" Cindy called Casey, who said she was away on a "mini-vacation" to Jacksonville, Florida. In fact, she was staying in town with a boyfriend, Tony Lazzaro.

After comparing notes with some of Casey's friends, Cindy had had enough. She barged in at Lazzaro's condo and told Casey she was bringing her back to the Anthony home, and if Casey didn't want to come, then Cindy would just take Caylee home. But the tiny tot with the huge brown eyes wasn't at Tony's. Casey got into Cindy's car, and they argued on the way home, with Cindy calling 911, stating she wanted to file a stolen vehicle charge against her daughter. At the Anthony residence, Cindy kept asking where Caylee was. Still not satisfied with Casey's response, Cindy called 911 again, mentioning the missing car and asking for a deputy to come to the home to question Casey about Caylee.[4] A third call, with Cindy in hysterics, kicked the case into high gear:

> 911 OPERATOR: 911. What's your emergency?
> CINDY ANTHONY: I called a little bit ago. The deputy sheriff—I found out my granddaughter has been taken. She has been missing for a month. Her mother finally admitted that she's been missing.
> 911: OK. What is . . .
> CINDY: Get someone here now!
> 911: OK, what is the address that you're calling from?
> CINDY: We're talking about a three-year-old little girl! My daughter finally admitted that the babysitter stole her! I need to find her!
> 911: Your daughter admitted the baby is where?
> CINDY: That the babysitter took her a month ago, that my daughter's been looking for her. I told you my daughter was missing for a month. I just found her today, but I can't find my granddaughter. She just admitted to me that she's been trying to find her herself. There's something wrong! I found my daughter's car today, and it smells like there's been a dead body in the damn car!

The operator asked to speak with Casey:

911: Can you tell me a little bit what's going on?

CASEY ANTHONY: My daughter's been missing for the last 31 days.

911: And do you know who has her?

CASEY: I know who has her. I tried to contact her. I actually received a phone call today now from a number that is no longer in service. I did get to speak to my daughter for about a moment, about a minute.[5]

Soon the home was swarming with law enforcement officers. The peaceful neighborhood around Hopespring Drive would never be the same. Detective Corporal Yuri Melich of the Orange County Sheriff's Office Criminal Investigation Division joined his deputies. Briefed at the scene, he became the lead investigator. He took Casey aside to review a four-page written sworn statement she had prepared for one of the responding officers. Melich told Casey her story seemed implausible and that lying to police is a crime. Given the chance to change her statement, Casey insisted she had told the truth. Now, on audiotape, Melich reviewed all the details with her. Casey claimed that on the morning of June 9, she had gone to work at the nearby Universal Studios theme park but had first dropped Caylee off with a babysitter, Zenaida Fernandez-Gonzalez, who lived at Orlando's Sawgrass Apartments. She said she handed off the baby to Zenaida at the stairwell outside unit 210, where Gonzalez lived. Casey claimed she had known Zenaida for four years, since the woman was hired as a seasonal worker at the park, but she said Fernandez-Gonzalez had been Caylee's babysitter only for the past year and a half. After work, Casey maintained, she went back to the apartment to pick up her daughter, but there was no answer at the door and no response when she called Zenaida's cell phone. Casey couldn't produce the phone number, stating it was on a cell phone she had lost at work. Casey explained that she drove to places she knew Zenaida frequented but didn't locate the sitter or the child, so she went to her boyfriend Tony Lazzaro's residence, where she could feel "safe." Since that day, Casey told Melich, she had been conducting her "own investigation" but didn't call law enforcement because she had seen movies about missing people who got hurt when police became involved. Casey said she had shared information about Caylee's disappearance with two co-workers who could confirm her account: Jeffrey Hopkins and Juliette Lewis, both of whose phone numbers were also saved onto Casey's missing cell phone.

At the conclusion of their interview, Melich drove Casey in his unmarked car to various places of interest. One apartment building where Casey said Zenaida stayed during 2006 turned out to be a seniors-only facility. Another address was where Casey said Zenaida's mother, Gloria, lived, and where Casey had dropped off Caylee on previous occasions. As they drove through the complex, Casey said she couldn't recall the unit, and when they knocked at three different doors, the tenants all said they had never heard of Zenaida or Gloria.

After Melich brought Casey back home, George Anthony took the detective aside and said he felt his daughter was holding back information. Both Cindy and George seemed fearful that something had happened to their granddaughter. Thinking perhaps that this could be some sort of family custody dispute, Melich asked the Anthonys about Caylee's biological father. George and Cindy informed him that they had never met or spoken with the man and that Casey had told them he was dead. Casey confirmed that to Melich, saying that Caylee's father was named Eric and that he had died in a car accident in Georgia in 2007. Melich and another officer drove to the Sawgrass Apartments and spoke to the manager and a maintenance man, both of whom asserted that they didn't recognize Caylee from a photo they were shown. Neither the manager nor the maintenance man knew any Zenaida, and both said that the unit Casey claimed Fernandez-Gonzalez lived in had been vacant for 142 days. The manager produced a list of people who had filled out applications for an apartment, and a "Zenaida Gonzalez" had logged in on June 17 but had not rented the unit. Melich obtained a copy of the information, including Gonzalez's cell phone number. When he called her, she said she had never heard of Casey or Caylee. Later, she gave officers a sworn statement and didn't recognize Caylee's photo when it was shown to her. She also said that "Fernandez" was not part of her name.

Melich then drove to Universal Studios and met with a personnel investigator, Leonard Turtora, who informed him that Casey had indeed worked there but had been fired in April 2006. Jeffrey Hopkins had been fired in May 2002, and there was no record of Juliette Lewis or Zenaida Fernandez-Gonzalez ever having been employed at the park. Melich called Casey and put her on a speakerphone so Turtora could interact, and Casey stated that she worked as an event coordinator and gave an extension for her office; Turtora said there was no such extension. Turtora also said the man Casey claimed was her direct supervisor was not on the employee roster, and when she gave the name of someone who headed her department, that man said Casey was not employed there. Casey couldn't remember the building number or location where she claimed to work, nor was she able to produce a worker identification card. Nonetheless, Melich sent two officers to pick her up and bring her to meet him at Universal. Turtora escorted her onto the property and to where Melich was waiting. Casey said she would show them exactly where she worked and, with purposeful strides, led the group into a building and down a corridor, until she stopped cold, put her hands in her back pockets, and admitted she didn't really work at Universal. Melich took Casey into a small conference room and recorded a new interview. She confided that the apartment she'd pointed out as Zenaida's was across from that of an ex-boyfriend named Ricardo Morales, with whom she had stayed some of the time since Caylee went missing. She again stated that she last saw Caylee on June 9, with Zenaida. Throughout all of Melich's discussions with Casey, she never cried or showed emotion over the loss of her child.

Back in the police car, an officer pulled up all the Zenaida Gonza-lezes in the state's Driver and Vehicle Information Database (DAVID), but Casey said none of the photos matched her babysitter. When shown the photo of the Zenaida who had signed the rental application, Casey said the woman was "too old." Cops would spend weeks interviewing women with various permutations of the name "Zenaida Fernandez-Gonzalez," but in the end, only Casey ever claimed to have known or spoken to such a person. Still, Casey stuck to her guns, suggesting that cops expand the search for Zenaida to Miami, New York City, and Char-lotte, North Carolina.

Police began getting sworn statements from Casey's friends, some of whom called police on their own. All claimed that Casey habitually lied and some said that she had stolen from them. Tony Lazzaro called to say he had learned of Caylee's disappearance only that morning when offi-cers came to his residence. He met Casey in May through Facebook, he said, and they started dating in June. On June 9, Casey moved into his place, alone, and told him Caylee was either with the Anthonys or with the nanny. The last time he saw Caylee was on June 2 at the pool of his apartment complex. He had never met Zenaida Fernandez-Gonzalez and didn't know where she lived. Lazzaro told detectives he was a college student who worked as a club promoter at Fusion Ultra Lounge, an Orlando sushi restaurant that turned into a disco at night. He got Casey work there as a "shot girl," one of the several young women who would wear sexy outfits and dance with men to sell them pricey drinks.[6] Laz-zaro said that he and Casey went to a Blockbuster Video® store to rent movies on June 16—the first night Casey spent away from her parents' home—and he furnished officers with receipts of his transaction; later, police obtained surveillance video from the store that confirmed his account. The two movies they rented were *Untraceable*, which happens to have a scene of a human body being put in a car trunk, and *Jumper*, which is about a mother who abandons her child. It was never clear which of them selected the films.[7] Lazzaro then spoke to Amy Huizenga, who lived with Casey's ex-beau, Ricardo Morales. Tony urged her to contact the detectives, so Amy made the call. Amy spoke of text messages she had received from Casey at the end of June, in which she complained that her father had borrowed her car and run over an animal, causing a foul odor to emanate from the car's engine area. Amy and some friends had been on a week's vacation to Puerto Rico; Casey had been invited to attend, but she declined because she couldn't afford to go. Amy allowed Casey to drive her car while she was away, and Casey used it to pick Amy up at the airport on June 15. Amy soon learned Casey found Amy's checkbook in the car and used it to write and cash hundreds of dollars' worth of Amy's checks; police charges against Casey would follow.

Jesse Grund was an ex-fiancé of Casey; he told Melich that Casey had called on June 25 to see if he wanted to get together. Casey mentioned that Caylee was with the nanny at the beach for the weekend. Grund also reported that he had a phone conversation with Casey on June 24 and believed he heard Caylee in the background with Casey; he would later revise that information to police, stating that he might have heard Caylee's voice during some other, earlier, phone call. He also said that Casey's online account had been updated to remove more than two hundred photos of her with Caylee. Kristine Chester called Melich after seeing the "Caylee's Missing" stories on TV. Chester said she was Casey's "best friend," and that she had seen Casey just days before, but Anthony never mentioned that her daughter was missing.[8]

Months later, audiotapes of Melich questioning Casey were released. In one he asked if Caylee is in "a better place," and Casey said, "No.... If she was with her family right now, she'd be in the best place. She's not. She's with someone that I absolutely do not trust." And when the detective asked when Casey stopped trusting the person who had been babysitting her daughter for a year, Anthony replied: "The moment that her phone was cut off and I couldn't get in contact with my daughter."[9] But shortly after making this statement, Casey added that she'd had a phone conversation with Caylee just the day before. The call came from a "private number," Casey claimed, and Caylee greeted her with "Hi Mommy!" Casey described the rest of the call: "She started telling me a story, talking to me about her shoes and books." Casey's phone records failed to list such a call.[10]

On July 16, Melich charged Casey with child neglect and providing police with false information and booked her into the local jail. He obtained search warrants to take Casey's Compaq laptop from the Anthony home, along with the Pontiac Sunfire, which had a child's car seat in the back passenger side. Adult shoes, a belt, and some DVDs and CDs were also collected from the car. Caylee's baby doll was booked into evidence, plus a Dora the Explorer™ backpack, a dinner knife, and a black leather bag with papers inside. And in case there would be a need to match DNA for identification, Caylee's toothbrushes, hairbrush, comb, and oral thermometer were also collected. Cindy had washed a pair of Casey's slacks found in the Sunfire, as well as clothes Casey's brother Lee had picked up from Lazzaro's home. Because the items had been laundered, their forensic value was diminished, so they were not processed by the crime lab. Casey was visited behind bars by a crime scene investigation (CSI) technician who swabbed the inside of her mouth and took hair samples for future use.

When investigators looked at Casey's laptop, they found video of Caylee with an elderly man, later revealed to be her great-grandfather, Cindy's father, who was living in a convalescent home. That video, which included a scene of Caylee reading a picture book and singing "You Are My Sunshine," was dated June 15, a full week after Casey and

Cindy separately said they had last seen the little girl. Melich later showed George and Cindy the video and was told that the date of the visit was, indeed, June 15, when Cindy and Caylee saw the senior citizen on Father's Day. It was a harmless mistake that both women made. Casey's computer also had an e-mail from someone purportedly named "Thomas Franck," who worked at Universal Events and had apprised her of when she was to show up for work. But a trace on the e-mail proved that it was a bogus address and that there was no employee at the theme park with that name. Casey's cell phone records showed no incoming or outgoing phone calls to Zenaida Fernandez-Gonzalez, Jeffrey Hopkins, or Juliette Lewis.

Melich, Sergeant John Allen, and Crime Scene Investigator Gerardo Bloise met at the lab's forensics bay to inspect the Sunfire. Upon opening the driver's door, they were bowled over by the strong smell of decomposition, an odor familiar to all of them. Orange County K-9 deputy Jason Forgey brought his cadaver dog Gerus to the bay. The animal was trained to detect the smell of human decomposition and no other biological scent. Opening each of the four car doors, one at a time, the dog sniffed but didn't alert—but when the trunk was opened, Gerus let the trainer know a dead human body had spent time in that part of the car.

Deputies also went to Johnson's Wrecker and spoke to the manager, Simon Birch, who told them about the Anthonys reclaiming the Sunfire. As Birch and George had walked to the car, Anthony mentioned that his daughter had been missing for a while, would not tell them where her daughter was, and had told several lies. Birch had opened the car door, and the odor of death poured out; it was the same odor he had smelled once before in a car in which a man had committed suicide. When they opened the trunk, flies swarmed out, and the two men saw a white garbage bag with paper, food wrappings, and maggots inside, along with an empty pizza box. The outside of the bag picked up some of the decomposition odor, but the smell inside the bag—where the trash was—was nothing compared to the car trunk's stench. Simon tossed the bag into the business's Dumpster, where it was retrieved by cops and brought to the lab.

Officers continued speaking to Casey's friends, including Tony Lazzaro, with whom she had been living before her arrest. He and his roommates let officers search the residence, but nothing was found. When police interviewed Danny Colamarino, owner of Cast Iron Tattoos, they learned Casey had been a regular customer for the last couple of years. On July 2, one of his employees had inked a new tattoo on Casey's left shoulder: the words *Bella Vita*, Italian for "Beautiful Life." She had another tattoo appointment scheduled for July 19 that she would not be keeping.

At the bond hearing on July 22, police revealed to the court that strands of hair that looked like Caylee's were found in the car trunk and that a trained dog hit on the scent of cadaverine—the odor of putrefied flesh—in the trunk. Bail was set at $500,000, which meant that Casey would have to post a bond of 10 percent, or $50,000, if she wanted to be released. Officials announced that they were treating the case as a potential homicide, and that Casey Anthony was a "person of interest."[11]

On July 24, Cindy Anthony phoned detectives and said there had been a Caylee sighting in Georgia, but police were never able to verify the claim.[12] That same day, George Anthony met with Melich and Allen, without telling Cindy. During the recorded interview, George disclosed that he'd had "bad vibes" when he smelled the car trunk. He acknowledged that the odor was from something dead, adding that he had whispered to himself, "Please don't let this be my Caylee." He recounted Cindy's comment, "What died?" and told the detectives he explained it away by telling her that rotting pizza had been in the trunk. But George was having dark thoughts, he said; he didn't want to believe he might have raised a kid who "could do something" to another person, but if that was the police theory, to please tell him so that he could prepare his wife. He apologized for Cindy's antagonistic behavior toward the detectives. (Taped interviews would later show Cindy's combativeness in support of her daughter, although on one occasion she referred to Casey as a "sociopath."[13] Cindy also told detectives that she had thrown a high school graduation party for Casey in 2004, only to learn on the day of the event that Casey was one-half credit shy of earning her diploma.[14]) George informed police that Casey had hired an attorney by the name of José Baez who was recommended by another inmate. George also complained that his daughter lived "on the edge," lied, took money from them, and has resented Cindy since the moment Caylee was born, when the nurse first handed the infant to Cindy instead of to Casey. Just before his wife saw Caylee for the last time, George said, Cindy had found the house's back gate open with the pool ladder down. The family had an above-ground pool and always made sure to keep the ladder out of Caylee's reach when the pool was not in use. K-9 deputy Forgey and his cadaver dog, Gerus, and a second cadaver dog, Bones— trained by neighboring Osceola County K-9 deputy Kristen Brewer— were brought in separately, during the early days of Caylee's disappearance. Both animals hit on areas near the child's backyard playhouse, leading investigators to think "something" had occurred there; there were no hits by the pool. Still, the detectives told George they had to consider that Caylee might have fallen into the water and died, or that Casey had drowned her defenseless daughter. If Caylee's death had been an accident, the natural thing for Casey to do would be to call 911. If emergency workers were unsuccessful in reviving the child, Casey should have let the authorities take over, and then be seen at the funeral, grieving. Concocting a fantastic story as a cover-up wasn't rational. But how could the deputies and George get Casey to reveal what she knew? George didn't have the solution. The meeting ended when he began trembling and vomited.

The Anthonys' next-door neighbor, Brian Mark Burner, would inform police that on either June 18 or 19, Casey borrowed a shovel from him; it was later booked in as evidence.[15] That news caused some to speculate that Casey had buried her daughter somewhere, and there were unsubstantiated rumors that GPS tracking of Casey's cell phone linked her to a location a few miles from her home during the time Caylee might have been killed. Searchers in the area kept their eyes peeled for recently dug graves or suspicious loose dirt. Police knew that the sooner a body could be found, the better. Forensic evidence can diminish with time, especially on and from the body itself—the best hope for determining cause of death.

Inmates at the Orange County jail have their visitor interviews video-taped, and many of those tapes, along with most legal filings and police reports, become available to the public, thanks to Florida's "Sunshine" law, which stipulates that such records are accessible to interested parties. Only attorneys are allowed to have private, unrecorded visits with clients. The Anthony case was quickly becoming the biggest media sensation in the country, with nightly coverage on the cable TV crime news programs—particularly *Nancy Grace* and *Issues with Jane Velez-Mitchell* on CNN's sister network, HLN (Headline News), each aired an hour per night with regular reruns. Within hours after visits between Casey and George, Cindy, or Lee, video of the meetings was played nationally, with pundits evaluating each hunk of conversation as if it were a sporting event.[16] Melich and his detectives also had live closed-circuit access to the family visits. During one session, Casey told Cindy she couldn't discuss the matter for fear of endangering the family, hinting that Zenaida had a key to the Anthony home.

The description of Zenaida became more detailed. Casey claimed that the missing nanny was about five-foot-seven and one hundred and forty pounds, with curly brown hair that had been straightened, brown eyes, and no tattoos. Zenaida's father, who was African American, was named Victor, and her Puerto Rican mother was Gloria and was in her fifties. Zenaida moved to Miami to go to the University of Florida, had a lot of money, drove a silver 2008 Ford Focus with a pink child seat in the back, and had an older half-sister named Samantha. Zenaida's room-mates—both of whom had family money—were Raquel Farrell and Jennifer Rosa, Casey claimed, adding that she knew where they both worked. Of course, none of these names were on Casey's cell phone list or logged on her ingoing or outgoing phone records, and neither of the roommates' alleged workplaces had employees with those names. Even Ryan Pasley, who Casey listed as her "best friend" on her cell phone, called police to say the nanny story was "crap," and that Casey had expressed to him that she wished she hadn't had Caylee because she was too young and couldn't go out and do the things she wanted to do. Ryan, who worked at the Sports Authority sporting goods store, learned Casey told her mother that she also worked at the outlet, which was untrue. When Cindy called Ryan to look for Casey, he mentioned that he had loaned Casey four hundred dollars he never got back. Cindy told him her daughter had stolen money from the Anthonys, as well as from Cindy's parents. Ryan told Melich that a week or so before Caylee went missing, Casey had called him and said she had been using drugs, which he found odd.

FBI agents Scott Bolin and Steve McElyea of the Tampa field office interviewed Cindy and learned that Casey had once described a car accident that Zenaida had been in that caused her to be hospitalized in Tampa, but authorities later found out there was no such accident. Cindy told the agents she had never met Caylee's father, Eric, but the family attorney had prepared paperwork that gave Casey full custody; a later check with that lawyer revealed he had never heard about Eric and had not worked on any custody issue involving Casey.

Police worked to pin down George Anthony's timeline. He said he last saw Casey shortly before 1 p.m. on June 16, before they both left for work. Casey was wearing a white top and gray dress slacks—similar to the pants Cindy found in the car and laundered—and Caylee had on a blue denim skirt and pink top.

The tabloid magazines published and TV crime shows aired photos of Casey that were taken at the Fusion Lounge, where Casey had partic-ipated in a "Hot Body" contest on June 20, after Caylee went missing. Melich contacted the two photographers of the images and received dig-ital copies with time stamps. In each of the images, Casey was drinking or dancing provocatively with other people. She looked like a woman who was enjoying life to the fullest. Investigators also had access to a handwritten diary Casey kept. An entry dated June 20 read: "I have no regrets, just a bit worried. . . . I just want for everything to work out OK. I completely trust my own judgment and know that I made the right decision. I just hope that the end justified the means."

No matter how many of Casey's friends police spoke to, not one had ever seen or spoke to Zenaida Fernandez-Gonzalez, nor did any of them hear that Caylee was missing during the month from when the child was last seen until she was reported missing. Many had seen Casey during that time and said she was her normal party girl self. Over five thousand tips came into the police CrimeLine during the first several weeks of the investigation, but there were no credible sightings of the tot.[17] On August 9, on what would have been Caylee's third birthday, crowds gathered in front of the Anthony residence, holding candles and posters in tribute to the missing and presumed dead little girl. Flowers and teddy bears dotted the sidewalk. Whenever there were such gatherings outside the Anthony home, protesters who believed Casey was guilty would nearly come to blows with supporters of the Anthony family; often George and Cindy would get into shouting matches with critics who taunted them. Someone would always be videotaping the events, and the footage would wind up on the nightly news.

According to the National Center for Missing and Exploited Chil-dren, two thousand children are reported missing every day—more than seven hundred thousand per year—and most of these cases don't turn out to be homicides. Yet there was something so gripping about this case. The media showed a procession of photos and videos of the dimpled moppet who always seemed to be on the verge of a giggle and her alluring brunette mother who must have looked just like Caylee at that age. The many images of the two together made one question how someone who seemed on film to be such a doting parent could commit an untoward act against her offspring. And Casey was adamant that she loved and missed her daughter, imploring through her jailhouse talks with her parents that whoever took Caylee should please bring her back. George and Cindy never missed an opportunity to publicly insist that Caylee was alive out there, somewhere, and they defended Casey's honor and parenting ability. But a reasonable observer might wonder: If Casey had nothing to do with her child's disappearance, why did it take thirty-one days for her to report the girl missing? And why did Casey seem to lie every time she opened her mouth?

Friends, relatives, and people who had opinions about Casey Anthony were all sought-after "gets" for media reporters. I made countless appearances on national television and radio programs and gave my co-author, Dawna Kaufmann, several interviews for her magazine articles. Whenever a new, official piece of evidence would be revealed, there'd be lively discussions about how it might affect the case. A photo of Caylee was released showing the child with what seemed to be a bruised eye, and some people asked me if that was proof of child abuse. Maybe it was, maybe it wasn't, I said, but I doubted the photo, on its own, would become a major court exhibit, if Anthony went to trial. Active toddlers get bumps and bruises during a number of innocent pursuits. Unless there was a witness to an act of Casey abusing her child, that photo couldn't be substantiated—and if there was such a witness, why hadn't he or she done something about it at the time? Some TV hosts expressed astonishment that a parent could kill her or his own child, so I had to explain that "filicide" is not uncommon. A recent Bureau of Justice study found that 66 percent of murdered children under five years of age were killed by a parent or close family member.[18]

In early August, initial reports from the FBI's Quantico, Virginia, laboratory started coming back to local FBI special agent Nickolas Savage and Orange County investigators. The single human hair with a purported decompositional band that had been found in the trunk was a likely DNA match to either Caylee or Casey; more testing would be performed. A chemical analyst with the FBI found residues consistent with chloroform in the trunk, as well as on the car trunk liner and spare tire cover. Dr. Arpad Vass, of the Biosciences Division of the University of Tennessee's Oak Ridge National Laboratory—more popularly known as the "Body Farm"—issued two different reports confirming his initial assessment that the car trunk was the location of a "decompositional event" that could be of human origin; he also ascertained that chloroform was present in the trunk.[19]

I was certainly familiar with the valuable research done by the Body Farm on behalf of various government agencies and to train law enforcement officials and medical personnel. Since 1981, when forensic anthropologist Dr. William Bass established the program, scientists there have used a 2½-acre plot of enclosed woods to measure decompositional changes on dead human bodies. The corpses are exposed to the elements, wrapped in blankets or plastic, buried or submerged in water, or put into car trunks or suitcases. Over a period of time, the experts chronicle the smell and appearance of each corpse, the speed of skeletonization, insect activity, plant growth, and environmental changes. Today, under the leadership of Dr. Arpad Vass—who has devoted his life to studying death—this remarkable program receives more than one hundred donated bodies per year. When reporters asked me about the wisdom of prosecutors bringing Dr. Vass into the case, I'd answer that he's the world's best expert for that discipline. I was eager to learn what exact experiments he'd conduct to get answers. In my own experience, I knew that in Florida's muggy June or July weather, a dead body put into a car trunk would become malodorous in as few as thirty-six hours.[20]

At some point, a search warrant was issued for the Anthony family's desktop computer, and Melich asked Detective Sandra Osborne to forensically review its contents. Specifically, he asked her to conduct a Google® search on the computer for the word *chloroform*. She reported that a search had been made for the chemical—and that an expert from outside her department had discovered a Wikipedia® entry for *chloroform*. There were searches for other keywords, such as *chest injuries, hand-to-hand combat,* and *ruptured spleen*—all within fifteen minutes of each other on March 17, 2008. On March 21, searches were made for *neck breaking, making weapons of household products,* and *how to make chloroform* and the ingredients necessary for doing so, including *acetone* and *alcohol*. These searches were made three months before Caylee went missing. In all, prosecutors would contend that there had been eighty-four searches for the word *chloroform*. Since there was no way to know which person in the Anthony home might have Googled the information, Melich compared the time of each listing with Cindy's and George's schedules. Cindy was at work during the times in question, so she could be eliminated, but George could not, because he had not worked that month. Casey was believed to have been home during the time of the searches.

Casey sent detectives a note asking them to set up a private meeting between her and her father at the Orange County jail. So, on August 15, Melich, Allen, and Bolin drove George to the meeting, surreptitiously recording him in the car as he spoke of hoping to get "closure" and some answers. The cops made it clear that they were not suggesting questions George should ask and that he was not acting as an agent of the state, which he said he understood. When they arrived, Casey was with José Baez's co-counsel, Adam Gabriel. George waited an hour and a half to speak to Casey, but he was taken home when she changed her mind about wanting to talk to him.

––––––––––––

Three days later, Osborne had another surprise for Melich. As she reviewed Casey's e-mails to and from her user name of "casey o marie," she found chat logs showing that Casey had communicated with someone whose user name was "nyitaliano3"—and that person was Anthony Rusciano, a probationary deputy sheriff with the Orange County office, the very team that was investigating Casey. Rusciano was brought in and told Melich and Allen he had "spent time" with Casey over a few months prior to her arrest. He saw Caylee with her only once, in 2007, and had "chatted" with Casey in May 2008. (Chatting is when two or more computer users communicate in real time, often employing text that is ungrammatical or misspelled for the sake of brevity.) Because a log remains on the users' hard drives, even if the texts are deleted, Osborne was able to make transcripts, which were then shown to Rusciano. The flirty texts from Casey mentioned that Caylee was with her nanny or that Casey couldn't find a babysitter. In one exchange, Rusciano invited Casey over, to which she replied: "ha, want me to bring the little snot head?" followed by "didn't think so."[21] Rusciano could have told his bosses about his friendship with Casey from the moment Caylee was reported missing, but he chose not to. His superiors considered that omission to be a lie. Confronted by the chat logs, Rusciano admitted he was culpable, and within days he was fired.[22]

On August 17, Leonard Padilla, a bounty hunter from Sacramento, California, and two associates, Rob Dick and Tracy Conroy, traveled to Orlando to post bond for Casey.[23] A frequent "talking head" on TV crime news shows and featured on several specials on the National Geographic Channel, he is usually seen wearing a black cowboy hat and sometimes has a blue and gold parrot on his shoulder. A bounty hunter since 1975, Padilla obtained a law degree in 1980. In 1982, he and some colleagues opened the Lorenzo Patino School of Law, named for a judge who was a partner, offering an affordable legal education; Padilla serves as chairman of the school's board of trustees. Padilla has also run for mayor of Sacramento four times—most recently in 2008—as well as for

Congress in 2005 and for a supervisor's seat in 2006. He expressed on TV his hope that by posting Casey's bond and meeting with her at her parents' home, she might feel comfortable enough to share any critical information she had. He admitted that finding the child would be good for his bounty hunting enterprise, and he considered the expenditure a reasonable risk. The bond was posted on August 20, and the defendant was allowed to leave the jail the next day for home confinement. Padilla's team was ensconced in an RV parked outside the Hopespring house and took part in meetings inside the residence for a total of ten days. Tracy, a female member of Padilla's team, stuck to Casey around the clock to protect his investment.[24] Padilla would later tell Nancy Grace that Casey never once showed any emotion about the loss of her child and "very seldom" mentioned the girl's name. Padilla recalled that Tracy had sat with Casey and Cindy as they looked through an album. When either Cindy or Tracy pointed to a photo of Caylee and commented on how cute she was, Casey pointed to a photo of herself and responded, "What about me? I look cute, too."[25]

The more time Padilla spent with Casey, the more he became convinced that Casey had passed the child off to a friend. He didn't want to believe Caylee was deceased. Casey kept giving him the same old nanny story, which he found ridiculous. Once, he claimed, she expanded the nanny narrative to include Zenaida's sister, Samantha, who grabbed Caylee and put her in a car with her own children, then handed Casey a list of thirty days' worth of instructions about what to tell people.[26]

Also on August 20, police made a recorded conference call to Rick Plesea, Cindy Anthony's brother, who had been writing about his niece online. Plesea had his own accounts of Casey's devious activities. He said a counselor had advised Cindy to kick Casey out of the house, but Cindy refused for fear that Casey would take Caylee away. Plesea said his sister was considering filing for custody of the little girl. He also revealed that his mother told him Casey was practically bankrupting her parents with credit card debt, and that she had stolen money from the family, including a $354 check of her grandparents, which she used to pay her phone bill. Casey resented Cindy, he said, because Caylee liked her grandma more than she liked her mother. He stated that no one in the extended family knew that Casey had been living elsewhere with the child until they heard about her arrest on the news. After that, Rick e-mailed his sister several times, urging her to "wake up" to Casey's involvement, but Cindy wouldn't budge. A measure of Cindy's propensity for denial came with Plesea's story of his June 2005 wedding, which Cindy, George, and Casey attended. Plesea said Casey wore a tight-fitting top with her stomach protruding and her belly button "sticking out at least a half inch." When she left the room, he turned to the Anthonys and inquired about Casey's pregnancy, but Cindy denied it, saying that she had just put on some weight. The rest of the family was laughing because Cindy was a nurse but couldn't see that her daughter was obviously pregnant. In fact, Cindy insisted to them that Casey was a virgin. Two months later, on August 9, Casey gave birth to Caylee, with Cindy at her side. Rick told the detectives that Casey, in an attempt to stop her parents from asking about Caylee's father, found a stranger's obituary and claimed he was the daddy. Plesea furnished police with copies of all the e-mails he had exchanged with Cindy. Soon after, cops went to the home of Shirley Plesea, the mother of Rick and Cindy. She confirmed that Casey had stolen checks from her, including some that Rick hadn't mentioned. Shirley never pressed charges, figuring Cindy and George had enough to contend with; she said Casey had stolen up to $45,000 from them. Shirley had never met or spoken to "Zanny the Nanny"—Casey's nickname for Zenaida—but she'd heard about her for more than a year.[27]

The Orange County Sheriff's Office announced that the hair found in the car trunk was likely Caylee's, and that the child was almost certainly dead. An FBI lab report stated that, under microscopic inspection, a dark band was found on the hair that was indicative of decomposition. DNA testing confirmed that the hair belonged to an Anthony family member. Since Casey, her parents, and brother were all alive—

and only Caylee was missing—the implication was that the hair was proof that Caylee was dead and had shed the hair while she was decomposing in the car trunk.[28]

When asked by media outlets about this finding, I admitted that the hair could provide fertile ground for forensic debate during a trial. I had never heard of "decompositional banding" being argued in a murder trial and wondered if such evidence would be admissible. I didn't go so far as to classify such testing as "junk science," but, I said, I hoped that there had been proper peer review for the technique.[29]

Although police continued to check out leads regarding live Caylee sightings, the science led investigators to conclude that the child was deceased. On August 29, Tim Miller, the founder of Texas EquuSearch (TES), officially joined the search for Caylee. Miller's sixteen-year-old daughter Laura had vanished in 1984. A year and a half later, her remains were found, along with those of two other missing girls, the handiwork of a presumed serial killer; no arrest was ever made. From then on, Miller, a horseman, turned his anguish to activism; every time a child disappeared in his area or was presumed to be dead, he would organize mounted search-and-recovery missions and offer comfort to the families whose pain he knew all too well. Eventually, he expanded his operation and began consulting on national and international cases, including the Aruba search for Alabama teenager Natalee Holloway, which brought him much media attention. Miller's work is now endorsed by law enforcement but is funded solely by public donations. He uses an army of volunteers, some of whom are civilians and some of whom have training in medicine or lifesaving skills or with cadaver dogs. As the need for TES's services has increased, so have the company's techniques: Volunteers use horses when needed and rely on state-of-the-art equipment for any kind of land, air, or water search. On any day, TES—based in

Dickinson, Texas—is juggling dozens of open cases, and their recovery rate is outstanding. To date, Miller and his crew have worked 1,232 cases.[30]

It was Cindy who originally phoned Miller to ask for help on the case. She persuaded him that the child was alive and that the sheriff's office was not pursuing solid leads. So he flew to Orlando and met with the parties. Very quickly, however, he came to believe the Anthonys were being evasive and that he'd be searching for a dead body. At the Anthony home, Casey laughed a lot—not the standard reaction he normally saw from grieving parents of missing children. José Baez thanked Miller for coming but instructed him not to talk to his client about the case or to talk to her at all unless she had counsel present; Miller had no option but to honor that request.[31] A cop friend of George's from Ohio visited the home and saw the problem Miller was having making progress in his search. At one point, Miller handed a map of the area to George and asked him to tell Casey to put an "X" on the spot where Caylee's remains might be found. Cindy became irate, and Casey ran off into her bedroom without touching the map. The cop remarked to Miller, "He knows the answer's in the bedroom and the fucking bitch won't talk."[32]

Miller had more cooperation from the sheriff's deputies, who showed him the pings from Casey's cell phone during the period of time they believed Caylee was murdered. (Any cell phone that is turned on—not necessarily in use—gives off recorded pings as it passes within a reasonable range of cellular towers, providing law enforcement with incontrovertible proof of the owner's movements.) Miller took a search party to a nearby swampland on Suburban Drive that he felt would be the logical spot for dumping a body, but it was water-soaked from a recent tropical storm; he didn't want his horse-mounted volunteers to accidentally trample on the remains. It would be better to wait for the waters to recede, he advised detectives.

After a few days, Miller and his team returned to Texas, having spent more than $100,000 on the effort and having nothing to show for the work. With so many families desperate for TES's assistance, Miller felt his time would be better served elsewhere.[33]

Leonard Padilla's employee Tracy saw George berate Casey, shouting, "Where's my granddaughter? You know!" and said he would have assaulted her had Cindy and his police buddy not pulled him away.[34] Over the next several days, as more results from lab testing piled up, Padilla stepped up his demands for answers from Casey. When she felt no compunction to furnish them and kicked him out of the house, he took his team and went back to California. He also felt that with the livid spectators outside the Anthony home, Casey would be safer in protective custody, so he rescinded her half-million-dollar bond. Casey was returned to custody on August 29, again for various financial crimes. TV cameras captured the spectacle of Casey being marched out of her parents' home. This annoyed attorney Baez, who told reporters a typical bond for what Casey was charged with would be three thousand dollars or less.[35]

Days later, Melich was contacted by Richard Grund, whose son Jesse had been engaged to Casey. In a recorded statement, he recounted a phone call he'd had with George Anthony, after Grund scolded him for not acting like an ex-cop should. George's response was that Cindy ruled the household and was giving him marching orders. "Whatever Cindy wants, Cindy gets," said Grund, adding that Cindy feared losing both Casey and Caylee. He also said that Jesse and Casey spent much time together at the Grund home, with babysitting duties falling to Grund family members. Although the family was beguiled by the toddler, Richard worked out of his home, and Caylee was a disruption. He asked Casey to line up a permanent sitter, and she soon told him about a nanny named Zenaida, who was bonding well with Caylee. Grund said Casey complained a lot about her parents—once stating that her father had gambling debts of $30,000. Richard also recounted examples of Casey lying and taking money from Jesse. Richard and Jesse had been told by bounty hunter Padilla that he had sat through meetings between the Anthonys and their legal team during which they said that if Caylee was dead, Jesse Grund must have killed her. Jesse had a key to Casey's car and could have planted evidence to frame her, it was claimed. Cindy went so far as to tell officers that Jesse might be "Zanny the Nanny," and that Casey could be covering up for him. Richard Grund didn't want his son to be falsely accused by anyone, especially since there were so many arrows pointing to Casey as the real culprit. Jesse had willingly taken and passed a polygraph test; why hadn't Casey taken one, too?

Jesse, according to his father, had received a call from Lee Anthony, stating that the night before Casey had left with Caylee, she'd had a fight with her mother. According to Lee, Cindy had wrapped her hands around Casey's throat in an attempt to silence her. Jesse would later confirm his conversation with Lee to police, speaking of Casey's resentment of her mother, which was based on Cindy's being handed the newborn before Casey got to hold her (this echoed what George Anthony had already told cops). Jesse told police that he and Casey began dating toward the end of January 2005; soon after, she announced that she was pregnant and that Jesse was the father. After she gave birth to Caylee in August, Jesse paid $550 for a DNA paternity test, which determined that he was not the infant's biological father; still, he continued dating Casey and treated the baby as his own. Jesse also told officers that Casey confided to him that when she was in her teens, her brother Lee had once attempted to touch her breasts. Detectives showed Jesse a chat log between him and Casey—where he used the screen name SpecialAgentJAG4—in which she wrote that she was going to try to obtain some Xanax® from a friend. Jesse said the chat looked familiar, but he couldn't recall the part about the pills; the only medication he knew she took was for birth control. He recalled one time, after they had been out late and fell asleep on his sofa, Casey had woken up, foaming at the mouth and shaking like she was having a seizure. He couldn't say whether it was drug-related, but she recovered quickly. Jesse also told detectives he had used the Anthony family laptop briefly. His romance with Casey ended in May 2006; that month she introduced him to her new boyfriend, Tony Lazzaro.[36]

———————

In early September, my co-author Dawna called me to discuss chloro-form. She had heard rumblings that the drug would be a significant factor in the case, although law enforcement wouldn't yet confirm it. Like most civilians, Dawna's knowledge of the drug was from movies in which a bad guy is shown soaking a rag with the liquid, then holding the cloth against someone's nose and mouth to knock them out. I answered her many questions with this explanation: Chloroform is a sweet-smelling, color-less liquid that combines methane and halothane atoms. Years ago, it was used as an effective anesthetic but was replaced by more predictable prod-ucts, like nitrous oxide. Today chloroform is mainly used as an industrial solvent, and even that is going out of favor. It's not a prescription medi-cine, nor is it available at drugstores, but some chemistry labs use it, and it can be ordered online. In more than fifty thousand cases, I've never per-sonally seen a death attributed to that compound. Dawna said there were high readings of chloroform in the car trunk and on the trunk liner, and since Caylee was still missing at that point, there was no way to know if she had inhaled any. If someone applied a chloroform-soaked cloth over your nose and mouth, you'd struggle and try to get away. Since there's no greater biological urge than the urge to breathe, you'd take even deeper breaths, which would cause you to pass out and go limp within about a half dozen inhalations. How long you'd be unconscious would depend on the dosage, your size, and whether you were in an open-air environment, where the gas would dissipate more quickly, or a closed chamber—like a car trunk—which would cause the molecular markers to remain in the air for a longer period. When you'd awaken, you'd have a sore, raspy throat and sinuses; watery, burning eyes; and possibly a rash or red skin where the liquid touched your skin. You might also vomit. In a fatal dosing, as your respiratory system would begin to fail, you'd suffer cardiac arrhythmia, and finally your brain would die from lack of oxygen. You might be alert for thirty seconds then spend the next few minutes unconsciously fading to black. Dawna said that a friend of Casey's informed detectives that she had attended a loud party with Casey where Caylee slept soundly on a nearby chair. Since Casey's apparent Internet searches for chloroform occurred three months prior to when Caylee went missing, might it be possible that Casey had been dosing her child so Mom wouldn't be disturbed by an inconvenient toddler? I replied that while I had seen many child deaths due to a mother dosing a child to make him or her sleep, the typical means were barbiturates or antihistamines in liquid or pill form and often put into juice or milk. Casey could have achieved the same goal without chloroform.

Dawna mentioned that some of the Anthony computer Google searches sought instructions for making chloroform, and that some web posters wrote about mixing various caustic household chemicals to get a type of chloroform. But those chemical cocktails aren't chloroform, and no lab—especially those of the caliber doing work on the Anthony case—would label it as such. Using a gas chromatograph mass spectrometer (GCMS)—specialized equipment used in toxicology labs—the scientist would isolate and measure the voluble organic compounds, breaking down the exact chemicals and their percentages.

We also kicked around another theory: that Caylee had somehow fallen into the swimming pool and drowned, and that a urine-soaked disposable diaper might have combined with the chemicals in the pool to give a reading that was mistakenly listed as chloroform. If that is what actually happened, I stated, Casey might have saved herself a lot of trouble—and a possible death sentence—if she had said so from the start. She could have made the legal argument that she didn't see her child go into the water, but when she fished her out and couldn't revive her, she panicked, put her in the car trunk, and drove around until she could think of a believable excuse. Had she used that story to cut an early deal with prosecutors, it's possible the state and feds wouldn't have performed the extraordinarily precise testing they undertook when they had to counter Casey's full-throttle defense.

Although Casey had so far been charged only with petty crimes, I anticipated that she'd soon be charged with the murder of her daughter. I was eager to see how things would play out in court, with the experts on both sides educating the jurors.[37] One indication of how a trial might proceed came from a publicly released forensic report that challenged the Anthony family claims that it was either rotting pizza in the car trunk or a dead squirrel under the car that produced the maggots and lethal odor. Oak Ridge National Laboratory performed comparative testing of a trunk carpet of similar color and texture from two other Pontiac Sunfires, which had been found in a Knoxville, Tennessee, junkyard and brought to the Body Farm. And even though no pizza was found in the empty box in Casey's trunk, to address her mother's claim that there was, the lab tested mushroom-pepperoni pizza as it decomposed for several days. It did not give off the same smell of chloroform or decomposition, and no maggots were found on the pizza. Casey told her brother and a friend the odor was from running over a dead squirrel, so the lab decomposed a squirrel over time but could not reproduce the same smell that was in Casey's car. The lab also had stats on a Montana case in which a small child wrapped in a blanket was left to decompose in a car trunk. No chloroform smell was discovered in that car's trunk. Oak Ridge was able to break down Casey's trunk smells to gasoline, Scotchgard™, decomposition, and chloroform; these were then compared with the other Pontiac trunk smells, which were broken down into magnesium, calcium, iron, and sodium. Bottom line: Nothing the lab reproduced had the same quantity of chloroform as was found in Casey's car trunk.[38]

On September 4, 2008, two Orlando-area bail bond companies (choosing to keep their names private) combined forces and posted a $500,000 bond to spring Casey once again from her twelve-by-eight-foot jail cell into house arrest. The next day it was revealed that George and Cindy Anthony had signed a promissory note for $50,000, 10 percent of the bond.[39] That same day, Melich learned that George had bought a Taurus® .38 revolver and ammunition from a local gun store and brought it home, a direct violation of Casey's home confinement policy. Officers went to the house and took the gun for safekeeping, and Casey was allowed to remain at home.

On September 8, Casey's boyfriend, Tony Lazzaro, came to police headquarters to elaborate on tape about things he had forgotten to mention previously; namely, that he once told Casey that if he had children, he wanted boys because, having had younger sisters, he felt girls were too hard to handle. In addition, he said that on June 23, Casey had told him she ran out of gas. Lazzaro picked her up and drove her to the Anthony home, where she made him break the lock on a backyard storage shed and take out two gas cans, which they used to get her car running. Four days later, he stated, she needed help with another empty gas tank. This time she was at the Amscot parking lot, and when he picked her up, she said her father would take care of her car. Asked about Casey's drug use, specifically Xanax, Lazzaro mentioned they would sometimes smoke marijuana, but he didn't know about her taking pills. Lazzaro added that on a couple of occasions in early July, when they were sleeping together, Casey would wake up, sweating, in the middle of the night. Detectives met with Lazzaro's roommate, Nathan Lezniewicz, who said he met Casey and Caylee at the apartment in late May or early June. But he added that after Casey moved in full-time, around the second or third week of June, he never saw Caylee again. In a separate interview, another roommate, Cameron Campina, told the same story but said that Casey was anti-drug and seemed happy; he was stunned to hear of her legal troubles.[40]

On September 15, Casey was rearrested on additional bad check charges but was bailed out the next day by her attorney with a $1,250 bond. Baez's argument about a more reasonable bail must have swayed the court.[41] Media types discussed whether authorities were offering Casey a deal to admit guilt about whatever happened to Caylee in exchange for a prison term instead of the death penalty. Maybe the discounted bond was to give family and friends a chance to talk some sense into her without the authorities listening to their every utterance.[42] Days passed and nothing happened, except more protesters showed up in front of the Anthony home, carrying picket signs and chanting that Casey was a murderer. One woman brought her two-year-old child who held a sign that asked: "Why would you wanna kill a child like me?" While Casey stayed housebound, George and Cindy tried to live normal lives, wearing T-shirts with "Where's Caylee?" logos and driving a car with the hotline number painted on the window, but more than once they had to call police for crowd control. A judge considered establishing a curfew or enacting a noise limit. Searches were still being conducted throughout the area, and items that were found by searchers were booked into the lab for analysis.[43]

A separate investigation was filed by the state Department of Children and Families, with Agent William Procknow asking Casey at her home why she needed a nanny if she wasn't working. She told him that the police got it wrong, that she did work at Universal Studios. Procknow closed his case with a report that verified "inadequate supervision and threatened harm."[44] On September 17, 2008, Orlando's 9 News reported a new theory about how Casey came up with the idea of "Zanny the Nanny," stating that "Zanny" was street vernacular for the antianxiety drug Xanax. This led people to wonder if Casey might have been in the habit of dosing her child with the drug so she could leave her alone and asleep while Casey went out.[45] Two days later, three more fraud charges were filed against Casey, bringing the total to fifteen, and raising to seventy-one years the potential time she faced in prison.[46] More police interviews, case documents, witness lists, cell phone and computer reports, and personal photographs were released, feeding the media. Perhaps the cops wanted Casey to feel the drip-drip-drip of water torture, so she would capitulate and tell them what they needed to hear.

Sometime after the Caylee case began skyrocketing, while the child was still "missing," I received a phone call at my Pittsburgh office from José Baez, the Kissimmee, Florida, attorney who was representing Casey Anthony. He wanted a bit of guidance in structuring his defense, insisting to me that his client had no idea what had happened to her daughter. He realized he had a tiger by the tail with this case and expressed that it was going to be well beyond anything he had handled before. He also knew that, although there was no proof that the child was dead, Casey could be charged with serious crimes, including murder. I admired his candor and, over a few conversations, tried to prepare him for what was to come. He had to believe in what Casey was telling him and adjust his defense accordingly. Should the state produce mountains of evidence against her, he might be able to spare her from death row by fashioning a plea bargain, but that would require her acceptance and admission of some involvement, and, from the comments her family had been making in the press, that didn't seem likely. Short of that, he had to go full steam ahead in exploring other suspects and getting access to every morsel of scientific evidence. If and when Caylee's body was recovered, I could perform a second autopsy, but in the meantime, I advised him to get a top-notch criminalist on his team at once to go up against the powerful experts on the state's side and assess the evidence that Florida had against Casey. I introduced Baez to my close colleague Dr. Henry C. Lee, chief emeritus for scientific services for the state of Connecticut and founder of the Henry C. Lee Forensic Institute at the University of New Haven. While I wasn't privy to what work Henry conducted on the case, I was certain he'd be a powerful asset to Baez.

On September 19, 2008, while I was in Orlando delivering the keynote address at the annual conference of the Florida Association of Private Investigators, José and I had a lengthy patio lunch at my hotel, and I got to know him better.[47]

Born in 1969, in Puerto Rico, José Ángel Baez was raised in the Bronx, New York, and south Florida by his mother. Fluent in Spanish and Portuguese, he dropped out of high school in ninth grade, married and had a child, then earned a GED diploma and joined the navy. José spent three years assigned to the North Atlantic Treaty Organization in Norfolk, Virginia, where he held a "Cosmic Top Secret" security clearance, the highest level attainable within NATO. Later, he divorced and attended Miami-Dade Community College and Florida State University, where he was a member of Lambda Alpha Epsilon, a fraternity for criminology majors. In 1997, he graduated from Miami's St. Thomas University School of Law. He operated several different businesses and nonprofit foundations, worked for the local public defenders' office in a nonlawyer capacity, as well as for the legal information company Lexis-Nexis®, was admitted to the state bar in 2005, and opened his own law firm. A black belt in the Korean martial art tae kwon do, Baez is also competitive in karate and marksmanship.[48] His legal work has included cases involving drunk driving, drug and sex offenses, domestic violence, white-collar and Internet crimes, as well as representing clients in juvenile, state, and federal courts.[49] Prior to the Casey Anthony case, some of Baez's high-profile defense cases included former Kissimmee mayor George Gant, who had been accused of sexual battery; Elvira Garcia, who was charged with kidnapping a roommate's baby (both of these cases were dismissed); and Nilton Diaz, who was tried, found guilty, and sentenced to fifteen years in prison for the manslaughter death of Noeris Vasquez, the two-year-old granddaughter of boxing legend Wilfredo Vasquez.[50]

On September 25, Zenaida Gonzalez, the woman who filled out the rental application at the Sawgrass Apartments, filed a defamation lawsuit against Casey for blaming her for Caylee's disappearance. Although contentious depositions by George and Cindy Anthony were held on the case, a judge ruled the matter would not be dealt with until the resolution of any criminal action that Casey faced.[51] The Casey Anthony drama merited major national coverage, with each scintilla of detail discussed ad infinitum in every possible medium. HLN's Nancy Grace dubbed Anthony "Tot Mom" and opened each show with a promise of "bombshells" and "breaking news," and her colleague, Jane Velez-Mitchell, devoted endless hours to the case on her own program. Caylee's disappearance was also widely discussed by Fox News' Geraldo Rivera, whose weekend program *Geraldo at Large* featured regular reports from Kimberly Guilfoyle; by Fox's nightly program *On the Record with Greta Van Susteren*, and by ABC News' Ashleigh Banfield on *Nightline* and *Good Morning America*. These journalists are tenacious advocates for crime victims; Grace, Rivera, Guilfoyle, and Van Susteren are also lawyers. Every new piece of information on the case was dissected by their respective panels of experts, who mulled over the possibilities as sports commentators do at Olympic events. On the Internet, the number-one true-crime forum is Websleuths.com, co-owned and operated by Tricia Griffith. Since 1997, nearly forty thousand members, using aliases as screen names and from all walks of life worldwide, have posted almost seven million messages on any and all homicide and missing person cases—but little Caylee and her controversial mother Casey have merited passionate and unprecedented attention there.[52]

On October 1, 2008, Casey was officially named a suspect in her daughter's disappearance. Twelve days later, she was charged with first-degree murder, aggravated child abuse, aggravated manslaughter, and providing false information to law enforcement.[53] And on October 14, the grand jury returned an indictment against Casey Anthony, charging her with the first-degree murder of her daughter. The next day, Baez and his client appeared in court, and Casey declared her innocence. She was remanded back to jail, with no bail. In Florida, a first-degree murder can be either premeditated or committed in the course of another, underlying crime.[54] Though it would not give Casey much reason to celebrate, the child neglect charge was dropped on October 21.[55]

The next weeks would see Baez criticized for hugging his client in court, Casey's mental acuity debated, release of a defense memo asking the prosecutor for leniency, and FBI divers going into an alligator-infested swamp from which they produced a bag of toys and tiny bones, only to learn later they weren't connected with the case. There were also more Caylee sightings across the nation, with George and Cindy Anthony insisting that their only granddaughter was out there somewhere, still alive.[56]

———

The big breakthrough came on December 11, 2008, when a tiny skull was discovered less than a half mile—fifteen houses—from the Anthony home, in a swampy, overgrown area near the intersection of Suburban Drive and Chickasaw Trail. Police locked down the area and said they were "somewhat confident" that the skull was Caylee's, but forensic testing would confirm the identity. Crime scene specialists had to use machetes to clear paths through the tropical foliage, where trash and beer cans had been tossed over the years, and snakes were prevalent. It was reported that Baez tried to gain access to the area for his defense experts but was denied by Judge Stan Strickland; Baez's team would later get its chance once prosecution experts had finished their work at the scene.[57] Reports surfaced that a jailhouse video captured Casey doubling over twice, hyperventilating, and asking for a sedative when she learned that unidentified remains had been found on Suburban Drive—and that she had had no reaction when she heard a previous news story about bones being found in a park. Calling the jailhouse video "highly inflammatory," Judge Strickland ordered it sealed.[58]

Public focus quickly centered on the person who made the finding, an Orange County utility meter reader by the name of Roy Kronk, whose route included the vicinity around the Anthony home. But Kronk didn't discover the skull in December—he initially happened upon it on a muggy day four months earlier. In an interview with ABC's Robin Roberts, Kronk explained that on August 11, he and two co-workers were on Suburban Drive, trying to beat the heat under some shade trees while on a break. Kronk walked several yards into the woods to urinate and noticed a bag with something "round and white" inside—he thought it looked like a small skull, but he wasn't sure. He had heard about the Anthony case from the news but didn't know much, other than that the child was missing. When he rejoined his friends, he mentioned the white object, but then the trio became distracted by a dead six-foot-long diamondback rattlesnake that was nearby. That took over the conversation, and nothing more was said of Kronk's sighting. The workers took the snake back to their office and photographed it. At about nine-thirty that night, Kronk called 911 and reported the round, white object, but he didn't leave his name. He would later learn that a deputy went to the area but wasn't sure where to look and found nothing. When Kronk didn't hear anything in the media about a skull being located, he phoned 911 again the next night. The dispatcher told him to call the tip into the police CrimeLine phone number, and someone from that service told him to call back the next day and an officer would meet him at the site. After work on August 13, Kronk phoned the tip line from Suburban Drive and was soon joined by deputy sheriff Richard Cain. The meter reader pointed out the general area of the bag, and Cain walked toward it, getting within six feet when he slipped in the mud. Using his expandable metal baton, Cain poked at the waters but saw only garbage. When Kronk showed him the photo of the snake, Cain had had enough. Kronk felt the officer was rude and dismissive, telling Kronk he was wasting the county's time and that the area had been previously searched. As they walked back to the street, another deputy pulled up. Kronk told her the story, but she didn't investigate. Deputy logs would report that only trash was found at the site. Just over a week later, Tropical Storm Fay hit, leaving that swampland knee-deep in fetid water for the next couple months.

By December 11, the water had receded. Kronk went back to the same area to urinate and to see if the bag and white object were still there—and they were. This time he stuck his meter reader wand into what appeared to be the skull's eye socket to get a better look before gently setting it down and calling for help once more. And this time, law enforcement leapt into action. The area was cordoned off as crime scene investigators collected the child-sized skull, as well as bones, hair, teeth, and physical evidence, which were then taken to the local medical examiner's office. It would later be revealed that K-9 deputy Jason Forgey had brought his cadaver dog Gerus to Suburban Drive in July, but not to that specific site.[59] As for Deputy Cain, his superiors determined that he had failed to do a proper search of the area and had lied to them about it. He was suspended and would later submit a letter of resignation, which was accepted.[60]

The world didn't wait for an official proclamation of who the remains belonged to—everyone just assumed that Caylee's body had finally been found. And there was an additional piece of information floating around: that pieces of duct tape were attached to the skull. I began fielding calls from journalists wanting to know if I had ever heard of someone using duct tape as a murder weapon. I replied that I, along with most medical examiners, have seen cases in which a homicide victim is found with duct tape over his or her nose and mouth. In such cases, the victim has usually been restrained in some way and the tape is to keep the person quiet—but it can also prevent the victim from being able to breathe, causing death by asphyxiation. I've seen this scenario many times, but never when the victim was a child. Many reporters commented that only a monster parent could kill a child in such a way, and I couldn't dispute that. Someone wanting to end the life of a two-year-old could do so with a pillow or some other means of suffocation; the child would not put up much of a fight. But duct tape over a baby's nose and mouth? And using chloroform, too? Then putting the child in a car

trunk? If these were the facts, it was such bizarre overkill. A child accidentally left in a hot car can die within a short amount of time without
any of the other elements that seemed to have befallen Caylee Anthony,
if these remains did indeed belong to her. Television news coverage
showed images of a lively, playful Caylee, and one couldn't help but speculate what her final minutes would have been like, or the terror she must
have felt as she looked into the eyes of her killer. If everything I was
hearing turned out to be true, a chilling degree of premeditation went
into this death—and it would be very challenging for the defense team
to argue that the demise was from some sort of accident. I warned all the
journalists I spoke with that if the remains were only skeletal, we likely
wouldn't learn the cause or manner of death. And unless the killer confessed, we might never understand which mechanism—duct tape, chloroform, car trunk, or something else—came first.[61]

––––––––––

Caylee Anthony's identity was confirmed via DNA testing, and on
December 19, she was officially declared dead. Around the same time,
the state attorney's office filed papers stating they would not seek the
death penalty against Casey Anthony, who remained behind bars.[62]

Media experts smelled the makings of a defense strategy: Baez's team
might argue that Roy Kronk had more to do with this case than he was
letting on. They might ask if he was involved in putting the remains at
the site and why the cadaver dogs did not alert at the location. And, if
the remains were placed there while Casey Anthony was in jail, might
she truly be innocent, as she had been claiming all along? Any criminal
attorney looks for an opportunity to convince a jury that his or her
client is innocent and that "some other dude did it." The "SODDI
defense" might give Casey Anthony another suspect to target besides
Zenaida Fernandez-Gonzalez. While these types of questions were
favorable to the defense, the prosecution had a problem: Did police offi-

cers fail in their duties to adequately investigate this location? Florida summers are hot, the dump site is prone to flooding, and a hurricane had come through in August, so might any of those factors have had a bearing on how and when the remains were found? Insects would be collected from the site; what might their growth cycle tell scientists about how long the remains had been in that location?[63] I trusted that both the prosecution and the defense were sending out investigators to lock down as many of these open questions as possible. With a jury of twelve individuals, it only takes one to find enough reasonable doubt to refuse to convict a defendant. These variables are what make forensic medicine and law so compelling.[64]

Reporters gathering information on a major crime case don't always get their leads in a linear fashion. When authorities release new public information, it can build on what the journalists have already reported, offering tantalizing updates. This was true for WDBO Radio's Nikki Pierce in early January 2009, when she learned that in addition to the Google searches already linked to the Anthony family computer in March 2008, other keywords were typed in at approximately the same time. One search was for the hundredth episode of the popular young-adult drama *One Tree Hill*, in which a little girl is kidnapped by a nanny who intends to change the child's hair color.[65] And Yahoo!® contributor Lori Lane added that keywords including *peroxide, shovel, inhalation,* and *death* were listed at the same time as the word *chloroform* (and the misspelled version *chloraform*) were typed. According to the time stamps, only Cindy, who was at work, could be eliminated as the party who conducted the searches.[66]

On January 21, WDBO Radio reporter Drew Petrimoulx announced that newly released documents showed that the duct tape that had been placed over Caylee's mouth showed the imprint of a heart-shaped sticker. A sticker that seemed to match the imprint was found at the site. There were also reports that a child's blanket with a Winnie-the-Pooh® design was found with Caylee's remains.[67] The *Nancy Grace* show featured video from Caylee's bedroom that had been taken prior to her disappearance; a Winnie-the-Pooh theme was noticeable. [68]

On January 23, George Anthony sent several suicidal text messages and was discovered in a Daytona Beach, Florida, motel room, reportedly under the influence of medication and alcohol. A five-page note was found in his car, saying that he wanted to be with Caylee in heaven. He was briefly hospitalized, then released. As my colleague Dawna monitored news coverage, she saw some people expressing sympathy for a man who had finally reached his boiling point. Others didn't believe George had seriously attempted to harm himself but that his actions were a ploy designed to save his daughter's life, since his mental and emotional condition would surely be brought up at her trial.[69] It was later disclosed on the *Nancy Grace* show that Cindy had also contemplated suicide, preparing notes for her family to find after her death. Casey, who was home at the time, in between her jail stints, talked Cindy into staying alive.[70]

Caylee's remains were returned to her grandparents and cremated, and on February 10, 2009, a memorial was held at the First Baptist Church of Orlando. Casey had petitioned the court to allow her to leave jail briefly to attend, but the request was refused. Nearly two thousand others gathered to mourn the little child most of them had never met. Casey's parents and brother all spoke, including these comments:

CINDY ANTHONY, CAYLEE'S GRANDMOTHER: It breaks my heart that Case's not with us today to honor her child who she loved so very, very much. Casey, I hope you're able to hear me today. I love you, and I wish I could comfort you right now. I wish I could take away all of your pain and wipe away your tears. I want to thank you for giving me the greatest gift that I have ever received, and that is for Caylee Marie. Caylee was so much like you. She's got your beauty and your compassion. She had your spirit. And she will always love you. She knows that she was loved by her family, and that's

all that's important. Stay strong, my child. God will keep you
safe. And Caylee is watching over all of us.

GEORGE ANTHONY, CAYLEE'S GRANDFATHER: To hear her call
me Jo-Jo—sure, I was Grandpa, but I was Jo-Jo to her. Some
days, when I wouldn't maybe just pay attention to her for
just a second, she would get right in my face and—Jo-Jo,
Grandpa, Grandpa Jo-Jo, George. She knew me. She knew
how to push me to smile at her and hug her.

LEE ANTHONY, CAYLEE'S UNCLE: This family is united, but this
family is incomplete. I am incomplete. I'm broken. C.M.A.—
C.M.A., each day, you continue to teach me about life and
about the way it should be lived. Each day, you give me the
ability to be strong or to be weak. It's been so long since I've
been able to see you or to hug you or to tell you how much
you mean to me. C.M.A., I miss you! I love you. C.M.A., I am
so proud of you! I hope you're proud of me, too. I need you
to know that I will never forget the promise I made to you. I
will never forget.

"C.M.A." is reportedly the nickname Lee used for Casey Marie
Anthony, although Caylee Marie had the same initials. He didn't publicly explain to whom he was referring or what he meant by his pride or
his promise; some observers wondered if he was trying to send a coded
message to his sister. Casey had not requested permission to watch the
memorial service on the jail television, and whether she listened to it on
radio in her cell is unknown.[71]

In February 2009, I was in Seattle attending the annual conference for
the American Academy of Forensic Sciences, of which I am a past president and where I was making a special presentation with Drs. Henry C.
Lee and Michael M. Baden, another long-time colleague and a forensic

pathologist from New York City. Caylee Anthony's body had been recovered about two months earlier, and José Baez was at the conference. Our paths crossed, and he told me that he had beefed up his legal team with defense attorneys qualified to handle death penalty cases, a requirement in most states to ensure that a defendant facing the ultimate punishment has duly experienced counsel. Although at that time prosecutors had taken the death penalty off the table for Casey, José knew there was a chance it could be reinstated. He had also brought onboard Michael Baden's wife, Linda Kenney Baden, a prominent defense attorney. The new attorneys had their own scientific experts, including eminent forensic pathologist and author Werner U. Spitz, MD, who had conducted a second autopsy on Caylee's skeletal remains. In honesty, I told Baez his court battle was not going to be over determining cause of death, which was unknowable, but rather over whether Casey was the person who caused her daughter's demise. That would be argued by experts in disciplines other than forensic pathology. So there was not much I could do for him, except to wish him well, and I told him he could certainly call on me if he had any questions. I haven't spoken with him since. In the many months ahead, Baez's team would endure dropouts and replacements, a common occurrence in cases that go on for a long while, especially when many people are working pro bono.[72]

For some time, an awkward rumor had been circulating that Lee Anthony was Caylee's biological father instead of her uncle. But officials obtained a DNA sample from Lee through a search warrant, and the FBI lab confirmed there was no paternal link.[73] It didn't bring anyone closer to determining who *was* the girl's father; no one to date had stepped forward to claim paternity. I often pondered why there had never been a greater effort on the part of George and Cindy, if not Casey herself, to establish that biological connection, regardless of whether the

baby's father was dead or alive. Even if the Anthonys didn't hope to collect child support, shouldn't Caylee have been given the right to know
that side of her family? Once Caylee went missing, from an investigative
point of view, the Anthonys should have wanted her paternal relatives to
be checked out, if only to eliminate them as suspects. And after she was
determined to have died, wouldn't the decent thing have been to include
paternal family members in the mourning process?

The Anthony family, annoyed by having video of their jailhouse
visits with Casey given to TV stations for broadcast, stopped going to
see her, although Cindy and George were often in the courtroom when
she made appearances for legal motions.[74] Reports stated that the
Anthonys had made considerable money by licensing photos and video
footage of Caylee and their family during happier times to news organizations, including $200,000 they were paid by ABC News for an appear-
ance—and they were criticized by some for that. This is a common
dance that happens in many major cases—network news outlets, who
boast of being on higher ground by denying they pay for exclusives, get
around it by licensing images for very large sums of money, then get an
interview "for free."[75] ABC News also paid Roy Kronk $15,000 for his
appearance on *Good Morning America*, but to preserve their premise
that they didn't pay for his interview, per se, they licensed the photo of
the dead snake he and his co-workers found on Suburban Drive and
aired it during his talk with Robin Roberts.[76] (ABC has since stated that
they will no longer pay for interview footage.) This is the world we live
in, and I don't think this practice should be viewed as shocking or necessarily harmful to a case. The public demand to see these stories makes
for a competitive atmosphere, so the bidding can go sky-high. Usually,
the people in the middle of a hot case have run up major expenses and
are relieved at the chance to recoup some funds. Even before she went to
jail, Casey was a financial burden to the Anthonys, but afterward their
lives were affected at home and work by protesters, which added to their
stress. So if they made a financial windfall by selling images, the accom-

panying interviews were a bonus that allowed them to reiterate their support of their daughter and cast doubts on the tsunami of evidence that seemed to increase each day. Without the photos and video, those interviews likely would not have taken place. It wasn't just the Anthonys and Kronk who made money on the Caylee case; Internet sites sold T-shirts, buttons, bumper stickers, jewelry, magnets, key chains, a Caylee doll, and even a Casey Anthony Halloween mask. And there was an Australian production of an original play titled "Tot Mom."[77]

WFTV's Kathi Belich reported on March 10 that Casey had filed a sworn affidavit, writing: "I did not commit the crime and the state is angry that I refuse to take a plea deal." But Belich's sources said there never was a plea deal; there was only, early on, a "limited time offer for limited immunity." If Casey would lead them to the body, authorities wouldn't use her words against her, but allegedly there was no guarantee not to prosecute her. For his part, Baez stated: "If they think this is going to make her plea, they're sadly mistaken. They have no witnesses, no confession."[78] Frankly, I would hope there were overtures for a plea deal. Taxpayers, after all, are paying the bill for trials; getting justice while saving citizens money seems a worthwhile goal. But if a client turns down such an offer, a defense attorney has no choice but to go to trial.

The state filed a motion to compel José Baez to disclose how he and his team were getting paid, seeking assurance that he wasn't making deals that could be harmful to Casey in the long run, such as selling the rights to her story for a movie, which might be more lucrative with a particular resolution—and which could also be grounds for an appeal if she were convicted. But Baez balked at giving out any information, correctly stating it was no one's business how he was getting paid and adding that he had no entertainment or book deals pending.[79]

April Fools' Day of 2009 brought a report that Baez's team was deposing Kiomarie Torres Cruz, a childhood friend of Casey's who had given a statement to police with several aspects the defense needed to hear for themselves. Cruz reiterated that Casey had told her she wanted to put Caylee up for adoption to spite Cindy; Cruz even offered to adopt the child herself, but Cindy put the kibosh on that. Cruz also claimed to have never heard about any nanny named Zenaida Fernandez-Gonzalez, and—perhaps most important—Cruz said the area where Caylee's remains were found was where Casey, Kiomarie, and other girlfriends from middle school would hang out and bury their deceased pets.[80] Cruz later told the *National Enquirer* that she and Casey affixed heart stickers to the pets' wrappings before the burials.[81]

On April 13, prosecutors sent a written notification that they'd had an about-face and planned to seek the death penalty against Casey Anthony. Despite the fact that Casey had never had any arrests or negative experiences with police, authorities stated that they found her alleged crimes against Caylee to be "heinous, atrocious, and cruel." That Caylee was under the age of twelve and dependent on her mother for her well-being also factored into their decision. In the months to come, the defense filed multiple motions asking that the charges be dismissed and citing a lack of evidence tying Casey to the crime.[82]

The one-year marker of Caylee's disappearance—June 16—passed with little fanfare, except that Brad Conway, the attorney then representing George and Cindy Anthony, announced that the family still didn't know what happened to the child but continued to believe in Casey's innocence. He said they expected she would take the stand in her own defense at her trial. I don't know if that was bravado on the part of George and Cindy, or naïveté, but with the number of tall tales Casey had told, I don't think there's any way her legal team would have wanted her to go before the jury and risk being attacked by cross-examination. Legally she couldn't be compelled to testify and face self-incrimination. Jurors are instructed to not hold it against a defendant who stays silent. Nonetheless, once in a while, an accused person overrules his or her legal counsel and gambles that straight talk to the jury is worth the risk.[83]

According to the official autopsy report, which was made public on June 19, 2009, Caylee Anthony's medical examination occurred between December 11 and December 23, 2008. The reason for the prolonged examination is that, while most of the remains were recovered on December 11, investigators—including chief medical examiner of Orlando, Jan C. Garavaglia, MD—continued poring over the site for the next twelve days, finding tiny fragments of bones and pertinent evidence that had been scattered by animals or the elements over almost an acre. It was the most highly publicized recovery operation in Florida history. Even though the professionals blocked off the area with crime scene tape and tarps, national press personnel lined the streets, reporting on the activities, and tearful civilians paid their respects. People knew in their hearts that the remains would be identified as Caylee's, but it wasn't confirmed until Garavaglia made the somber announcement at a brief press conference.

Garavaglia—who performed the autopsy of Colonel Philip Shue (discussed in chapter 2)—wrote a taut report that demonstrated the mere facts she had to work with. A piece of the body's right tibia (lower leg) had been sent to the FBI's Quantico laboratory for nuclear DNA comparison and was matched to Caylee. Garavaglia determined the cause of death to be "Homicide by Undetermined Means" and included the dates when Caylee was last seen alive and when she was reported missing. The doctor listed the key experts with whom she worked on the case: Gary Lee Utz, MD, deputy chief medical examiner; John Schultz, PhD, who led the scene dispersal examination; and Michael Warren, PhD, a diplomate of the American Board of Forensic Anthropology, who worked on the osteological examination. The toxicology examination was performed by Bruce A. Goldberger, PhD, a diplomate of the American Board of Forensic Toxicologists.

The report describes the remains of a child, approximately three years of age, discovered in an overgrown wooded area and intermixed with two black plastic trash bags with yellow handles and large tears, and a tan-colored canvas laundry bag with a metal ring fastener and long canvas handles. The skeleton was disarticulated—the bones were separated from the joints—with no soft tissue and only a minimal amount of adipocere—the waxy by-product of decomposition—on several bones. The skeleton showed no evidence of antemortem trauma or damage prior to death, such as from a fracture.

The skull, which had been inside the three bags, was wrapped with several overlapping pieces of duct tape, around the anterior portion of the lower skull, keeping the mandible (lower jaw) and a portion of the maxilla (upper jaw) in place. Garavaglia wrote that the duct tape was "clearly placed prior to decomposition." She also stated her view that the remains had been placed at the site soon after Caylee was last seen alive, noting roots from the area's foliage that were wrapped around some bones and growing into the canvas bag. The bags had no odor of cadaverine. Vertebrae clusters outside the bags indicated animal activity after decomposition started, but before complete disarticulation, indicating that "the body was put in the location prior to complete skeletonization." Also collected were sandy dirt, insects, pupae, silverfish, and spiders by renowned forensic entomologist Neal Haskell, PhD. In a trial where post-mortem interval would become a critical issue, Garavaglia and her team were taking a stand.

Garavaglia detailed a day-by-day recovery of body parts. Each item collected would be brought back to the lab, where experts would lay them out as if they were working a jigsaw puzzle. An ulna and radius (forearm bones), fibula (lower leg bone), scapula (shoulder blade), two iliums (pelvis bones), two clavicles (shoulder bones), a piece of pubic bone, and numerous vertebrae, ribs, hand bones, and fragments were accounted for. Missing were small bones of the wrists and hands, fingers, ankle, hyoid (U-shaped cartilage at the base of the tongue), and a patella (knee cap). Nearly all teeth were recovered, either from the jaw structure and cranial cavity, or from the ground; only one incisor was never found.

Adhered to the tape were medium-brown scalp hairs, swatches of which were sent to the FBI laboratory for toxicology testing, along with the left femur (thigh bone) and soil from the hair mat and saline washing of the cranial cavity.[84] The report on the conclusions of the hair mass, written by forensic examiner Madeline A. Montgomery of the Quantico chemistry unit, was dated March 13, 2009, and showed a negative reading for the presence of the following medications: alprazolam (generic name of Xanax), clonazepam (Klonopin®), flunitrazepam (Rohypnol®), diazepam (Valium®), ketamine, lorazepam (Ativan®), mida-zolam (Versed), nordiazepam (Valium metabolite), oxazepam (Serax®), triazolam (Halcion®), temazepam (Restoril®). Montgomery's unit did not address the chloroform, which was tested in another unit of the lab.[85]

Inside the three bags was a baby blanket with the faded image of Piglet riding on the back of Winnie-the-Pooh. Multiple roots were woven into the fabric. Material likely from a pull-up-style diaper was also present, rec-tangular and purplish. A multicolored pair of cotton toddler shorts, with an elastic waistband and four empty pockets, was also collected.

Scattered amid the vegetative debris were four sets of glittery pink letters. The letters "B," "I," and "G" were about two inches in height. Slightly smaller were letters that spelled out "T-R-O-U-B-L-E." Less than an inch tall was a hunk of connected letters spelling "COMES," with a similar hunk nearby that spelled "SMALL." A garment tag with pink stitching stated: "3 Toddler, 100% cotton, Made in El Salvador."[86] In a publicly released memo to the FBI evidence analyst, lead detective Yuri Melich wrote: "It would be pretty awesome to have a photo of what the shirt used to look like." He got his wish when the *Globe* tabloid later published a photo of the lettering booked into evidence, and another one of Caylee smiling broadly and wearing a pink T-shirt with decal let-ters that spelled "BIG TROUBLE COMES IN SMALL PACKAGES" in a photo snapped by Casey's ex-boyfriend, Ricardo Morales. Docu-ments released later listed dozens of other *Globe* stories that Melich found significant. In separate police interviews, which were released online, George and Cindy Anthony denied knowing anything about the distinctive pink T-shirt, even though the little girl had lived with them, and Cindy did all of her laundry.[87]

Casey's defense team fired off some grenades at the prosecutor's alleged "rush to judgment" against Anthony and close-mindedness toward other possible suspects, citing several deficiencies with the state's evidence. And they were supported, somewhat, by documents made public that revealed that when the duct tape was sent to the FBI lab, no fingerprints were found, but female DNA not belonging to Casey, Caylee, or Cindy Anthony was left behind on the tape. When workers in the lab were tested to have their DNA compared to find the source, the results were linked to a questioned document examiner. It has not yet been disclosed how the contamination happened—it could have occurred when an eyelash or skin cell fell onto the sample—but it's the kind of blunder that makes one wonder why a document examiner would ever be allowed to handle physical evidence outside her area of expertise. Also, the outline of the heart-shaped sticker found on the duct tape had been covered over by the powder used in the fingerprint tests.

WFTV's Kathi Belich explained that another duct tape battle would be fought over whether the tape over Caylee's mouth is "microscopically similar" to tape found on one of the gas cans from the Anthony family storage shed and on "Missing Caylee" posters the family put up around town. The impact of months of outdoor exposure and extreme weather conditions on the skull's duct tape would be evaluated by experts on both sides, no doubt. Belich's news crew looked at old footage of the posters and saw a distinct black oval logo from Henkel, the tape manufacturer, that matched those on the Anthonys' gas can. The specific Henkel product had been off the market for years; it was so rare that less than 1 percent of all national duct tape sales between 2002 and 2007 were from that product. FBI documents indicated that the

Henkel logo was also found on the tape stretched across Caylee's mouth, and there are photos that support their claim. (Forensic matches can often be made between plastic garbage bags found at a recovery site and those found in a suspect's home, comparing striations and batch numbers. That didn't happen here, likely because too much time had passed between when Caylee went missing and when her body was found; families tend to go through boxes of plastic bags with regularity. A match with any plastic bags collected from the Anthony home would have been mentioned in a criminalist report.)

But one of the newly released documents gave the defense a tough challenge. The carpet of Casey's car trunk was stained with what arguably could have been a silhouette of a child in the fetal position, which the FBI believed signified where Caylee had lain while decomposing. If shown in court, these photos would surely remind observers of the grisly death that child suffered as her mother reportedly drove around in the car, looking for fun.[88]

New documents from the FBI showed a plastic Gatorade® "Cool Blue" sports drink bottle that was also collected near the scene where Caylee's remains were discovered. Inside the bottle was a plastic bag labeled "Disposable Syringe Kit" and a syringe, and chemical tests showed the presence of chloroform, testosterone, ethanol, and water.[89] Since there was no flesh on Caylee's remains, her autopsy would have shown no possible injection site, although testing on the needle for skin cells or blood might reveal whether she had been injected. These items, if linked to Caylee, would certainly boost the argument that there was premeditated intent on the part of whoever killed her.

With Casey still in jail, drama roiled in the case. Baez told the court that his client was indigent and the judge approved funds for the defense; George and Cindy both got tattoos of their granddaughter's face; and

Cindy wrote her daughter in lockup, saying that she looked forward to being reunited with both Casey and Caylee—who she stated was still alive—when the trial was over.[90] And a woman named Krystal Holloway—who also uses the pseudonym River Cruz—gave a number of interviews insisting that she had been George Anthony's mistress. She claimed she met him when she volunteered on a search team. They became friends, then had sex at her condo on multiple occasions. Detectives found out about her when they found text messages on George's cell phone to and from her, including one that said: "I need you in my life." Holloway told investigators that in November 2008, George confided to her that Caylee's death was "an accident that snowballed out of control."[91]

In mid April 2010, a scandal broke involving Internet blogger David L. Knechel, an Orlando-based writer, graphic artist, and barbecue aficionado, whose website is called MarinadeDave.com. Intrigued by the Anthony case, Knechel began attending many of the court hearings and writing about them on his blog, attracting about a hundred thousand visitors per month. According to one of Knechel's posts, Judge Stan Strickland recognized the blogger in the courtroom, telling him, "I must say that you have the best website regarding this case. You investigate and are very fair to everyone." Knechel would later tell a reporter that he didn't feel the conversation created any judicial bias.[92] But Baez's team filed a motion calling Strickland a "self-aggrandizing media hound," which the judge vehemently denied, firing back with "the irony was rich." Nonetheless, Strickland recused himself from the case and was replaced by the presiding chief judge of the ninth judicial circuit, Belvin Perry Jr., whose reputation showed he had scant patience with shenanigans in his courtroom. One of Judge Perry's first rulings was to deny a defense motion that tried to prevent George and Cindy's comments about the death smell in the car from being admissible at trial. Perry said jurors would hear those statements and could weigh their value.[93]

Controversies brewed over various letters that, due to Florida's Sunshine law, were released to the public and can be found online. In one, dated July 22, 2009, a Florida inmate named Jerry L. Jackson, wrote to "whom ever [*sic*] is representing Ms. Anthony," stating that the person responsible for Caylee's death is not Casey but her boyfriend, who had a history of child molestations and bragged of "how he did the little girl and how her mother got stuck with the charge." The boyfriend wasn't named in the letter, but Jackson said that he would furnish the name provided he was contacted within the next three weeks.[94] In another letter, dated June 8, 2010, a Michigan inmate named Curtis Jackson wrote to lead prosecutor Linda Drane Burdick, stating that he and Casey had been pen pals in early 2008. Jackson claimed that Anthony was fascinated with his criminal convictions, asked if he had ever killed anyone, wondered what he would do to get rid of a child he didn't want, and asked whether he knew anyone who could be paid to kill someone. Casey wrote that she felt too young to have a child, Jackson said, and asked his advice about how to properly dispose of a body, and whether he could recommend poisons that were untraceable. Jackson did not include the purported letters in his communication with the prosecutor, nor did he say if he could produce them, but he offered to testify against Casey—provided the state attorney put in a good recommendation at his next parole hearing. The files do not indicate whether either letter received a response.[95]

Casey's own jailhouse missives, also publicly released, showed a potential disconnect from reality. While segregated from the other inmates, she was able to communicate with a convicted drug dealer and mother of two named Robyn Adams by hiding letters in a book they would pass back and forth. Casey referred to herself as "Muffin," and called Adams "Cookie" and "Sister," and frequently made religious references, suggesting that she and Adams should get a recreational vehicle so they could preach the word of God in Costa Rica. Writing that she was "a GREAT Mom!" Casey expressed remorse that she couldn't protect her daughter better but stated: "In a lot of ways, I'm content by the fact that she will never have to have her heart broken or see the constant negativity that our society breeds, nor will she ever be abused or taken advantage of. The clock is ticking and the end of days is near. I can feel it." Anthony also wrote to Adams and another inmate named Maya Derkovic that she had sometimes used chloroform to help Caylee sleep so that she could go out. In a letter to Adams, Casey complained about the men who wrote to her, calling her "hot" and "sexy," then asked: "Is this what 'celebrities' have to deal with?" Casey's letters included claims that her brother, Lee, and their father, George, both molested her. One passage included: "My own brother walking into my room at night and feeling my breasts while I slept." Police confirmed Casey told another inmate that she had had "sexual intercourse" with her brother over a three-year period, beginning when she was twelve. Another passage to Adams stated: "I think my Dad used to do the same thing to me, but when I was much younger." When the unsettling disclosures hit the media, Casey's relatives released this statement: "The Anthony family denies that there was any improper sexual behavior in their family, nor was there ever a time when Casey told them of sexually inappropriate conduct by her brother or father." After jailers found the letters, Adams was moved to a federal prison to serve out the remainder of her ten-year sentence.[96]

José Baez and his co-counsel, Andrea Lyon, appeared on the *Today* show to announce they had taken a sworn deposition from someone who believed that meter reader Roy Kronk might be Caylee's killer. In a video clip they aired, Kronk's former wife, Jill Kerley, stated: "The more I think about it, the more my gut's telling me he had something to do with it." Kerley described an occasion during their four-and-a-half-month-long marriage when Kronk allegedly restrained her. "He duct-taped my hands one time," she said, adding, "I was sitting in a chair and he told me if I moved that he would beat me and he would know if I moved." Baez told anchor Matt Lauer that Kronk had "a possible history of inappropriate behavior with young girls, a history of abusing, restraining, and holding women against their will, and had, in the past, used duct tape to restrain women against their will." While Baez maintained he wasn't saying that Kronk killed Caylee, he felt police should have investigated the utility worker to a greater degree. Asked for comment, Kronk answered: "I haven't done anything wrong, so I don't have a reason to be fearful or troubled by any of this." And Kronk's attorney, David Evans, asserted that his client "has become a witness and become a victim. They just dumped a big pot of mud on his head and said, 'Look at this guy.' Having mud dumped on your head when all you did is find a young girl's remains is pretty hard for him to take."[97]

In an interview with Jane Velez-Mitchell, Baez stated that his team was reviewing more than twenty-three thousand documents and over three hundred hours of audio and video, and that "[e]very alphabet of law enforcement has taken part in this case."[98] My old friend Geraldo Rivera pulled no punches on the "40th anniversary of his career" show when he called Casey a "selfish, self-involved dimwit" and "clearly guilty," but he said that prosecutors seeking to execute her were "more concerned with scoring cheap political points than attaining justice. It's an absurd overprosecution." Rivera also pointed out that the death sentence might be more likely to put the state's case in jeopardy and cause jurors to acquit her than if there was a more realistic sentence on the table. He felt a more fitting punishment for a child murder would be "fifteen or twenty years," less time already served.[99]

The State of Florida vs. Casey Marie Anthony—officially logged as Case Number 48-2008-CF-015606-O—got under way in Orange County's ninth judicial circuit courthouse in the spring of 2011. In April, Judge Perry made a number of important rulings: deemed admissible to be heard by jurors would be the MySpace messages of Cindy and Casey Anthony, Casey's history of lying and stealing, Casey's comments to law enforcement before she obtained counsel, and some details of her sexual history. Annoyed by squabbling between prosecution and defense members, Perry announced that any future outbursts would cost that particular lawyer one hundred dollars, to be donated to the United Way charity at the end of the trial. Perry reviewed a request by Michigan inmate Curtis Jackson to remove Baez as Anthony's counsel. Jackson claimed he wrote the request on Casey's behalf since she was "not competent" to file it herself, but Perry decided Jackson lacked status to be involved with the case. On the forensic front, the judge allowed the jury to learn about the stain on the car trunk liner, the residue from the heart-shaped sticker on the duct tape that was found on Caylee's skull, the alerts by the cadaver dogs, the hair found in the trunk that appeared to have post-mortem banding, the chloroform levels in Casey's car trunk, and the keyword searches on the family computer.[100]

Judge Belvin Perry received undergraduate degrees from Alabama's Tuskegee University and earned his Juris Doctor from the Thurgood Marshall School of Law at Texas Southern University in 1977.[101] A member of the bar in both Texas and Florida, Perry worked his way up the ladder as a prosecutor, having a 100 percent conviction rate on his numerous death penalty cases. His most infamous capital case was that of the "Black Widow," in which Judi Buenoano—the first woman put to death by the state of Florida in 150 years—was convicted in 1985 for fatally poisoning her husband, a boyfriend, and her paralyzed adult son who had been poisoned and drowned. When Buenoano went to the electric chair in 1998, Perry, by then a judge, attended the execution. Perry has been the chief judge of the ninth judicial circuit since 1995, with a two-year stint as an Orange County civil judge between 1999 and 2001.[102]

The Anthony trial's lead prosecutor was Linda Drane Burdick, assisted by Jeff Ashton and Frank George. Ashton was the forensics expert on the team; he was the first prosecutor in the nation to use DNA in a criminal trial and would now be the first to argue decompositional odor.[103] Casey's defense team consisted of lead attorney Baez, assisted by Cheney Mason, Dorothy Clay Sims, Charles Greene, and, in the event of a conviction, Ann Finnell, a death penalty specialist.[104]

If convicted and sentenced to death, Casey Anthony—or, as she was known in Florida, Inmate #08049710—would have the option to face death by lethal injection or electrocution.[105] Currently, there are four females on death row. Tiffany Cole was sentenced to death for the 2005 double murder of a Jacksonville couple who were duct-taped, put in a car trunk, driven out of state, and then buried alive. Emilia L. Carr received the death sentence for the 2009 kidnapping and murder of her boyfriend's ex-wife; Carr and her lover lured the woman into a trailer, duct-taped her to a chair, and suffocated her with a plastic bag. Margaret A. Allen faces execution for the 2005 torture and strangulation murder of her housekeeper, who Allen believed stole money from her. And Ana Maria Cardona is on death row for the 1990 beating death of her three-year-old son, whose body was dumped in the woods.[106]

There could be little doubt that, on the cusp of her criminal trial, Casey Anthony was the most hated woman in America. Protests were still taking place around Orlando, and the Internet was ablaze with negative postings about her, declaring her guilty before she had her day in court. I have performed autopsies and assisted on many cases in which an unlikeable person is tried and convicted for a homicide—even death penalty cases—and I'm professionally comfortable dealing with someone vilified by the public. That's how the system works; the science is the science, and if my opinion happens to help to put away a remorseless murderer, at least that person's conviction likely won't be overturned for lack of adequate counsel. So I supported Baez in his attempt to give Anthony the best possible defense. I also can't criticize any work done by Florida or federal authorities, and I looked forward to seeing how the forensic evidence—particularly the unique presentations—would play before a jury.[107]

There was a preview of things to come on April 16, when attorney

Linda Kenney Baden appeared on the CBS News show *48 Hours Mystery*. Although she had formally left the case seven months before, she had continued making various TV appearances to give a general sense of how Casey's defense might react to new rulings and expected testimony—but what she said to CBS's reporter Troy Roberts was a game changer. Followers of the case were expecting that the defense was going to pin the crime on Zenaida Fernandez-Gonzalez, the nanny Casey told cops had kidnapped Caylee. Detectives, of course, maintained there was no such nanny, and a woman with that name (sans the "Fernandez") was suing Casey, claiming that she had never met the defendant who spotted her name on a rental application and manufactured a story. Kenney Baden boldly stated to Roberts that the "Zanny the Nanny" excuse was, indeed, a fabrication. "Everyone knows that was a lie. . . . Because of who she is, because of her upbringing, because of how she was treated, she lies. But being a liar does not make you a murderer." José Baez, on the same program, refused to tip his hand about defense strategies—including a prevalent rumor that George Anthony would be targeted for blame—saying it would all be explained in his opening statement.[108] I didn't see the broadcast, but the next day my co-author, Dawna Kaufmann, called me to discuss it. Dawna had been closely following and regularly writing about the case for *Globe* magazine. She asserted that it seemed as if Casey's team was not going to try the case the way the defendant might have wanted them to, and since it was a death penalty case and she was so roundly despised, perhaps a decision was made to save Casey's life the way the lawyers saw fit. For Kenney Baden—an officer of the court, whether or not she was still an active defense team member—undercutting the "Zanny" avenue would have required her to have permission from Baez and probably the Anthony family. It was a most curious development that neither Dawna nor I had ever seen played out in a case before. We'd learn soon enough if that theory was correct.[109]

    In order to seat a jury that hadn't been subjected to months of news saturation about the case, Judge Perry decided to hold voir dire, or jury selection, in Clearwater, Florida, in Pinellas County, about one hundred miles southwest of Orlando. That process began on May 9 and lasted eleven days. During pre-screening, the judge explained to each citizen that this was a capital case, and, while a conviction of Casey Anthony wouldn't automatically result in the death penalty, any juror chosen would have to accept that she could get that ultimate sentence if the jury entered into the second phase of determining her punishment. Once the twelve jurors and five alternates were seated, they were bused to Orlando and sequestered at the Rosen Shingle Creek Hotel until the trial was complete. The panel of twelve was composed of seven women and five men, and included two retired nurses and a nursing student, three communications workers, and two chefs, among other occupations. Most were married or divorced, and half of the jurors had children. Three men and two women were seated as alternates; they would hear all the testimony but wouldn't be able to deliberate on a verdict unless any of the panel of twelve had to be replaced. The judge estimated that the trial would last six to eight weeks, and to speed things up, Saturday sessions would be necessary.[110] Jurors would be paid thirty dollars each day, including weekends, for their service, with an additional fourteen dollars in quarters per week for the hotel's laundry facilities. Meals would be furnished, sometimes at local restaurants; phone calls, Internet use, television, and reading materials would be monitored by sheriff's deputies. Sundays would be set aside for family visits, if relatives cared to travel to Orlando.[111] To protect their identities, Perry ordered that their names would not be released until October 2011; after the trial, if a juror cared to speak publicly, he or she could individually decide whether to provide a name.[112]

The press corps was out in full force for the Anthony trial. Attending some, if not all, of the proceedings were national figures including Nancy Grace, Jane Velez-Mitchell, Jean Casarez, Beth Karas, Geraldo Rivera, Greta Van Susteren, Ashleigh Banfield, and Diane Dimond of thedaily beast.com, as well as local print, television, and radio journalists—among them blogger "Marinade Dave" Knechel, who covered the case for

Orlando magazine. Gavel-to-gavel coverage was aired on TruTV's *In Session*, HLN, local television and radio, and the Internet. Enterprising case fanatics on Websleuths.com not only gathered to talk about the trial in real time; some volunteered to do rough transcripts of the testimony, the notes of which can be found on the site. Civilian spectators lined up starting at 2 a.m. for the fifty courtroom seats set aside for the public, with occasional fisticuffs occurring when rogue individuals tried to cut in line. Many reporters compared the frenzy to the 1995 double-homicide trial of football legend O. J. Simpson, suggesting that Casey Anthony's was "the trial of *this* century."[113]

The role of the prosecution and defense differs in a criminal trial. The burden of proof is on the part of prosecutors, who must convince jurors beyond a reasonable doubt that the defendant committed the crime he or she is charged with. If that standard is met, the jury will continue on to the sentencing phase; only then is the panel allowed to consider the appropriate punishment for the defendant. It is not necessary for the state to show motive for the crime, although juries—made of twelve peers of the defendant and invested in the process—naturally like to learn the reason, if possible. The defense's job is to prevent the client from going to prison or death row by mitigating the defendant's responsibility in the crime. Defense counsel must impress upon each juror that he or she is to keep an open mind regarding the fact that someone besides the person on trial could have committed the deed. The defense doesn't need to "prove" anything; they just need to cast doubt on the prosecution's claims. Both sides call witnesses to testify under oath, produce evidence in the form of numbered exhibits that are projected on a big screen to the courtroom (and broadcast, if the imagery isn't too graphic), and attempt to poke holes in their opponent's arguments. In case they wish to chronicle the testimony, jurors are given pens and notebooks. After the trial is over, the notebooks are collected and destroyed, lest any of the jurors want to use the fruit of their labors for a book. (Jurors can write books, of course; they just can't use their trial notes as research.) Witnesses called by one side or the other give testimony, then opposing counsel asks them rebuttal questions; sur-rebuttal questions are allowed to counter rebuttal testimony as long as they hew to only the issues being discussed. The judge reminds jurors that the defendant has a Fifth Amendment right not to testify or to be a witness against himself or herself, and that no guilt should be inferred if that right is invoked. Then jurors—who have heretofore not been allowed to talk about the case to each other—go into a conference area outside the courtroom and take as long as they need to deliberate and find a verdict they can all agree on. They can ask the judge for a read-back of testimony or clarification of terms, and they can inspect exhibits. Failure by the jurors to arrive at a verdict will produce a mistrial, resulting in the state likely re-filing the same or lesser charges and re-trying the case before another jury. It's the American way, and it's a pretty great system.

A criminal trial begins with opening statements, during which each side lays out a road map of what it intends to prove. The prosecution begins, the defense comes next, and then prosecutors—having that burden of proof—get one last turn. (The same process occurs during closing arguments at the end of the trial.) Opening statements are not considered evidence, and claims made during such statements are expected to be elaborated on during trial. It's fair to say that in a case that was already teeming with emotion and controversy, José Baez's opening statement left jaws agape.[114]

Casey Anthony's homicide trial began in the twenty-third-floor court-room of the Orange County Courthouse on Tuesday, May 24, 2011. Linda Drane Burdick told jurors in no uncertain terms why they were there: Caylee Marie Anthony had been brutally murdered by her mother, the defendant, but jurors would be able to serve as the dead child's voice as she cries for justice. With a steady demeanor, the lead prosecutor gave a timeline of the crime and its aftermath. She delivered a capsule version of Casey's many lies; when she spoke of the imaginary Zanny the Nanny, Casey could be seen shaking her head as if to say, "She's not imaginary." Finally, Drane Burdick played the last video of Caylee, in which she was smiling and singing on Father's Day with her great-grandpa. She then juxtaposed the video image with an extreme close-up photo of Caylee's denuded skull. "This is the last picture ever taken of Caylee Anthony—on December 11, 2008," Drane Burdick whispered. Jurors sat spellbound; Casey Anthony sobbed. After lunch, Casey fixed her long brown ponytail into a demure bun, which she would continue to wear through most of the trial.

José Baez's opening statement began: "This is not a case of first-degree murder. On June 15, 2008, Caylee Marie Anthony died in the family swimming pool." He added that drowning deaths are the leading cause of death of children in Florida. It was an accident, he stated, abandoning the "Zanny the Nanny" canard, as his former co-counsel Linda Kenney Baden had hinted he would. Then he tackled why Casey was such a liar and why she waited thirty-one days to tell anyone her daughter was missing without mentioning that she was dead. Caylee's death caused Casey to hide her pain and retreat into a "dark corner" to escape her ugly life and dysfunctional family, he explained. She was warped by a lifetime of childhood sexual abuse, first by her father when she was eight, and then by her brother as a preteen. "She was taught to keep the secret and to lie," Baez stated dramatically. "At 13, she'd have her father's penis in her mouth and then go to school and play as if nothing was wrong." Baez's scenario of events had George Anthony finding Caylee's dead body in the pool, yelling at Casey that her mother would "never forgive" her and that Casey would wind up in jail for the rest of her life for child neglect. Baez next smeared Roy Kronk, who he claimed was "morally bankrupt" and wanted the $250,000 cash reward in the case, sketchily suggesting that the meter reader somehow obtained and kept Caylee's corpse until disposing of it in December 2008 and "finding" it.[115] How the lawyer intended to prove those claims was the subject of much media discourse. The only sources for Casey's sexual abuse claims would be friends that she told or wrote to, which would make the comments "hearsay" and therefore inadmissible. The sole option for supporting the abuse would be to have George and/or Lee admit it under oath, which didn't seem likely, or for Casey herself to take the stand and tell what happened. But if she took the stand, she'd also be questioned about every action she took since the beginning of the crime and beyond, and that would definitely open doors she might not want opened. We would find out much later that Baez's statement shocked Drane Burdick, who, savoring the chance of grilling Anthony on the stand, spent considerable time readying for that possibility.[116]

Judge Perry granted special permission to allow George and Cindy to sit in the courtroom, even though they were to be witnesses who usually have to remain outside. But they would not be able to say anything or even wave at their daughter; the Anthonys had not had an actual conversation with Casey since October 2008.[117] Two broadcast cameras were in the courtroom. One would cut between whoever was speaking—the lawyers, the judge, or the witnesses—while another captured reaction shots of Casey or panned into the spectators to show the often anguished faces of George and Cindy. Images of the jury were never broadcast during the trial or as the panel entered or left the courtroom.[118]

The prosecution's first witness was George Anthony, who testified about the last time he saw his granddaughter. Although he might be considered a "hostile witness" whose testimony could convict his only daughter for the murder of his only grandchild, he presented himself professionally. The next witnesses were a succession of friends who had known Casey and didn't hear from her that anything was amiss during the thirty-one days before Caylee was reported missing. Many of them talked about the partying they engaged in with her during that time, and some spoke of their victimization by Casey, who stole money from them. Most of them were told by Casey that she worked at Universal as an event planner and that she had a nanny who took care of Caylee when the girl wasn't with her. On cross-examination, Baez scored points when he got several of Casey's pals to admit she was a "good mother" who seemed devoted to her daughter and never lost her temper with the toddler. He also got a former girlfriend of one of Tony Lazzaro's roommates to acknowledge that, shortly after the time we now know Caylee was last seen, she rode around in the backseat of Casey's Pontiac Sunfire and didn't smell any bad odor. The same woman testified that Casey told her George and Cindy would be moving out of their home in the near future and would give it to her and Caylee.

The Anthony's next-door neighbor testified about seeing Casey's car pulled up backward to her garage door and that he loaned her a shovel— but conceded that when she returned the tool she didn't seem sweaty or dirty. Casey's last boyfriend, Tony Lazzaro, testified that he and the defendant had dated for only a few weeks but were falling in love, and that he planned to move back to his home state of New York when he finished school. Lazzaro said that while he didn't see that much of Caylee at his apartment, he noted that she could count to forty in Spanish, which she learned from the TV series *Dora the Explorer*. Lazzaro also didn't smell anything foul in the car trunk when he and Casey got the gas cans from the Anthony shed, but it was Casey who put the cans in the trunk; he was a few feet away. Casey's previous boyfriend, Ricardo Morales, testified that during the three-month period when they dated, beginning in February 2008, Casey would bring Caylee over and they would all sleep in his bed. Morales admitted making $4,000 from *Globe* magazine for photos he took of Casey and Caylee, including one showing the child wearing the pink T-shirt and another showing Caylee with a bruised eye. Before that photo was displayed, Judge Perry had both sides stipulate that Caylee's eye had not been injured by her mother. Morales also stated that on his web page was a "joke" photo that Casey might have seen. It showed a man hugging a woman from behind with a rag in his hand and the caption "Win her over with chloroform."[119] At the end of that court session, many observers wondered if the photo was what put the idea of chloroform in Casey's mind, causing her to do the Google searches in March of that year—assuming she was the person who performed those searches. Morales said he never searched for *chloroform* on the Anthony family computer.[120]

The district manager of the Amscot business testified about calling police regarding the abandoned Sunfire in her parking lot. She noticed a foul smell around it but assumed the smell came from a nearby Dumpster. Simon Birch of Johnson's Wrecker impound yard spoke of accompanying George Anthony to the Sunfire and smelling the unmistakable stench of human decomposition in the trunk. Despite the fact that George had told him Casey was a liar and that Caylee was missing, Birch said he didn't feel compelled to call police and report the conversation. George Anthony took the stand again to describe finding the toolshed broken and his gas cans missing, and how when he tried to get them back from Casey's car trunk, she blocked him and got them herself, snarling, "Here's your fucking gas cans."[121] George described the panic he felt when the Sunfire trunk was opened and he smelled the strong odor. "Please God, don't let this be Casey or Caylee," he prayed. But, like Birch, he didn't call police with his suspicions.[122]

Linda Drane Burdick gently questioned Cindy Anthony about her MySpace post and her futile pleas to get Casey to tell her where Caylee was. Cindy admitted feeling betrayed by her daughter's distance but accepted that Casey was trying to forge her own way in the world. Casey had also told her she was hooking up with a former boyfriend who was wealthy and had a child Caylee's age; Cindy didn't know that was all a lie. When Cindy's three 911 calls were played for the jury, she collapsed in tears on the stand—but she explained that she told the dispatcher "It smells like there's been a dead body in the damn car" only to get officers to respond more quickly. During cross-examination, Cindy didn't want to make eye contact with Baez but called Casey a "very loving, very caring mother." Baez got Cindy to reaffirm that she had been unaware of Casey's pregnancy and that she wasn't sure who the biological father was and had never tried to find out. He also took her through a number of people who Casey said existed but didn't, including Zanny the Nanny, Zanny's sister and mother, and friends of Casey's, supposedly from her job at Universal. Before the summer of 2008, Cindy said, she never had a reason to not trust what her daughter told her.

Lee Anthony testified about how he and his fiancée went to various nightclubs to look for Casey during the time she was missing from the family, hoping that she would tell him what was going on—but she wouldn't. On the night of July 16, when Casey was brought to the home, he observed his sister and mother arguing. He took Casey aside and asked why she wasn't cooperating, and Casey told him, "Maybe I'm a spiteful bitch." Soon she would mention that the nanny had taken Caylee; Lee had never heard of Casey having a nanny. It was his first realization that the child had been missing for thirty-one days.

The Orlando sheriff's officers who responded to the 911 calls testified about statements and behavior they witnessed at the home and at the Sawgrass Apartments when they took Casey there to find Zenaida Fernandez-Gonzalez. Detective Yuri Melich became the lead investigator at 3:53 a.m. on the morning of July 16, after being briefed by officers at the Anthony home. Audio from his questioning of Casey was played for the jury. On cross-examination, Baez asked Melich if he ever used the name "DickTracyOrlando." Prosecutor Jeff Ashton protested, the jury was removed from the courtroom, and questioning continued. Melich explained that while he was laid up with a broken leg, he had gone online at Websleuths.com and signed up under that screen name. He posted once under a Caylee discussion thread, not identifying himself as anyone connected with the case. His post read: "A true missing persons investigation is akin to a homicide investigation without a body." Baez claimed that the comment was proof that Melich believed Caylee had been murdered rather than dead as the result of an accident, and that it showed he was biased. Melich said that in the initial hours of his involvement in the case, he viewed Caylee as having been abducted and Casey as the mother of a missing toddler. And Ashton argued that Baez had not yet offered information to sustain an accidental death scenario, so Judge Perry ruled in the prosecution's favor. Baez dropped the matter, and the jury never learned about the posting.[123] What the posting is proof of, however, is the modern interest in Internet crime forums, not only on the part of civilians but also for law enforcement and defense counsel. It seems that everybody goes online to measure the pulse of a case.[124]

The jailhouse videos of meetings between Casey and members of her family were played for jurors and broadcast, although fans of the HLN crime shows could repeat them verbatim, having seen them so many times. In one, Casey told her family more details about Zenaida Fernandez-Gonzalez's appearance and warned that the Anthonys might be in jeopardy from the kidnapper. And in others, Casey fluctuated between giving her family hope that the child would be returned—"I know in my heart she's not far"—and shrieking and cursing at her parents for not believing her when she said she didn't know where Caylee was. Casey was also seemingly jealous of the media attention the Anthonys were getting and suggested that the funds being raised as a reward should be cashed in to spring Casey from jail, to allow her to look for her daughter. One video featured Casey speaking to George about what a wonderful father he was.

Melich took the stand again to describe the walk he took when Casey marched him across the lot at Universal, only to admit she didn't work there. When Baez asked why detectives didn't take more seriously the idea that Caylee might have drowned—since the ladder was up and near the pool—Melich explained that the notion was scoffed at by Casey, who insisted Zenaida kidnapped Caylee. A succession of crime scene technicians followed, informing jurors how they collect and process evidence, including the car trunk trash, clothing, hair, and buccal swabs (used inside the mouth) for DNA testing. Gerardo Bloise testified about processing the Sunfire and described his familiarity with the scent of human decomposition, something he had smelled "thirty-five to forty times" throughout his long career. In subsequent testimony, Bloise listed the items found in the trash bag in Casey's car: soft drink cans and bottles, napkins and food wrappers, an empty box of cigarettes, a broken plastic coat hanger, a receipt from Fusion Ultra Lounge, a flyer from an online media education university, and an empty pizza box. There was no food or organic material.

FBI forensic scientist Karen Lowe testified that a single hair found in the car trunk was microscopically similar to Caylee's and not to Casey's, and that it had a black band on it consistent with being from a deceased person. A sheriff's deputy testified about observing a stain on the car trunk liner and taking air samples from the trunk that he then sent to Dr. Vass at the Body Farm. Vass was next, explaining his credentials and the pioneering work he established at the research facility. Using a graph, he stated that the levels of chloroform in the air sample were "shocking high"—higher than anything he had experienced in his twenty years of doing this work. Vass added that it was one thousand times greater than what he'd expect in a decomposition case. And when he opened a can that contained air from the trunk, the stench was so powerful, he jumped backward. Nothing other than a dead and decomposing human body could have given off that odor, he testified.[125] Several of the TV reporters in the courtroom would later comment that very few of the jurors took notes during the prosecution's case, and only slightly more did so during the defense's, but Vass's science lesson seemed to get them writing in their notebooks.[126]

A forensic chemist from the FBI testified that he examined the car trunk liner and found high levels of chloroform, which was especially surprising to him since the box in which the material was shipped to him had not been sealed adequately and some of the compound would have dissipated. However, he had to agree with Baez's statement on cross-examination that chloroform can be found in certain household products like detergent.

Jason Forgey, Gerus's trainer, testified how his German shepherd could distinguish between the smell of a human cadaver and that of a dead animal, a ham bone, garbage, and pizza. Gerus, who also had training experience with a faux drowning victim, had 187 successful finds, only a few misses, and one false alert. He has since been retired due to a degenerative spinal condition. Kristen Brewer, Bones's trainer, echoed Forgey's testimony about where in the Anthony's backyard her dog alerted—by the playhouse, not the pool.

Sandra Osborne testified about finding deleted spaces on the Anthony's desktop computer; she had the technical ability to read the deleted space where she found the *chloroform* search. Prosecutors had alleged that there were eighty-four searches for *chloroform*. Osborne found only one reference to the name "Zenaida Fernandez-Gonzalez," on July 16; it would later be revealed that Lee Anthony looked that up when he was visiting his parents' home and was trying to get Casey to talk. Osborne's supervisor confirmed her work. A former law enforcement officer named John Bradley testified that he had been asked to help the Orange County detectives. Bradley owns the Canadian software company SiQuest, which offers a program called CacheBack® that was used to read the Anthony computer's files. He produced the list of keywords he found on his search of the hard drive, as well as the dates and times. Baez cross-examined him by saying there were also searches for zombies, self-defense, and kung fu, but Bradley said he only reported what was there and didn't analyze it for content. Bradley admitted that he was promoting his company by mentioning that he had worked on the case, but that was a recent development unrelated to the work he did for detectives two and a half years before.[127] Post-trial, Bradley went public with the revelation that his software program had computed some data incorrectly and that there was actually only one search for the word *chloroform*, not eighty-four. He claimed to have tried to tell law enforcement during the trial, but the lawyers never amended their record—yet the number eighty-four was never mentioned during the prosecution's closing argument.[128]

Despite defense objections, a brief animated video was played for jurors demonstrating the state's concept of how the three pieces of duct tape fit across a living Caylee's face. It began by showing a close-up photo of Caylee and Casey smiling, then digitally morphed the skull photo they had seen over the image of Caylee, adding the duct tape over what would have been the girl's nose and mouth. The expert who made the video testified that without the tape over the lower jaw, the skull would have separated into pieces. The video was so unnerving to Casey that she became ill, causing court to be halted for the day.[129] That evening, crime news programs featured commentators friendly to the defense who asserted that the video was offensive and so over-the-top it would be grounds for reversible error if Casey were to be convicted. What they failed to mention was that, for the last couple decades, videos have been used by both sides in US courtrooms to prove points in circumstantial cases. When there is no actual witness to a crime, it's reasonable for trial lawyers to want to physically show jurors their theory of how the crime occurred. Instead of the defense acting like this was an action worthy of a mistrial, I told reporters that I would expect the defense would rally back with their own edgy imagery when it was their turn at bat. And that's just what happened.

———

I was particularly eager to hear the testimony from the Orlando medical examiner's office.[130] Dr. Gary Utz, the deputy chief medical examiner, led off that portion of the prosecution. He had assisted in the collection of the skeletal remains found on Suburban Drive and described the days-long process of gathering bone fragments and other physical evidence. Forensic anthropologist Dr. John Schultz spoke of the various bones he examined and spoke of marks on some of the bones that signified that they had been gnawed on by small animals. Chief Medical Examiner Jan Garavaglia, MD—aka TV's "Dr. G"—testified about the three reasons she classified Caylee's death as a homicide and not as an accident: The thirty-one-day delay in reporting Caylee missing was a "red flag" to the doctor; the body was hidden in bags before being dumped in a swampy woodland; and there was duct tape on the skull—something that should never be put on a child's face and that would never be necessary to put on a body after a victim had died. She also stated that chloroform could have been a possible cause of death for Caylee. Addressing the defense theory, she said that in her experience, when a drowning victim is found, in 100 percent of the cases, somebody calls 911, no matter how grave the situation seems to be. "No person would make a drowning death look like a murder," she averred.[131] Garavaglia had a pleasant manner of speaking to jurors and smiled on the way out of the courtroom, as if she felt she had hit a home run. But, in all honesty, given the totally skele- tonized condition of the remains, I'm not sure why she didn't make a determination of "inconclusive," instead of "homicide." To have arbi- trarily eliminated "accident" from the mix seemed shortsighted; "incon- clusive" would have been a better call, in my view.[132]

The prosecution called an expert witness in entomology, Dr. Neal Haskell, whose home base is in Indiana but who has vast experience in cases all over the country. Haskell determined that insect evidence from the car trunk proved to him that a dead body had been in that location for a brief period of time—perhaps three days—and his analysis of insects at the dump site proved to him that the body had been in that location for "many, many months." Haskell explained to the defense attorney the difference between "trash" and "garbage"; the latter includes organic material, such as food. Very credibly, he took jurors through the life cycle of flies and beetles, who exist only to feast, lay eggs, and leave behind their casings in a predictable, measurable way.

There was powerful testimony by two FBI scientists who examined the heart-shaped imprint on one of the pieces of duct tape, and who stated that a book with heart stickers was recovered from Casey's bedroom. The agents also testified that the tape lacked fingerprints or DNA.[133] Tape samples might preserve trace evidence even years after an event, if carefully preserved, but here you had samples that were exposed to extreme climate changes, including a hurricane and heavy waters. Anyone who thinks those elements didn't have a detrimental effect on the tape is dreaming. But the beat-up condition of the tape does prove one thing: that it hadn't been recently placed at the dump site, as the defense tried to suggest. The tape, as well as the skull and the rest of the remains, had likely been on Suburban Drive for months.[134]

The state finished its case by recalling Cindy Anthony, who confirmed that she had similar duct tape, garbage bags, and a laundry bag in the home as were found at the dump site, and that Caylee's Winnie-the-Pooh blanket from her bedroom went missing from around the time she last saw her granddaughter. As she left the stand and walked by Casey, Cindy mouthed the words "I love you," but Casey turned her head away from her mother.

Local tattoo artist Bobby Williams described the July 2 inking he gave Casey's left shoulder—*Bella Vita*, in a feminine font. He testified that Casey told him Caylee was with her nanny, but that she would bring the little girl with her for her next appointment on July 19—a date she never kept because she was arrested.[135] The prosecution rested after eighteen days of court testimony and testimony from fifty-nine witnesses, some of them called more than once.[136]

––––––––––

The defense began its case by pointing out that the date was June 16, exactly three years after little Caylee drowned in her family pool. Baez called to the stand an FBI lab serology supervisor who testified she failed to find blood in any of the items she studied from the case, including the car trunk and its liner. She also obtained no DNA profile from the items she tested, including the shovel and Casey's clothing. Cross-examining her, Jeff Ashton ascertained that she didn't test for decompositional fluids. Two Orlando CSIs testified about the heart-shaped sticker that was found at the dump site, establishing that it was approximately thirty feet from where the skull and duct tape were recovered, in an area that was full of debris. Baez's point was that there was nothing to concretely link that sticker with the imprint on the tape, and that there was an elementary school nearby where many students might have used stickers of widely divergent shapes and sizes. It was later determined that the sticker found at the site had a slight padding that did not match the stickers found in Casey's bedroom.

Baez's entomological and anthropological experts interpreted the post-mortem interval in a vastly different manner from the prosecution's witnesses. Dr. Tim Huntington testified that the lack of hundreds, if not thousands, of blowflies—nature's first responders to decomposing flesh—in the car trunk or at the dump site suggested that Caylee's body was never in the trunk and was placed on Suburban Drive much later, perhaps just a couple days before she was recovered. Huntington never analyzed the actual stain in the car trunk, but he tried to replicate it with an experiment using a dead pig. But Jeff Ashton battled back, stating that conditions in the Nebraska winter, where Huntington did his test, were much different from a June or July heatwave in Florida, and Huntington agreed. Huntington also conceded that when he inspected the Sunfire, it still smelled bad, and that he understood that while there was trash in the trunk, it was not from foodstuff.[137] Criminalist Dr. Henry Lee never testified for the defense, nor did forensic anthropologist Dr. Kathy Reichs, both of whom had visited the dump site after the state's experts completed their work.[138]

Forensic pathologist Dr. Werner Spitz's testimony for the defense brought fireworks into the courtroom. He described his long career to the jurors and explained how he had performed a second autopsy on

Caylee's remains. He was irate that he was not invited to do his autopsy at the same time Dr. Garavaglia did hers, saying that had never happened to him in his decades-long career. Most importantly, he criticized Dr. Garavaglia's autopsy as "shoddy," stating that she failed to saw off the top of the skull so she could see inside. "The head is part of the body and when you do an examination, you examine the whole body," Spitz said in his thick Teutonic accent. When Dr. G. was on the stand, she had said she didn't feel the need to saw off the top of the skull because there was no brain in the skull and she could look inside from the bottom, once the mandible was no longer in place with the duct tape. She also said that she had washed the cranial cavity and sent the liquid to a toxicology lab for drug testing. But Spitz wasn't giving her any breaks. He also sniped at her declaration of homicide, when he believed the case was more likely an accident, and stated that there should have been some DNA on the tape if it had been over the child's mouth. Spitz even found fault with one of the crime scene photos of the hair on the skull, intimating that it might have been staged—"It wouldn't be the first time, sir. . . . I can tell you some horror stories," he raged at prosecutor Ashton.[139]

I can't speak for Spitz here, but my own lengthy career lists many secondary autopsies that I performed that were separate from the primary ones; sometimes doctors don't like to have someone else in the room, and that's fine, as long as the materials are accessible to the second doctor.

I will have to agree that Dr. G should have used a saw to take off the top of the skull, and I can't fathom why she didn't do that. She might have found some evidence of staining from old bleeding; an epidural hemorrhage lining the inside of the calvarium—the top of the skull; or a fracture of the skull, especially the basilar skull, the bony floor heading back from the eyebrow level. Such a fracture can occur with no injury seen externally, even on a body that has scalp and soft tissues. In addition, with an asphyxial death—such as from drowning—changes may occur from lack of oxygenation into the sphenoid ridges, the bony prominences behind the ears. But rather than label Garavaglia's autopsy as shoddy, I would call it incomplete. As I mentioned before, I also share Spitz's view that the case should have been categorized as something other than a homicide, though I'm not committed to his belief that it was an accident. And while I, too, have seen shameful stagings of crime scene photos, it hardly seemed to be the case here.

I saw a transcript of Spitz and Dr. Michael Baden on a TV appearance before the trial, and they complained that the state failed to test for the presence of diatoms—one-celled plants that naturally occur in water. Spitz felt that microscopic study might have found diatoms that would prove Caylee drowned in pool water. That struck me as a meaningless argument since there was no lung tissue to work with that could have shown diatoms. I can't eliminate the idea that Caylee drowned, but she also could have died accidentally in her mother's hot car, and then been put in the trunk to decompose. At that time of year, temperatures in Florida typically reach in the nineties, so a closed car trunk in direct sunlight would spike the temperature to approximately 170 degrees, and in that environment the body would liquefy, then decompose, within about three days.

Also, in the televised interview with Spitz and Baden, both wondered why the maggots found in the car trunk weren't tested for DNA, which could have linked to Caylee. (This would be via a common technique of putting the maggots in a blender and then testing the liquid for DNA; if they had feasted on Caylee, that proof would be in the liquid.) But Spitz had access to all the maggots, too. Why didn't he send them out to an independent lab himself? I can only assume it's because he didn't want to know the answer. And Spitz, who claimed on the stand that he believed there was brain residue on the inside of the skull that could have been detected had Dr. G. sawed the skull—and who shouted at Ashton that he was a forensic pathologist and not a chemist to explain why he didn't do the testing himself—certainly could have ordered that test. Nobody expects an autopsy doctor to have a toxicology lab at hand—the tests are always conducted by a reputable outside lab. Spitz well knows these things. I just think his opinions were worth presenting without the bias and bombast.[140]

———————

The issue of plant growth at the dump site got attention during the defense case, with Baez seeking to minimize prosecution claims that the plant tendrils growing through the skull and bags were proof that the body had been there for months. A forensic botanist testified that she felt by looking at the "leaf litter" nearby, the remains could have been there for only two weeks or so. On cross-examination, she admitted not being an expert on bones, and when asked by Ashton how she'd explain a leg bone that was buried four inches deep in the mud, she offered that a dog might have buried it. Ashton practically spat his contempt at the woman and dismissed her. An expert from the Netherlands was the defense's DNA pointman, but he ended up conceding that hot and moist weather conditions could cause the DNA to break down, which might be why it wasn't found in the car trunk or on the items tested. Detective Melich was recalled, and he admitted that his early search of the house didn't produce chloroform or any homemade concoction, but he also said that search was during the time Casey was viewed as a parent of an abducted child, not as a potential killer. Baez called another scientist from the Oak Ridge National Lab who attempted to minimize Dr. Arpad Vass's testimony by stating that Vass was not a chemist; of course, Vass never portrayed himself as a chemist, only as a PhD whose sole work is on body decomposition. Another chemist who once worked at Oak Ridge testified that his independent testing of air samples also found chloroform, but in levels that could be from common household products. An FBI trace evidence expert testified that she found no soil on Casey's shoes that matched that at the dump site, but on cross-examination she stated that just because soil isn't on an object when tested doesn't mean it wasn't there at some earlier point. A sheriff's department CSI employee identi-fied photos of the Gatorade bottle and laundry bag, and a recall of the FBI evidence tech cast doubt on the linkage of the duct tape to the home and reinforced that there was only one hair that had the purported decompositional banding. A hair and fiber expert with the FBI testified to the process of checking a hair for banding, and the subsequent heated exchange between lawyers left observers wondering if that was, as the defense claimed, "junk science." An expert from National Medical Labs in Willow Grove, Pennsylvania, reviewed the Body Farm scent docu-mentation for the defense and found it substandard; he also testified that chloroform is a by-product of chlorinated pool water.

In what might have been the most divisive testimony yet, Cindy Anthony testified that it was she, and not her daughter, who had per-formed the computer search for "chloroform." Cindy explained that one of her Yorkie dogs had been sleeping too much, and she wondered if it was from eating bamboo. She had meant to look up "chlorophyll" but misspelled it, she said under oath. She also justified the "neck breaking" keyword from being something she remembered seeing when she went online in March 2008—it was from a pop-up ad about skateboarding. On cross-examination, Drane Burdick asked why she was just now remembering this information, and Cindy answered that medication she had been on before clouded her memory. The lawyer also reminded her of all the other keywords that were significant—including *how to make chloroform, inhalation, ruptured spleen,* and more—but Cindy wasn't claiming responsibility for those. And there were no searches found that mentioned bamboo or Yorkies.

The next day, Baez recalled Cindy and finally brought out one of the ideas he suggested in his opening statement: that Caylee had drowned in the pool. He got Cindy to talk about how much Caylee loved playing in the pool and that she and the little tot would go in almost daily. She also emphasized how careful she and other family members were to put the pool ladder away so Caylee couldn't get into the pool by herself. Then the coup de grâce: a never-before-seen photo and video footage of Caylee standing on her toes and seeming to be able to open the glass door to the patio; Caylee climbing up the ladder, with Cindy's hands barely touching her—demonstrating how adept the child was on the stairs, even at a younger age than when she died—and happily splashing in the water with her grandma. According to Cindy, the only day the ladder was ever accidentally left up was on June 16, the day the defense said Caylee drowned. Cindy sobbed, and so did Casey. Cindy also denied that she got into a choking fight with her daughter on the night of Father's Day.

Lee Anthony was next and testified that he was the former owner of the Pontiac Sunfire before he handed it off to his sister. He knew that stain in the trunk, he said; it was there when he bought the car. He also broke down when he recounted how his family had not included him in the loop when Casey had given birth, and he claimed he wasn't very involved with his parents and sister for a while afterward. Lee said that he didn't want to be in court and didn't want his parents or sister to be there either. Despite being on the same page with his parents on that issue, some of his testimony was in direct contrast to things they had claimed, such as whether or not Cindy had hired a private eye to search Suburban Drive on the advice of a psychic.[141] If Baez wanted to show that the family was often dysfunctional, getting them to refute each other about matters that weren't very crucial was a clever tactic.[142]

Bad guy or fall guy? That was the question trial watchers had to consider when Roy Kronk took the stand for the defense. Under questioning by Cheney Mason, Kronk recited his three attempts in August to alert authorities to the round, white object he saw in the woods. He acknowledged knowing that there was a quarter-million-dollar reward, and admitted to receiving five thousand dollars from a private attorney who felt badly for him after Caylee's body was identified and to reaping the $15,000 from ABC when he and his snake photo appeared on *Good Morning America*. Kronk conceded that he had hoped his ex-wife wouldn't find out about his financial windfall and denied telling his son that he was going to be rich and famous—in subsequent testimony, Kronk's son, Brandon Sparks, disputed that. During cross-examination, Kronk testified that he did not know any of the Anthony family members and did not have access to their home, garage, or car.

With the jury out of the room, Judge Perry allowed the defense to call Casey's former fiancé, Jesse Grund, who said she had once told him that her brother groped her. Cindy was also called to refute that Lee had ever acted inappropriately with his sister. Judge Perry ruled that if Baez wanted that information in front of the jury, he'd have to find a way that didn't involve hearsay. The jury did hear Cindy respond to a jailhouse video in which Cindy told Casey of a media theory that Caylee drowned in the pool, and Casey's response was a bored "Surprise, surprise." The prosecution suggested that if Caylee had died in the pool, Casey would have jumped on that idea as a means of mitigating her responsibility.

Next came George Anthony, who told the jury of a suicide attempt he made when he became overwhelmed. He went to a motel with alcohol and pills and wrote a series of text messages saying good-bye to his wife and son. "I didn't want to think my daughter could be responsible for taking the life of my granddaughter. . . . I wanted to go be with Caylee," he said as he fought back tears. One of the final witnesses in the defense case was a grief counselor who said that people handle tragedy in different ways, including denial and "retail therapy." When asked if that could include going thirty-one days without telling anyone of a daughter's death, partying at nightclubs, renting videos, and getting a tattoo, the expert admitted, "That's very complex."[143] Orlando attorney Mark NeJame, who had followed the case closely and at one time had represented George and Cindy, used his Twitter account to write: "Find me one other person out of 6,000,000,000 in (the) world who went boozin', stealin', screwin' and tattooin' after their child died."[144]

Prior to the end of the defense's case, Judge Perry questioned Casey about whether she wished to testify in her own behalf and she said,

"No." She affirmed that that was her own idea and that she hadn't been coerced. Just a few days earlier, Casey had undergone three checkups by psychological specialists to evaluate her mental status, and all found her capable of making sound decisions. While the need for those tests wasn't announced, it was widely presumed to have been in anticipation of her decision not to take the stand.[145]

Krystal Holloway (aka River Cruz) testified to her purported romantic affair with George, which, she told jurors, consisted of "about twelve" sexual encounters. She asserted that a devastated George told her that Caylee's death was "an accident that snowballed out of control." She also spoke of a text he sent to her that read: "Just thinking about you. I need you in my life," and she admitted selling her story to the *National Enquirer* for $4,000. While Holloway testified, George and Cindy sat in the gallery, looking stoic. George was recalled to the stand to counter her testimony, telling the jury that he did not have an affair with Holloway and that she had a criminal record. He also claimed that he sent that text to all the people who helped him search for Caylee. Judge Perry advised jurors to only consider Holloway's testimony as a means of weighing George's truthfulness on other testimony, not as a basis for judging Casey.[146] It must be noted that Holloway's testimony seemed genuine, while George's was—perhaps justifiably—hostile. She left the courtroom and made the rounds of TV appearances, complaining that prosecutors had many more texts between her and George, which would have buoyed her story, but they chose not to discuss them in court. She said the stress of the case and not being believed had made her feel suicidal at one point. And she maintained that while she got money from the *Enquirer*, she had given that same amount to George as a gift when he told her he couldn't work.[147]

George was called to the stand once again, this time with Baez questioning him about all the deceased pets the family had and how they disposed of them. One by one, George spoke of dogs and cats who had died and been buried in the family backyard. Baez asked if they had been put in plastic bags sealed with duct tape, and George couldn't recall. Ashton countered by asking if any of them had been tossed in a swamp, and George said no. Next, Cindy was called to confirm what George said; she added that duct tape was used to keep the bags from opening. Lee Anthony said much the same thing.[148] I found this questioning particularly helpful to the defense because it put into jurors' minds the concept that perhaps the duct tape on Caylee's skull had transferred there after originally being on the bag. It also meant that there was likely no need for either lawyer to call Kiomarie Torres Cruz, Casey's childhood friend who claimed the two kids buried their pets on Suburban Drive. The jury, by the way, was never given an outing to visit the dump site, as is done in many cases. I presume it was because the area had been cleaned up so extensively after the recovery, it just didn't appear to be the same swampland as it was in the summer of 2008.[149] The defense rested its case after eleven days of testimony, having gone through forty-seven different witnesses.[150]

The prosecution rebuttal case then ensued, with the most explosive testimony coming from an attorney and supervisor at Gentiva, the home healthcare corporation that employed Cindy until the summer of 2008. Provided with the dates and times Cindy claimed she made the home computer searches, the executives described the process the home office uses to establishes computer use at work: There is a distinction between people who use a desktop and those who use a laptop, and—due to patient privacy concerns that require top-of-the-line tracking—every time an employee hits the "enter" key, the function appears on his or her permanent record. Thus it was relatively easy to determine that on the precise moments Cindy claimed to be searching online for *chlorophyll* or *chloroform*, she was actually at work, entering other data on her password-protected account.[151]

Out of presence of the jury, Judge Perry warned defense and prosecutors not to refer to Casey having been an incest victim during closing arguments. Since Baez failed to establish that through testimony—even when he had George and Lee Anthony on the stand—it could not come into his wrap-up. (The prosecution had asked both men briefly if they had molested Casey and got "no" for answers, but they didn't go further on the topic.)[152]

Then jurors were marched back into the courtroom for what would be the sprint to the finish line. Mindful that the panel would be sequestered and deliberating over the Fourth of July holiday, Judge Perry thanked them for their service and promised that the end of the ordeal was nigh. Closing arguments began on Sunday, July 3, 2011, with Linda Drane Burdick calling Casey Anthony "the most well-documented liar ever seen in a courtroom" and re-establishing the timeline that she had used in her opening statement.[153] Counting down the infamous thirty-one days, Drane Burdick asked: "Where is Caylee?" At the end of her presentation, she stated: "The question is no longer 'Where is Caylee?' We know where Caylee Marie Anthony is." Casey Anthony's actions and responses "answer for you the only real question left at this stage of the proceedings, and that is who killed Caylee Anthony . . . and left her on the side of the road, dead." Slowly and deliberately, Drane Burdick asked: "Whose life was better without Caylee?" Then, with a split-screen shot of two photos— one showing Casey at the Hot Body contest and the other with her *Bella Vita* tattoo—the prosecutor said simply: "There's your answer."[154]

José Baez's closer was no less touching, using plenty of images of Casey in loving embraces with her little girl. "To paint Casey Anthony as a slut, as a party girl, as a girl who lies, has nothing to do with how Caylee died," he said. "You would dishonor the law and Caylee Anthony's memory if you were to base your verdict on anything but the evidence and to use your emotion to get you angry is improper."[155] Baez used poster boards with big photos of all the witnesses who offered testimony that supported his side, an excellent way of reminding jurors of who, among the more than one hundred witnesses, said what. Piece by piece, he exposed what he called "fantasy forensics," such as the phantom heart sticker, the carpet stain that had been there for years, and the

Internet search that he maintained was made by Cindy. For an attorney who modeled himself after O. J. Simpson's lead counsel Johnnie Cochran—and whose pals jokingly call him "Juannie Cochran"—Baez didn't have his icon's catchphrase, which was used after the debacle when prosecutors told Simpson to try on a too-small glove, and Cochran warned the jury, "If it doesn't fit, you must acquit." But Baez's "fantasy forensics" is guaranteed to be around for many trials to come. At one point, Baez showed a poster board with all the imaginary characters Casey had confabulated, from Zenaida Fernandez-Gonzalez and her family, to Casey's rich boyfriend and co-workers. In the center was a photo of Casey—one that had to be changed at the last moment, when prosecutors complained that the image Baez chose was from when she was a teenager; he updated the board with a more recent shot. In the middle of his impassioned speech, the camera cut to Jeff Ashton, who sat with his hand over his mouth, chuckling. Baez mentioned that, and the judge called a sidebar and scolded both sides. It was a painful display with a bully prosecutor treating a colleague with disrespect, and a defense advocate being thrown off his stride. At Ashton's final time up at bat, he mentioned how Caylee had been becoming more verbal—sealing her fate with a mother who knew she would soon blow her secret about not having a job or money or a nanny.[156]

———————

And then . . . it was over. After thirty-three days over six weeks of testimony, twenty-five thousand case documents, and four hundred pieces of evidence, the Casey Anthony jury went behind closed doors to deliberate. And there they stayed for a period of ten hours and forty minutes over two days.[157] They did not ask for read-backs of any testimony, they did not request bailiffs to bring them any exhibits, they did not ask the judge for clarification of any definitions or points of law. On July 5, 2011, the original twelve jury members sent word out that they had a verdict—and the media and interested parties had thirty minutes to get back to the courtroom to hear it.[158]

Outside the courthouse, throngs of people held "Justice for Caylee" banners, while the cable news hosts speculated about what such a short deliberation might mean. Surely, all agreed, Casey would be convicted of something major, but the wise money was that she wouldn't be found guilty of first-degree murder, thus saving her from a date with death row. Even former members of her defense team admitted they would be pleased just to have her life spared.

Judge Perry asked the defendant and her counsel to rise as the clerk read the verdict for the seven charges she faced. On the felony charge of first-degree murder of her daughter: Not guilty. On the felony charge of aggravated child abuse: Not guilty. On the felony charge of aggravated manslaughter of a child: Not guilty. And of four misdemeanor counts of providing false information to a law enforcement officer—including that she worked at Universal Orlando in 2008, that she left Caylee with a babysitter named Zenaida Fernandez-Gonzalez, that she told Jeffrey Hopkins and Juliette Lewis that Caylee was missing, and that she received a phone call from Caylee on July 15, 2008: Guilty on all charges.[159]

Inside the courtroom, for one brief moment, you could have heard a pin drop. Then Casey dissolved into tears, gratefully hugging her lawyers, while her parents quietly slipped out of the courtroom. On the airwaves and Internet, the reaction was anything but relief. My co-author, Dawna Kaufmann, tells me that she heard screams of protest out the window of her Los Angeles home and, as she channel-surfed, she saw crime news hosts who were angry, crying, and slack-jawed. I was in Oslo, Norway, at the time, and when I learned the news I was incredulous. It would take a few days before I had all the facts to form an opinion.[160]

Judge Perry sentenced Casey to a maximum of one consecutive year each for the four misdemeanor charges, and after calculating time served, Anthony was allowed to leave the jail on July 17. She was also fined a total of $4,618, which covers one thousand dollars per count, plus court costs.

She will be expected to establish a payment plan of twenty dollars per month, beginning February 15, 2012.[161] She will also be required to reimburse the county for some of the costs of the investigation.

As this book goes to press, "Where is Casey?" is on everyone's lips. Whether she will attempt to cash in on her notoriety with big bucks paid for interviews is a good question, but for now she's gone underground to see what opportunities develop. Surely, she could use the money—but the public view of her making money off this tragedy is enough to make citizens furious and even boycott any outlet considering paying her. Vivid Video, a leading X-rated production company, offered, then immediately retracted, a lucrative deal for her to star in one of their films, and *Playboy* magazine founder Hugh Hefner said that he won't do a pictorial of her, stating: "I wouldn't reward someone like that for what happened."[162] *Hustler* publisher Larry Flynt, however, welcomed the controversy, offering Casey a million-dollar paycheck and a cut of royalties to appear in his magazine. Possibly some producer or publisher will buy the rights for her to tell "her story." Since she was acquitted on all major charges and can't be retried, she could use a megaphone in Time Square to confess every detail and not face prosecution again.

When I think of Casey Anthony, I'm reminded of the film *The Usual Suspects*, the 1995 neo-noir film that won Oscars for Best Screenplay for Christopher McQuarrie and Best Supporting Actor for Kevin Spacey. In the movie, Spacey's character, Roger "Verbal" Kint, gives a lengthy police interview about an elaborate violent crime that contains multiple flashbacks, fleshing out his recollection. At the end of the film, the cops realize he has made up the entire thing—based on items, photos, and notes Kint saw in the interview room, all woven together by a master liar. Perhaps that film inspired the lies that toppled Casey's house of cards. Did she pick up little things, like a name on a rental application, and weave a tapestry of lies? Did her father and brother molest her? Who knows? Are her parents and brother also liars who were in on a plan to smear themselves if it would save her life? Are they truly dysfunctional or sly as foxes? Did they follow a script that was as detailed and fanciful as one that might win an Academy Award? Prosecutors have admitted they won't be filing charges of perjury against any of the family members. And now that Casey's free, what will her relationship with them be? Can they all forgive and forget? Should they? Only time will tell, and maybe not even then.

Casey's legal team has filed appeals against the four misdemeanor charges, a seemingly puzzling action until you understand that it will prevent her from having to appear in any depositions or courtrooms for civil actions she is facing—from the real Zenaida Gonzalez who believes she was maliciously hurt by Casey naming her as a kidnapper, depriving her of jobs and a way to support her children; to Tim Miller of Texas EquuSearch and bounty hunter Leonard Padilla, who seek to recover hard costs for their efforts, since—if one accepts the drowning story— Casey knew all along that her child was dead.

While most of the jurors have continued to remain silent and unidentified, a couple have spoken out so far to explain what led to the unpopular verdict. The predominant theme is that they didn't feel comfortable possibly sentencing someone to death when the state hadn't proved its case. At least one even stated that there was no cause of death, no blood, no DNA, and no fingerprints that could be linked to Casey. The same person said they were "sick to their stomachs" because even though they acquitted Casey of the major charges, that doesn't mean she is innocent. An alternate who spoke out said he agreed with the verdict of his colleagues, and while he couldn't say whether Casey's father molested her, he felt George Anthony acted like he was "hiding something."

All I can say is that there was no way for this group to have reviewed six weeks of detailed scientific data and witness opinions in under eleven hours. They may think they did a good job, but they shortchanged the process. As reported, many of them didn't even take notes, so their collective level of understanding was compromised. They apparently swallowed up most everything José Baez said—even the parts that didn't make sense or weren't supported by evidence. And while they praised all the attorneys, at least one had a negative reaction to Jeff Ashton when he smirked and got caught. Perhaps a lesson for future litigators is to use more low-tech poster boards and don't take cheap shots at your opponents. I also believe that prosecutors felt overconfident in their case and didn't adjust appropriately to read their jurors. When a jury isn't taking notes, it's a sign that your high-concept ideas may just be too lofty for them. It's Darwinian: Adapt or die. Although to most trial observers, Drane Burdick and Ashton were stellar in their ability to streamline their case and present the science wisely, it may have fallen on deaf ears. What a shame that relatively new forensic techniques—air sampling, postmortem hair banding, and computer software analysis—will be argued in future courtrooms as "junk science," instead of regarded as the potent tools they can be. Back to the drawing board, then, and let additional peer review make the disciplines too impressive to ignore. And it's a certainty that jurors didn't comprehend when the judge directed them to not consider punishment until after any felony conviction. Maybe prosecutors were so sure of their case they didn't feel it was necessary to reiterate that there were lesser charges that the jury could have gone with—ones that involved a prison sentence and not execution.[163]

Dawna Kaufmann co-wrote an article for *Globe* that listed "five crucial clues the Casey jury never heard." The cover story got such good reviews that Nancy Grace even built an episode of her show around it. The five clues were: (1) The jailhouse video showing Casey's collapse over the discovery of Caylee's remains before they were positively identified, along with testimony from jailers who said Anthony hadn't reacted that way when another child's remains were found elsewhere; (2) Testimony from Casey's friend who had tried to adopt Caylee—the same childhood pal who used to bury pets with Casey on Suburban Drive; (3) More details on the physical fight between Casey and her mother, Cindy, when the older woman said she'd seek custody of her granddaughter; (4) Casey's shocking "confession" in her diary on June 20 when she wrote that she'd made the right decision and hoped "the end justified the means"; and (5) Testimony from the two jailhouse snitches who claimed Casey said she had chloroformed Caylee.[164]

Finally, I get dismayed when I hear people in the media suggest that this case was unwinnable because it was based on "circumstantial evidence." This is what I and others refer to as the "CSI Effect" because it gives an unrealistic look at forensic evidence that, unlike on TV, is not solved at the end of an hour. Autopsy analysis, DNA, toxicology, and other scientific methods are the building blocks of cases, and it sometimes takes weeks to get results. Also, very few crimes are captured on surveillance video, leaving no doubt about who the perpetrator is—meaning we must embrace circumstantial evidence to fill in the blanks. Police officials know that circumstantial evidence is more reliable than most witness testimony, which can be erroneous, vague, and/or forgotten in time. When some critics charged that Casey walked free because there was no certain cause or manner of death, no blood, DNA, or other trace evidence, I reflected on the many, many cases I have worked—including those in which a killer ended up on death row—when there was never even a body. The case of Laci Peterson and her unborn child was a purely circumstantial case, and her husband Scott is on death row. Laci's body had no head, was missing most of her limbs and all her flesh and organs, except for her uterus, and there was no firm cause or manner of death and no slam-dunk forensic link to Scott. But a discerning jury paid attention to the trial testimony and was able to put together the pieces. Sometimes we'll never know every detail of a crime, but "reasonable doubt" doesn't mean finding a reason *to* doubt—it means using logic and evidence to create a plausible scenario.

The Casey Anthony verdict was a bizarre aberration. The best news is that it will be discussed in law schools and in the media for years to come. It's not justice for this poor, slain child, but it will have to be enough.[165]

CHAPTER TWO

USAF COLONEL PHILIP MICHAEL SHUE

Suicide or Murder?

This next case is one of the most vexing to me for two reasons. First, the brutal nature of the crime itself is so appalling, and second, it illustrates how intractable some bureaucrats can be about correcting the status of a case when new evidence emerges.[1]

United States Air Force colonel Philip Michael Shue was a genuine American hero and had the awards and decorations to prove it, including honors for Meritorious Service, Achievement, Training, and Organizational Excellence; Expeditionary, Long Tour and Longevity Services; Bronze Stars for National Defense and Small Arms Expert Marksmanship; and medals from the United Nations and NATO.[2] That he died in such a horrific way, casting doubt on his mental acuity, is a shame. I hope to restore his reputation here and now.[3]

Colonel Shue was only fifty-four years old when his speeding 1995 Mercury Tracer veered off the westbound Texas Interstate Highway 10 and slammed into two trees. His death devastated his wife Tracy; they had such a bright future planned out. The attractive pair met in 1988 at Eglin Air Force Base in northwest Florida where Tracy served as an air force nurse and Phil worked as the chief medical director of inpatient mental health, and soon became board certified in psychiatry and neurology. "He was a great doctor," Tracy remembered. "Everybody loved him." They began dating, slowly at first because Phil was going through a difficult separation from his first wife, Nancy, and was headed for divorce. He didn't talk a lot about it to Tracy, except to say it was a love-less marriage. But Tracy helped put that behind him, and by 1993, when his divorce was finalized, Phil and Tracy wed. The two really clicked: the mild-mannered midwestern guy who grew up in Ohio, and the New York gal who was outgoing and fearless.[4]

Throughout the nineties, the colonel's deployments included Bosnia, Croatia, and the Persian Gulf, where he served as chief medical officer and flight surgeon for flying squadrons and task forces. In 1998, he entered a three-year air force residency in aerospace medicine and occupational health at Brooks Air Force Base in San Antonio, Texas, and earned his master's degree in 1999 in public health from the University of Texas, San Antonio. His specialized military training was in hyper-baric medicine, critical incident stress management, hostage negotia-tion, wilderness medicine, global medicine, land survival training, water survival training, and arctic survival training. In 2001, Phil Shue was reassigned as a staff psychiatrist/aerospace medicine physician at the Wilford Hall Medical Center at Lackland Air Force Base, also in San Antonio. He and Tracy, who had by then retired as a lieutenant colonel, bought a home twenty-five miles northwest of San Antonio in the bed-room community of Boerne, Texas.[5]

In October 2002, Shue was selected for a prestigious civilian forensic fellowship program in psychiatry at the University of Alabama in Montgomery that would begin when he retired from the military in the fall of 2003. It was to be a "new adventure, a new chapter," Tracy explained. On April 15, 2003, Shue took and passed a cardiac stress test at work, ordered new contact lenses, and picked up his lawnmower from a repair service. That same day, the Shues put a deposit on their dream house in South Lake, Alabama, where they planned to sit on the porch, watch ducks fly over the pond out back, and contemplate their good life together. Their dream would perish the next day.

———————

On the morning of April 16, Phil got up around five in the morning to get to his office an hour earlier than usual to do paperwork. He dressed in his fatigues, then brought Tracy her customary cup of coffee in bed, as well as a cup for himself. They discussed their new home and chores he planned to do at their current home, then he kissed her and left just before the clock struck six. "I love you" were the last words Phil said to Tracy. Within two and a half hours, he was dead.

According to an incident report filed by sheriff's deputy Clint Bass, he responded to a call for a single-car accident on a frontage road near the IH-10; already onsite was Boerne police officer Larry James. As Bass roped off the accident scene, they were soon joined by state trooper Al Auxier, Constable Don White, and other Boerne police officers. Bass's boss, Lieutenant Roger Anderson, arrived and was irate to see Auxier and White inside the crime tape, "destroying evidence," as he would later call it. Sniping began among the personnel over who had jurisdiction over the site; Auxier would have, had the accident been on the highway, but since it was on a road, the sheriff claimed control. Auxier, Anderson, and White all separately left the scene for a while.

Bass remained and took statements from two witnesses who told him the driver appeared to be "falling asleep at the wheel or intoxicated," almost driving into oncoming traffic at one point. They watched as the car, going an estimated sixty to sixty-five miles per hour, traveled into the center median of the freeway, struck an object, went airborne, and came down on all four tires. The car continued on the highway for a few more minutes, then drifted to the slow lane, went up a small grassy hill, smashed its right front bumper into the first tree, then spun around, flew a number of feet, and hit the second tree, seriously denting the driver's side door and causing a branch to enter the passenger side of the car. The witnesses did not see the car's brake lights being used, and there were no skid marks on the road, which you'd see if someone tried to slow down a runaway vehicle. The crash occurred on the route Shue would have taken to come home from work, but well past the exit to his house.

There is no information about where Shue had been after he left home that morning, and no one claimed to have seen him at work.[6]

According to what Tracy Shue told my co-author, Dawna Kaufmann, Bass looked through the car's windshield and observed that the air bags had deployed. The driver, bleeding from the head and face, appeared to be deceased. When the Kendall County emergency medical technicians arrived, they did not touch Shue's body, not even to take his pulse. No resuscitative measures were attempted, even though that should have been standard procedure. Death was assumed, with one EMT writing "Obvious Death" on a report. Noting that the driver's right wrist had four or five inches of silver duct tape hanging from it, Bass contacted dispatch and asked for a criminal investigator. The investigator, Luther VanLandingham, soon joined the EMTs, followed by Constable Don White, who returned with his wife, Nancy J. White, the coroner/justice of the peace for that jurisdiction. Texas has no statewide medical examiner's office, and in its smaller cities, a coroner system is in use. Justice White called Trooper Auxier to return to the scene and assume jurisdiction again, which he did. She would later admit that she never spoke to the EMTs but checked Shue's pulse by placing her hand over his wrist, which was covered by his clothing and duct tape.

Colonel Shue's body was not taken out of the car until nearly eleven in the morning, about two and a half hours after the crash. Eventually, using the Jaws of Life®, EMT crewmembers proceeded to cut the driver from the vehicle. He was then laid on the ground, as can be seen in a photograph taken at the site. Personnel there noticed that strips of duct tape similar to what was around the deceased's wrists were also wrapped around his boots, and that the front of his shirt was stained with blood.[7]

Kendall County is divided into four precincts, each with an elected justice of the peace, who typically will adjudicate small claims matters, issue warrants for searches and arrests, conduct preliminary hearings, administer oaths, perform marriages, serve as a coroner, and investigate "unattended deaths."[8] Nancy White was the justice in Precinct 1, but she was not a physician, had no medical credentials, and had no training in forensics or crime scene investigation. Nonetheless, she made an immediate determination that the collision was not a criminal matter and that it should be processed as a fatal accident. The death was a suicide, White decided. It was a snowball of an error that would lead to an avalanche of injustice. White accompanied the body to the nearby Vaughn Funeral Home where she observed Shue's injuries; more photos were taken. Someone must have suggested that a forensic pathologist should perform an autopsy because late that evening Shue was transported to the county morgue. There was no chain of custody or guard for Shue's body, nor was there a list of all the personnel who might have come into contact with his remains.[9]

Around 3 p.m., some seven hours after the crash, Kendall County sheriff Henry Hodge and others notified Tracy Shue that her husband was deceased due to an auto accident. It would be another three and a half hours before she was told the news by anyone from the air force. When a military member dies, there is a written protocol for notification: The Command Center notifies the Casualty Affairs and Mortuary Affairs Offices, which alert the Command Chain and the Casualty Notification Team, who then contacts the next of kin. In the Shue case, the Casualty Affairs office claimed to know nothing about Philip's death until late afternoon on April 16. Shue's duty station was not notified until around that time. The Casualty Notification Team, which included Shue's commander, also did not know until that time. Months later, Tracy said, when she questioned the Casualty Notification officer regarding the sequence of events and why it took so long for her to get the bad news, the officer admitted to "never having seen anything handled in this matter." The Mortuary Affairs officer stated the same; neither could understand why there had not been timely notification within the usual chain.

Tracy also asked Trooper Auxier about the delay, and he replied that it took time to identify the body. In the months to come, no matter who

Tracy asked, she received the same pat response. "Nothing made sense," Tracy would tell me later. "My husband was wearing his uniform with his name embroidered on it, and he was driving a car that was registered to him. I assumed he had his wallet and identification on him, and was not told otherwise. This happened in the wake of the Iraq War, and we live in a military-rich suburb, so I believe the state troopers would have automatically notified the military. But I was too frazzled to protest."[10]

When Tracy learned where the accident had taken place—beyond their home exit from the highway—she was more confused. And things got even more confounding when she was told duct tape had been wrapped about the colonel's wrists and boots. All Tracy knew at this time was that Phil Shue had died of head wounds; she did not know about any other injuries.

Col. Shue's body was brought to the neighboring Bexar County morgue in San Antonio, where autopsies for Kendall County are accommodated. On the morning after Shue's death, then-medical examiner Jan C. Garavaglia performed the procedure. (Days later, she would move to Florida to become the Orange County medical examiner and host of the *Dr. G* cable television series for the Learning Channel, featuring some of her cases. She also performed the autopsy on Caylee Anthony, which was discussed in chapter 1.) At the time of the Shue case, Bexar County's chief medical examiner was Vincent J. M. DiMaio, whom I've known for decades. His father, Dominick, was a mentor when he served as New York City's chief medical examiner in the 1960s, and father and son would later co-author a seminal textbook titled *Forensic Pathology*. Vince is a former professor at the Department of Pathology at the University of Texas, author of the textbook *Gunshot Wounds* and several forensic manuals, and a frequent expert witness in cases involving questionable deaths. We have often testified in the same court cases, sometimes on the same side of the aisle and sometimes on opposing sides, and we share leadership roles in many professional medical organizations.

Friendship aside, however, DiMaio and Garavaglia made an unfortunate call on the Shue case when they trumped Justice White's opinion, making things worse.[11]

Dr. Garavaglia's autopsy report notes that the deceased measured five foot eight and weighed one hundred and fifty pounds. The colonel's camouflage shirt—decorated with the US Air Force emblem and the name "Shue"—was open, with its bottom either cut or torn and buttons partially torn off. His olive T-shirt was tucked into his waistband, neatly cut from neck to navel and covered in blood. Much of his chest hair had been shaved, with stubble present. His camouflage pants were zippered closed and had a canvas belt in place, but the left back pocket had an L-shaped cut or tear. In the pants' right front pocket was a dollar and seven cents in change and a money clip with forty-two dollars in currency. A small flashlight was in the lower storage pocket of the right pant leg. Shue wore black military lace-up boots and white socks. After his pants and Jockey-style undershorts were removed, a small amount of white fiber material consistent with a disposable diaper was noted. Gel-like material adherent to the skin of the scrotum and penis was consistent with that from the absorbent area of a diaper.

Cut pieces of duct tape were wrapped around the tops of Shue's boots, with two small gray hairs on the left boot's tape; forensic testing would later prove the hairs were Shue's. Duct tape was also wound around both wrists, with the right one wrapped three times and smeared with blood, its loose end dangling. The duct tape on the left wrist was looped three times and covered Shue's watch; the end of that piece of tape hung four inches and was slightly wadded into a ball at the end. Both sides of the hands revealed dried blood; blood was underneath the fingernails, and the left hand also had glass on it. Numerous areas of body trauma were identified internally and externally. There were two versions of Garavaglia's report; one questioned whether the whites of Shue's eyes showed petechiae, or small blood spots, and the final report stated that there were none present. The face showed multiple abrasions, or scrapes, and contusions, or bruises. X-rays revealed fractures of the facial bones on both sides, and a displaced mandible, or lower jaw bone. There was a 7½-inch gaping, deep laceration of the right cheek extending to the scalp, with a displaced fracture of the skull beneath. Both ears were torn down to the cartilage, with a 2½-inch gaping, deep laceration behind the left ear, exposing a skull fracture. Upon examining the scalp, many soft tissue hemorrhages were noted, and there were multiple lacerations of the brain. Sectioning of the brain revealed petechiae in the white matter, contusions throughout the gray matter, and deep lacerations.

Garavaglia's report describes a 5¾-inch vertical gash that went down the colonel's sternum, with five linear abrasions on one end, which she interpreted as hesitation marks—the kind of minor, self-mutilating wounds often seen by a person who is testing the waters before going through with an act of suicide. On the other end was a ¾-inch abrasion, and next to the incised wound were at least two other similar abrasions, one that dug into the flesh by an ⅛-inch. Both of Shue's nipples and areolae had been excised, leaving two open wounds and sharp, though slightly irregular, edges. The right nipple removal had no associated abrasions or contusions, while the left had a blood clot adherent to it measuring 1½ × 1 inches. Bruises were found on his left wrist and arm, right hand and wrist, left knee, and shinbone area. His left pinky finger had been severed at the first knuckle, leaving contusions. There were also scratches on the left hand, right arm, and left knee, and a sizable irregular laceration with underlying puncture wound defect on the side of the right lower leg. Internally, there was no evidence of trauma. His vital organs were unremarkable, as was the interior portion of his neck.

The toxicological results revealed a reading of 0.49 mg/L (milligrams per liter) of diphenhydramine, which is the active ingredient in Benadryl®, used for allergy relief. There was also a minute reading of 2.4 mg/L of the anesthetic lidocaine in Shue's femoral blood sample. In addition, 1 percent carbon monoxide saturation in the heart blood was present, which is normal. While Shue had prescriptions for two medications—clonazepam, a benzodiazepine sold under the brand name Klonopin® and used for sleeping and to reduce panic disorders, and venlafaxine, an antidepressant sold under the brand name Effexor®—neither was in his system at death. It would have taken five to seven days of being off the latter medication for it to not show up in a toxicology screening.

The FBI laboratory repeated testing on small samples of Shue's blood and urine, finding only a trace amount of the clonazepam. They also determined a very low reading of gamma-hydroxybuterate (a stimulant better known as GHB), an odorless and colorless drug that, in higher levels, can be surreptitiously dropped into someone's drink and used as a "date-rape" drug. But GHB is also something that occurs as a natural result of decomposition, and since there was such a low level, there is no doubt how it came to be in the colonel's bloodstream. The medical examiner's office issued a deferred manner of death, pending the results of a number of probes by state and local police, Justice of the Peace White, and the military's own investigatory unit, the Armed Forces Institute of Pathology, whose own report would follow much later.[12]

Immediately after the Bexar County autopsy was completed, Shue's body was released to Tracy, who had it shipped to a private funeral home in Brookeville, Ohio, near where Phil's elderly parents lived. The mortuary, which often performs work for military personnel, embalmed Shue's body. Tracy had planned to have the colonel cremated, followed by a local memorial service and burial with full military honors at Arlington National Cemetery in Virginia. At this point, Tracy assumed Phil died wholly because of the car crash; she still did not know about the stab wound to his chest, the excised nipples, or the missing part of his finger.

A few days later, sheriff's investigator Luther VanLandingham called Tracy and said that the initial toxicology screening showed the presence of EMLA cream in Shue's system, and did she know why? EMLA is a popular topical anesthesia, obtained through prescription, that contains two active ingredients: 2.5 percent lidocaine and 2.5 percent prilocaine. Tracy explained that both she and Phil would occasionally use the cream—she for tiny spider veins on her face, and Phil for rosacea. A local dermatologist had suggested they try the cream, so Philip wrote the prescription and filled it at the Lackland AFB pharmacy. They'd only bought a few tiny tubes, each approximately the size of a Krazy Glue® container, which the Shues kept in a bathroom drawer. Tracy mentioned that on Philip's last night, he had complained of itching from where his chest had been shaved for the monitors from the cardiac stress test, so maybe he used some of the cream on his chest. She added that she didn't see Phil use the cream, nor did he tell her he had used it. But the EMLA answer seemed to satisfy the officer, so Tracy put the conversation out of her mind, at least for a while.[13]

Tracy couldn't have known it, but the EMLA information was something Dr. DiMaio needed to promote a theory he was leaning toward: that Col. Philip Shue had mutilated himself before committing suicide. If Shue used a numbing agent, he could have performed the nipple and finger excisions and could have stabbed himself before he crashed his vehicle. When DiMaio learned about the EMLA cream, he became convinced that Shue had rubbed it on his own chest, thus introducing it into his bloodstream. However, DiMaio's assumption was flawed because while the Bexar County toxicology lab had gotten a reading for lidocaine, it had not tested for the presence of the co-ingredient in EMLA—prilocaine—which would have had to be there if EMLA were used. I don't know why that test wasn't performed after the office learned Shue had access to EMLA, but the absence of the test allowed a wrong conclusion to fester. Even more astonishing was that in October 2003, Elizabeth "Betsy" Spratt, director of toxicology at New York's Westchester County Medical Examiner's office, and a friend of Tracy's sister, asked Bexar County's chief toxicologist, Gary W. Kunsman, PhD, whether he had tested Shue's blood and tissues for the presence of prilocaine, and he said he had not. He then conducted that test, found there was no prilocaine—which meant the EMLA cream had not been used—and informed the sheriff's department. Kunsman then sent samples to the FBI laboratory at Quantico, Virginia, which confirmed his analysis.

Despite feeling pressure from the military to schedule the cremation, Tracy told the funeral home to stop all plans and hold the body in a refrigerated crypt until she gave further instructions. Although she didn't know yet that DiMaio was formulating a manner of death of suicide, "things just didn't feel right," she confided to friends. A very experienced, retired Dayton-area police chief, George Brown, who was also Phil's best pal, suggested that Tracy ask a nationally renowned forensic pathologist to perform an independent autopsy. He had heard about me through various professional conferences he had attended over the years and made the first call to my office, speaking to one of my staffers. Told that I frequently do consultations for out-of-state cases, he gave my contact information to Tracy Shue. Because she had no legal counsel, except for a probate attorney, Tracy called me herself. I told her that I could do an ancillary autopsy, but since there was no rush, she should obtain the police files and photos before we scheduled the procedure. She would keep Phil's body at the Ohio funeral home.[14]

Back in Texas, Tracy pleaded with Kendall County attorney Don Allee and district attorney Bruce Curry to conduct a public inquest hearing, but was turned down, she said. When she brought her complaints to then-Texas attorney general Gregg Abbott, he declined to get involved, stating that it would be "inappropriate" for his office to intervene in local government's investigations and procedures, and suggested that if she didn't like the politicians in her community, she should "vote them out of office or go to the media." And the military brass, with whom she and her husband had both served with distinction, seemed annoyed by her refusal to move on. It wasn't until June, when she received a phone call from Zeke MacCormack, a journalist with the *San Antonio Express-News*, that she learned the full extent of her husband's injuries—something every person at the accident site, the funeral homes, and the morgue all knew but never bothered telling her. She thought MacCormack was making it up, but when she realized he wasn't, she felt sick.

Toward the beginning of August, Tracy began making almost daily drop-ins to the Kendall County sheriff's office, hoping to find that they were investigating the death as a homicide. Lieutenant Roger Anderson had been the top-ranking official at the crash site on the morning of Phil's death, but when he didn't like the way it was being handled, he backed off and turned the matter over to a deputy. But Tracy's pleas resonated with Anderson, so he allowed her to come to his office and review documents, which was acceptable since she was Phil Shue's next of kin. One day, he mentioned that the medical examiner's autopsy report had come in. As Anderson read the report aloud to Tracy and Investigator VanLandingham, all were appalled that the official manner of death was listed as suicide. Tracy Shue was offended at the idea and decided that if local authorities and the military weren't up to doing a proper investigation, she would grab the helm herself. Perhaps it was Tracy's own training as a nurse, or her innate curiosity, but from that day forward, she would take on duties a grieving widow should never have to contend with, including poring over graphic crime scene photos and police and medical reports, assessing new pieces of evidence as they came in.[15]

The Bexar County medical examiner's autopsy report was signed by Drs. Garavaglia and DiMaio, along with deputy chief medical examiner Dr. Randall E. Frost and medical examiner Dr. Suzanna E. Dana. Shue, they wrote, had died as a result of massive craniocerebral injuries from the car accident. His chest wound and nipple excisions were not part of the trauma of the accident but were self-inflicted. It was unclear to the doctors whether or not the missing finger portion was related to the accident. They found no evidence that any other individual was involved in Shue's death or in the infliction of his excised wounds.[16]

Tracy agreed that her husband died in the car accident, but she firmly felt someone had put into play a series of criminal actions that led to his death. That made it murder. She believed that he had been kidnapped, duct-taped, and tortured, then he somehow broke free, got into his car, or was put in the vehicle by someone else, and passed out before his car went off the highway and into the trees. She stated that Phil might have thought the witnesses who ended up giving statements about his car leaving the road might have been his abductors chasing him, and that, combined with compromised consciousness from his painful chest wounds, could have led to his reckless driving.[17] However, in an interview, DiMaio countered that Shue's natural reaction, had he been on the run from attackers, would have been to drive to the closest police station or hospital; instead the colonel was driving away from San Antonio and the hospitals there, and he passed three exits beyond his home town of Boerne. "This action is not consistent with someone fleeing an assailant," DiMaio said. He also noted that there was a working cell phone in the car, with no record of calls made for help.[18] But Tracy, whose neighbor Nina Woolard recovered the flip phone from police, maintained that blood was outside and inside the phone, as if Shue had attempted to make a call. The phone had been sitting in its charger in the car, but the route he was on had many drop-out spots where cell phones would lose signals or not work at all. Phone records proved that no successful phone calls were made, but failed attempts are never reflected on a call list.[19]

As noted earlier, DiMaio's theory was enhanced by the toxicology report that showed lidocaine in Shue's bloodstream. He went from initially claiming that Shue had rubbed the EMLA cream on his chest, to suggesting it was squirted directly into each wound, and finally—after he learned there was only lidocaine and no prilocaine, hence no EMLA—to positing that Shue injected liquid lidocaine into his own nipples before surgically removing the skin, and into his chest before plunging in the knife or scalpel to make the long wound.[20] The use of lidocaine proved

that no kidnapper was responsible, DiMaio stated, because anyone tor-
turing an individual would want them to feel the pain. The doctor felt that
Tracy's rejection of his suicide notion was due to her being "distorted by
her love," a reaction he termed "perfectly reasonable."[21]

DiMaio, in a 2005 civil deposition that is posted online, elaborated
on his opinion of two years before, stating that with all his experience as
a forensic pathologist, he had never "in our society" seen a case of physical torture. "This case is supposed to be a torture homicide, some
people say, with professional killers and things like that. That's all a fanciful, Hollywood, pulp fiction thing. It doesn't work that way in real life.
Contract killers virtually don't exist," he said, adding: "The only time
people get tortured, generally, are females and it's usually in sexual
assaults, if you want to consider that torture."[22] Well, I would have to
dispute both parts of Vince's statement. While contract killings are rare,
they do exist, and not just in the movies. As for sexual torture and homicide, it *is* torture, and it's not just females who are victimized, although
that is indeed more frequent. But to dispute that it happened in the Shue
case is shortsighted. If Col. Shue's torturer wanted something from
him—perhaps to sign something or to make a financial arrangement—
there likely would have been a systematic plan of torture, increasing the
level of pain to gain whatever was desired. Also, to my mind, the elements of a sexual assault were very much present, including Shue's
clothing being torn off at some point. Nobody put match sticks under
his fingernails, as we see in war torture scenarios and Hollywood movies,
but Phil Shue's nipples were removed, and nipples are an erogenous
zone. Who knows how much further the physical persecution would
have gone had he not escaped? We can guess that the assailant wanted
him to talk or scream since there was no duct tape residue on his mouth,
but it's also possible he had a ball gag in place, which may have even
caused some of the injury to his ears. The ripped duct tape on his wrist
indicates that he broke free from something he was bound to, perhaps a
chair. We don't know the sequence of injuries, but a logical scenario

might have been taking off his clothes, restraining him, the finger excision, some menacing but mild stabbing of the chest, then the nipple excisions, which caused him to react in such a forceful manner that he loosened one hand, maybe frightening his assailant. The chest wound could have occurred when Shue's captor tried to stop him from bolting. Of course, this is speculation; we'll never know the exact circumstances unless the perpetrator decides to talk.

DiMaio's controversial stance that Shue committed suicide convinced District Attorney Curry to convene an investigative grand jury of twelve citizens who would hear top-secret evidence and decide whether they agreed with the doctor or if there should be any kind of felony prosecution. When Curry found out that Tracy had been told what was in the autopsy report, he purportedly encouraged Justice of the Peace White to release the report to the media.[23] One week before the first hearing began, Zeke MacCormack was given a copy of the report. The headline for that day's *San Antonio Express-News* blazed: "Duct-Taped Driver's Death Was Suicide."[24] So much for the sanctity of the grand jury system.[25]

It was a struggle for Tracy to get Curry to present the grand jury with any witnesses who would suggest Shue was murdered and not suicidal. Not one person who knew Philip was invited, including family, friends, treating physicians, or co-workers. Even Tracy wasn't subpoenaed, but she requested a time and date and was eventually allowed to give testimony. Tracy read to the jurors a statement from a family friend, Nancy J. Haley, PhD, who was a vice president and forensic specialist with Metropolitan Life Insurance Company. Haley had studied the case file, felt Shue's death was a homicide, and outlined her reasons. During Tracy's time on the stand, she mentioned that I would be performing a second autopsy, which was a bombshell to Curry, who thought the colonel had already been cremated. Curry was so angry that, as he walked Tracy out of the room and to the stairwell, she says he hissed, "Since you like to testify so much, perhaps I should accuse you of the crime and have you end up in the defendant's seat." Not intimidated by his threat, Tracy told him she wouldn't back down.[26]

But the deck was unfairly stacked. The grand jury process was extended a total of three times before the panel was able to reach a decision in the case in November 2003, echoing Curry's and DiMaio's views that no crime had occurred. With the absence of critical witnesses and documents, and a blatant misrepresentation of the scientific findings from the experts who favored the suicide angle, the grand jurors reached the end of the line. There would be no further investigation by law enforcement, and the case would be closed.[27] Without redress in criminal court, Tracy would have to pursue the matter in a civil venue. "I couldn't allow such an injustice to have happened not only to a wonderful person, but a person that I loved," she said.[28] Shortly thereafter she retained legendary attorney Jason M. Davis, a former federal prosecutor and the 2001 Texas Prosecutor of the Year. Davis's laser-like litigation skills are on display in deposition clips on the Internet, causing Tracy to remark, "He reminds me of Tom Cruise's military lawyer character in *A Few Good Men*, which was Phil's and my favorite film."[29]

I get a lot of calls from family members requesting that I perform a repeat autopsy. Often it's because a medical examiner has determined the decedent died of a suicide when the next of kin is confident that the person had to have been murdered. Claims fly that authorities missed obvious signs of homicide and that there was a conspiracy to protect those who made errors, leaving a killer free to commit other crimes. More likely the parent, sibling, or spouse doesn't want to admit to having missed clues that their loved one was seriously depressed enough to take his or her own life. Denial helps mask the guilt. Of course, sometimes there are cases where I can find a significant factor to wake up a dormant investigation. When I consult on a case, I do not go into it with a preconceived viewpoint, no matter who is paying me; that would not be a scientifically principled approach. I endeavor to respect that the person reaching out to me is suffering and in need of honest advice, whether what I have to say ends their quest or opens new doors.

I had not heard about Philip Shue's death when Tracy had first phoned me, and I encouraged her to collect evidence before I proceeded to a second autopsy. But I was impressed by the work she had gathered in the months since we spoke. I told her that an ancillary post-mortem exam would either get the case reclassified as a homicide or confirm DiMaio's analysis, meaning Philip Shue had deadly ideations he hadn't shared with his wife. Either way, I knew the case would be intellectually challenging.

I studied the law enforcement reports, crime scene photographs, newspaper articles, and the Bexar County medical examiner's reports and X-rays. I also had lengthy conversations with Kendall County sheriff lieutenant Roger Anderson, whom I came to appreciate. Although he had been the lead investigator at the site, he admitted that he lost control of the case due to internecine squabbling between his department, the Boerne police, and the military. From the moment he could see the body in the car with duct tape on its wrists, he complained that there was more to this case than a vehicular death; he practically came to blows with some of the others and yelled at them to "get the hell out of my crime scene." But he was overruled and left the site in disgust. He was told later that the body and vehicle were taken away and the scene went unprocessed. I could understand his fury. Even if the case didn't end up being a suspicious death, that crime scene evidence should have been collected and preserved because once gone, it couldn't be replicated. To Anderson's credit, he has since been outspoken in support of Tracy Shue's quest to have the case viewed as a homicide. Still haunted by the case, he told me and would later repeat on television: "I believe Col. Shue was intercepted on his way to work, taken to some location unknown, and tortured and terrorized. That's what the evidence suggests to me, but because the crime scene was compromised, I can't prove a thing."

Shue's missing body parts—his nipples and the tip of his finger—

were not recovered from the car, nor were they with his body. While the colonel had money, as previously noted, in a front pants' pocket, his dog tags and wallet were missing. Of course, those items could have been tossed out the car window with zero chance of recovering them, as no one was sure what his route had been before he left the IH-10 and smashed into the trees. Shue's car featured an automatic seat belt harness that crosses the driver's body when the door is closed, but the belt that crosses his lap was latched. No forensic testing was done on the metal buckle to reveal fingerprints or DNA, from Shue or anyone else. A photo of the car's glove compartment showed a straight razor that seemed to have a bloody discoloration on the edge, but forensic testing proved it was rust. And a police report stated items inside the car included two small pocket knives and an unused latex glove, but the crime scene photos did not support some of that information. For example, only one knife—of a Swiss Army style—was shown in the photos, and its blade did not appear to be sharp enough to have created the surgical incisions on Shue's body. DNA analysis showed the presence of Shue's blood on one of the knives, the glove, and the car's steering wheel, and no one else's blood or fingerprints were on the items. Neither the colonel's, nor anyone else's, fingerprints were on the duct tape, which could be consistent with a killer wearing gloves. Also, Kendall County investigators reported there was an unopened box of small-gauge needles in the glove compartment, but they were not evident in any photo, and there was no hypodermic syringe photographed or reported. Those were just some of the frustrating issues I encountered as I went through the files.

In August 2003, Colonel Shue's body was shipped from the Ohio mortuary to Carlow University in Pittsburgh, a world-class Catholic teaching school at whose Gross Anatomy Laboratory I conduct my independent autopsies. The wooden casket containing the remains was well sealed, with no insects or fungal growth inside. Shue was clad in a dark-blue air force jacket and pants with silver buckles. Numerous medals were affixed to the left upper chest. He also wore a short-sleeved blue shirt, white T-shirt and Jockey-style shorts, black socks, and black military-type shoes, with white gloves on his hands. Lying on top of his chest was a hat with the markings of a colonel rank. His scalp was covered by neatly combed, moderately long, straight, graying, dark hair. Evidence of recent embalming was present, including heavy cosmetic material on the face and plastic cups over the eyes; the color of his irises could not be ascertained. The upper and lower gums were wired together, and various incisions had been closed tightly with thick, white string. I opened each of them to do my own inspection.

The body was nicely preserved. There was a minor amount of decomposition—which begins at the moment of death and continues to some degree, even if a body is kept in a cool environment—but I accounted for that as I proceeded in my task. Using a magnifying glass on the unclad corpse, I made a visual inspection of the chest and areolae areas, looking for the injection sites DiMaio insisted were there, but there were none. Had lidocaine been administered with a needle to those areas, there would have been tell-tale pricks and discoloration, even if they were very shallow injections. In fact, I could see no pinpoint injection marks anywhere on Shue's body. Also, as stated in the toxicology report, the lidocaine present was not of a high enough level to have acted as an effective anesthetic for such delicate surgeries as occurred on the nipples, and there was no proof of, or sensible reason for, Shue having put a huge gash in his own chest.

As is typical in an ancillary autopsy, the internal organs and tissues were placed in a plastic bag within the reopened chest cavity, with the bag surrounded by sawdust material to absorb moisture. I removed the organs and tissues and conducted my own examinations. There was no evidence of hemorrhages, tumor, infectious process, or other abnormalities on the lungs, heart, aorta, spleen, liver, kidneys, gastrointestinal tract, tongue and oropharynx, larynx, and trachea, or adrenal glands. I also removed the testes from the scrotal sac and noted no injuries to them.

My final pathological diagnoses detailed massive and extensive cran-iocerebral injuries: lacerations, abrasions, and contusions to his face; multiple and bilateral fractures of facial bones; subgaleal and sub-periosteal hemorrhages (bleeding between the skull and scalp); multiple, extensive, and bilateral fractures of the calvarium (upper part of the cra-nium, from the eyebrows up and back) and basilar skull (floor of the skull); and extensive subdural hemorrhages. There was epidural and sub-dural hemorrhage of the cervical (neck), thoracic (chest), and lumbar (back) spinal canal. His sternum (breastbone) was fractured, along with his left ribs 2, 3, 4. I noted the incised wounds of his anterior chest wall, which I measured to be 6¼ inches, which is one-half inch longer than what Dr. Garavaglia wrote in her report. I agreed with her basic findings about the excision of Shue's right and left nipples and the traumatic amputation of the distal phalanx (left fifth finger), as well as superficial contusions of his arms and legs. There were also extensive and bilateral fibrous plaques of his diaphragm (rib cage), a natural disease process having nothing to do with the traumatic injuries.

As I compared my findings to those signed off on by the Bexar County medical examiner team, I noticed glaring omissions or irregu-larities made by Dr. Garavaglia. There was no list of all the people who attended the autopsy, which is typically provided when military per-sonnel are autopsied. Tracy Shue later learned that uniformed officers were in attendance, but she was not told who they were or what rank they held. Colonel Shue was in his military clothing when Garavaglia got the body, and, in her report, she refers multiple times to how neatly his T-shirt was tucked into his pants. He had been examined and pho-tographed previously at the funeral home, so it seems he was re-dressed, but it is unknown who would have done this. This should have been specified in the report. And there were other signs of re-dressing. While Garavaglia observed that Shue's right calf had a puncture wound deep enough to go into the underlying musculature, there was no corre-sponding tear or puncture in the right pants' leg. A photo shows that one of Shue's boots was laced poorly—hardly the way a colonel would leave for work. To me, that photo could indicate re-dressing, but it raised no questions to the medical examiner, who did not mention it in her autopsy report. More disturbing was the fact that both of Shue's boot bottoms were caked with mud and a white, powdery substance, which could have been a clue to where he had been in the missing two hours. No samples were taken and sent to the crime lab for analysis.

The Bexar County report acknowledges the diaper-like material found in Shue's Jockey-style shorts, but Tracy was never questioned about it. She would later tell me that Phil had had some recent history of prostate enlargement with frequent urination, so he would cut up pieces of diaper to line his underwear. This matter was not given appropriate analysis in the report, which struck me as a lack of scientific inquisitiveness on the part of the doctor—and there were similar failings. An autopsy room photo shows Phil's canvas belt looped through his pants and a pager attached to the belt. But there was no mention of the communication device in Garavaglia's report. The pager vanished without being entered into evidence or forensically analyzed to see who might have contacted Shue in the hours leading up to his death. A similar blunder occurred with Shue's Palm™ Pilot, a handheld personal computer that had been collected from the Shues' home office by state trooper Al Auxier, who scrolled through its planner. The device should have been turned over to the Kendall County sheriff's office and entered into evidence, since those personnel were the lead investigators at that time. Instead, Auxier turned it over to someone from the Air Force Office of Special Investigations and got a receipt. But the PalmPilot was never seen again and is not mentioned in any report.

Shue's blood was found on the inner aspect of the duct tape—the portion that adhered to the skin of his left wrist or arm—but there was no significant blood in the surrounding area. Garavaglia's report didn't offer an interpretation, such as that the colonel may have been bleeding at the time the duct tape was applied. And while the report notes the back of Shue's wrist showing a faint, semi-circular bluish contusion underneath his wristwatch, there was no comment, such as how that could indicate pressure while the tape was applied. Information of this nature could have been helpful in determining the order in which the injuries were sustained.

Garavaglia's final report stated that Shue's eyes showed no petechial hemorrhaging, even though her previous draft said there was. When I inspected the eyes, the telltale red marks were quite apparent. She also tied the hairless spots on Phil's chest to the injuries he sustained, but had she called Tracy, she would have learned that the shaved patches were from the day before, when Shue took a cardiac stress test in preparation for retirement. Tracy also would have explained the presence of three small, aging contusions found on his abdomen, which were from breaking up their dogs from roughhousing weeks earlier. The doctor wrote that Phil had no previous surgical scars yet acknowledged that his appendix "could not be identified." That's because it had been taken out surgically years before, leaving a very obvious scar on his lower abdomen. While Garavaglia described Shue's coronary arteries as "without athero-sclerosis," I found a minimal, focal amount. Trauma marks on upper extremities were noted but, oddly, were not viewed as defensive wounds. Blood beneath his fingernails was noted and identified as Shue's, but his nails were not scraped for DNA and analyzed at the laboratory, a standard procedure in assault cases. Often forensic pathologists assessing stabbings will fill the wounds with plaster of paris to make a cast that can show the type of knife or instrument used in the attack. Very specific information can be obtained in this fashion, including the length, width, and shape of the blade; whether it was sharp on one or both edges; if there was a hilt at the top of the blade; the angle and depth of attack; whether it went in and out more than once or was twisted; and even whether the individual wielding the tool used a right or left hand. But none of this analysis was possible in the Shue case because the Bexar County experts did not cast or give much detail about the chest wound, and Tracy was never asked whether Phil was right- or left-handed (he was right-handed).

I concurred with the Bexar County autopsy doctors that Phil Shue died as a result of the grave head injuries sustained in the car accident. Beyond that, I reported that his chest gash and other wounds would certainly have been uncomfortable for him but were unlikely to have caused immediate death. The incision to his chest missed vital organs. The loss of blood would not have caused a quick loss of consciousness; it would have more reasonably led to the diminishing degree of motor coordination and sensory perception that was consistent with his driving before he hit the trees.

I did not reveal my findings to Tracy Shue until January 2004, when she and her attorney, Jason Davis, and their private investigator, a retired FBI agent named George Parks, visited my office in preparation for the civil lawsuit they were pursuing. Meeting Tracy in person resulted in mixed feelings for me; I knew how she had led the brigade over the last few months, yet she seemed almost fragile. I decided that the first order of business was to order in lunch for everyone, thereby earning gratitude from my guests. Then, in a very productive meeting, I outlined how I added up all the puzzle pieces to scientifically arrive at my determination. I concluded that Colonel Philip Shue had been ritualistically tortured and murdered. The Bexar County autopsy report should have listed the manner of death as "homicide" or, at the least, "undetermined" or "pending further investigation." But who was Shue's killer? My visitors had a theory for that, and I listened in fascination. They said that there was a very good suspect—and, according to them, the motive was money.[30]

Nancy Shue is Phil's first wife; they were high school sweethearts, although she was one year older than him. The pair married in January 1970, with George Brown, the former police chief who suggested I do a second autopsy, acting as best man. Nancy was six months pregnant when they wed, and, as she told military investigators looking into

Shue's death, she wasn't sure who the baby's biological father was; while dating Phil, she was also seeing an NFL coach. Phil raised the boy, Jeffrey, as his son, and never felt the need to confirm paternity with a DNA swab, despite the fact that the boy looked nothing like him. The Shue family was based in Dayton, Ohio, where Phil graduated from the medical school of Wright State University in 1984 and was accepted into a four-year psychiatric residency program at Wright-Patterson Air Force Base Medical Center. Nancy worked as an elementary school teacher. In 1988, they moved to Fort Walton Beach, Florida, when Phil took an assignment at Eglin Air Force Base, and Nancy quit teaching. Jeff's teenage years were thorny; his activities included hanging out with known marijuana dealers. Phil and Nancy's marriage became strained to the point that Phil wanted to move out but was advised against that by Jeff's therapist.[31] In early 1990, they legally separated, and Phil moved into an apartment; several months later, he began dating Tracy. Phil and Nancy agreed to remain married until he finished his service commitment in June 1992; Nancy, who wasn't working, would retain all military benefits until then. Phil's monthly paycheck as a military physician went to her, while he lived off a moonlighting job as a private psychiatrist in Dothan, Alabama, during the estrangement. Once the couple divorced, Nancy started taking psychology classes, eventually earning a master's degree and becoming a licensed counselor.

The most contentious part of the Phil and Nancy breakup was over two insurance policies that she held on his life, worth a total of one million dollars. When the divorce became final, she retained ownership of the policies. And she wasn't about to give them up, even though Phil made many requests during the late 1990s.[32] In the heat of the battle over the policies, Phil received a letter that frightened him, according to Tracy. Computer-generated, undated, unsigned, and filled with grammatical errors, the letter read:

Dear Dr. Shue,

Please read this letter. You may be in danger.

I'm writing because I remember you as such a kind and caring doctor. And I can't sit by and not help you by telling you what I know. I'll try to keep it short so your certain to read it.

A friend of mine who worked with Don (your ex wife's husband) told me some skary things. I don't know Don or your ex wife myself (sorry, I don't even know her name). My friend told me they wish you were dead so they could collect life insurance. I don't understand why they would have life insurance on you, but that's what my friend told me. My friend things they may actually be planning something.

I don't know if they would actually hurt you, but please be careful. I had to write. If I didn't I couldn't bare the thought of something bad happening to you that I could have prevented by telling you what I heard.

If I hear anything more specific I will let you. Please be careful. I'm sorry to worry you, but I just couldn't not write and find out later that I could have stopped a bad thing from happening.

Donald "Don" Timpson, an air force special forces pilot, was Nancy's current husband. Phil confided to Tracy that there was another other equally ominous letter; only after Shue's death did Tracy find out there was a similar third letter. Phil wrote to Nancy, pleading with her to drop the policies and declaring that he felt like a sitting duck if she "should hire good assassins." Nancy wrote back that she had nothing to do with any letters, which "may be someone's terribly sick idea of a game or a joke." And no, she wouldn't give up the policies.[33] Regrettably, nobody at the Bexar County Forensic Center tested the letters for fingerprints or DNA. They were kept in the Shues' bank safety deposit box where sheriff's investigator Luther VanLandingham lifted and looked at them with his ungloved hands. There was also no linguistic testing of the documents against known samples of any of the people involved in the case to determine if there were similarities of content that could identify the author. The Shue home computer was checked to see if Phil Shue himself had written the letters, but when that search came up empty, investigators lost interest in the subject.[34]

Phil tried to make an end run around Nancy and began dealing directly with the insurance companies, showing the agents the letters and demanding that they cancel the policies. But even if the companies understood his alarm, they were powerless to do anything. Nancy owned the policies, and as long as she kept paying the premiums, which amounted to twelve thousand dollars per year, no one could wrest, cajole, or sue the policies away from her.[35] Following military protocol, Shue advised his commanding officer of the predicament. Soon Phil, the quiet, steady man—a trained psychiatrist who solved everyone else's problems—began to come apart at the seams. He became depressed and couldn't sleep, and Tracy maintained it all started with that first letter.[36]

I asked Tracy why her husband had not reported the threatening letters he believed were from Nancy to the Boerne police, instead of telling the military. The answer, she told me, was because Phil had a top-secret clearance, a fact that Drs. DiMaio and Garavaglia never knew or asked about. The military has laws and a firm set of rules for reporting incidents, even those that happen outside of one's official duties. Both active duty personnel and those who are retired are subject to this requirement, and the higher the rank, the bigger the mandate for secrecy. This was a common theme throughout the case; military personnel were even required to seek and obtain permission from the top brass before being allowed to speak to civilian investigators or testify in court. Due to nondisclosure rules, anything Philip Shue told his commanding officers about the letters or anything else cannot be made public or cited in court. While officials have admitted that Shue confided in them, Tracy's representatives could not access any associated documentation to confirm it.[37]

Tracy had another reason to point her finger at Nancy, and it had to do with the cruel nature of Phil's injuries on the last day of his life. Unbeknownst to Phil or Tracy at the time, Nancy had begun a career as a board-certified sex therapist whose duties involved bondage role-playing with clients. She studied under William Granzig, PhD, founding president of the American Board of Sexology and author of the preface of a book titled *Screw the Roses, Give Me the Thorns: The Romance and Sexual Sorcery of Sadomasochism*. Nancy's training was both extensive and expensive. In July 2000, she borrowed over forty-five thousand dollars, at 8 percent interest, against one of Phil's life insurance policies. And in September 2002, just months before Shue's death, she owed more than thirty-two thousand dollars on her credit cards.[38] It wasn't an accident that Shue's nipples were removed with surgical precision. It was torture, perhaps the handiwork of someone who had expertise with acts of sadism. Phil did not enjoy that kind of fetishism or fantasy in his sex life, Tracy assured me.[39] Military police questioned Nancy, but she and her husband both claimed to have been at work that morning. According to Tracy, Nancy had witnesses for her alibi, but Donald's whereabouts reportedly could not be verified. Nancy was invited to take a police polygraph but declined. Donald, who held a top-secret clearance in the air force, wouldn't have been allowed to take a polygraph and thus wasn't even asked. The Department of Defense was monitoring the case and may have given Timpson instructions to not participate.

Shortly after Shue died, Tracy's probate attorney, Bob Ogle, filed paperwork with the court to block any payoffs from the two insurance companies—USAA and Northwestern Mutual Life—until the case could be properly investigated. Later, Tracy's civil litigator, Jason Davis, took over the case and filed lawsuits against the two companies, naming Nancy Shue Timpson as a defendant and Jeffrey Shue as a third-party defendant. Tracy's position was that the companies were told that Nancy had threatened Phil's life and did nothing to cancel the policies, which made them liable. Tracy told me she felt that Nancy and possibly Jeff had knowledge, if not complicity, in Phil's death, and she didn't want them to be able to cash in on the policies they never should have been holding in the first place.[40] Davis salivated at the chance to put Nancy under oath and depose her, but when she appeared for the videotaped deposition—which is posted online—Nancy refused to say a thing beyond confirming her name and status as Shue's first wife. Davis asked her: "Were you responsible for the death of Colonel Philip Shue?" And Nancy replied, "On the advice of counsel, and pursuant to the Fifth Amendment of the Constitution of the United States, I assert my right against self-incrimination and refuse to answer this question on the grounds that any answer might incriminate me." A basic premise of pleading, or "taking the Fifth," as it's known commonly, is that once that plea is invoked for a question, it must be invoked for all subsequent questions. So when it came to all questions regarding murder, motive, or torture, Nancy Shue Timpson took the Fifth—more than twenty times. Donald Timpson was neither deposed nor named in the lawsuit.[41]

Tracy told me she was disappointed when Jeff Shue refused to talk to local law enforcement or military investigators about the colonel's death. "You'd think he'd be outraged that his father died under such mysterious circumstances and everyone seems to be covering it up," she said. Both Phil and Tracy had taken pride in Jeff's accomplishments, even paying for his pilot training, which led to his being hired by Delta Air Lines for its commuter routes. At the time of Phil's death, Jeff was on his second marriage and had a young son. He also had a 2002 bankruptcy, thanks to debts of about one hundred thousand dollars, twenty thousand of which were gambling losses. For that reason, Phil had recently rewritten his will to exclude Jeff—but it's unknown whether Jeff knew about that. The younger man was not deposed in the civil suit because he filed an affidavit, invoking his Fifth Amendment privilege. Since he never made himself available to speak to police, he never refused to take a polygraph examination. Such exams, of course, are not admissible in court, and most defense lawyers advise clients not to take them. But accepting a police-administered test is a way for an innocent person to prove his or her innocence, at least to law enforcement. And passing such a test signals to investigators that their time might be better spent looking elsewhere for a suspect.[42]

I proffered my written opinion on the case in April 2004 to Tracy Shue and her attorney Jason Davis and promised I'd be ready and willing to testify if they ever needed me to. I knew that there were still outstanding facets of the case that could send things in a new direction. One such facet came the next year, with the release of the twenty-page "psychological autopsy report," prepared by two outside experts for the Armed Forces Institute of Pathology (AFIP): Dr. Gerald F. Donovan, deputy chief medical examiner of the Behavioral Science Division in Rockville, Maryland; and Dr. Elspeth Cameron Ritchie, associate professor of psychiatry of the Uniformed Services University of the Health Sciences in Bethesda, Maryland. The document—which was dated May 4, 2005—was requested by the Lackland Detachment of the Air Force Office of Special Investigation (AFOSI), and it described how Colonel Shue had consulted psychiatric colleagues about his depression and panic attacks. The report also mentioned my second autopsy findings, noting that I disagreed with the Bexar County ruling of suicide and stating that I felt that "another person may have been involved" in this death. They also listed my reasons for believing Shue was not suicidal: imminent retirement from the military, acceptance to a forensic psychiatric fellowship program, the purchase of a new home, and lack of suicidal ideation at the time of death. They might have also cited his positive cardiac stress test of the day before he died; his new contact lenses; the chores he planned to do at his current home, including using the lawnmower he had just picked up; and his loving marriage with his wife, Tracy. I told the interviewer that the fatal car accident was far more likely the result of passing out behind the wheel, rather than a purposeful collision into a tree, which might not have guaranteed death and could have led to severe paralysis, something someone suicidal might have considered the worst possible outcome.

On the face of it, this AFIP report should have been the most comprehensive investigation to date; most of the key players in the case were interviewed, with the exception of Nancy Shue Timpson, her son Jeffrey Shue, and her husband Donald Timpson. And one section was terribly shocking. It recounted statements from Dr. Douglas Dionne, Shue's personal psychiatrist at the Brooke Army Medical Center, who described the panic attacks the colonel had experienced after receiving the anonymous threatening letters. Dionne noted Shue's emotional expressions while talking about the letters, which Dionne found consistent with the story being true. But the worst part happened six months before Shue's death, according to Dionne's statement. He quoted Shue as having a "dissociative episode" in which he "imagined his car went out of control on the way to work" and "great violence was done" to him while he was in uniform. That would be a staggering admission, if true. The problem is, it wasn't true. As Tracy Shue's attorney learned directly, Dr. Dionne never told that story to the AFIP interviewer and was never told that story by Colonel Shue. There is no documentation in any of Dionne's notes that reflects Shue's telling that story. Moreover, Dionne is willing to clarify that to any official at any time, in an interview or under oath. Why would someone in the military attribute a fabricated statement to one of his own? Others can speculate about that. But what seems apparent to me is that there was a pronounced need to make Phil Shue seem psychiatrically unstable by the authors of this report—a bitter irony when applied to a man whose entire career was in service to the psychiatric well-being of his fellow enlistees and who reached out to them during their most difficult wartime crises.[43]

In June 2008, the civil lawsuit Tracy and attorney Davis filed finally went to court, with some changes. Nancy Shue Timpson was no longer named as a defendant, nor was her son Jeffrey; in 2005, there had been a million-dollar settlement agreement between Nancy Shue Timpson,

Jeffrey Shue, and Northwestern Mutual Life. Two years before that, Tracy Shue received a $1.8 million award from her husband's military death benefits, and policies from Midland Life Insurance and TransAmerica Life Insurance. The only defendant that remained in the Shue lawsuit was USAA Insurance.[44]

I was on the plaintiff's witness list, awaiting the call to fly to Texas and testify, but I didn't get the opportunity.[45] Also waiting to testify, having flown to Texas from Ohio and unhappy that he didn't get the chance, was Phil Shue's best friend, former police chief George Brown.[46] In an unusual move, Judge Bill Palmer excused the jury and announced that the parties agreed that he would rule on the case himself. He dropped all charges against USAA, stating the company did nothing wrong in refusing to cancel its policy, then he said the words that Tracy and her attorney had waited years to hear. "The evidence considered by the court substantiates a finding that Colonel Philip Shue was murdered," Palmer stated, adding: "The court therefore finds that the April 16, 2003 death of Colonel Philip Shue was a homicide."[47]

At this point, it should have been an easy request for Col. Shue's death certificate to be changed to reflect Judge Palmer's decision—and in Kendall County, Precinct 1, the justice of the peace in charge of that decision was Larry James—the first cop at Shue's crash site—who was voted into that office after Nancy White lost her reelection bid. He has so far refused to update the certificate—and even if it's changed, it wouldn't automatically mean a criminal homicide investigation would follow. Also, the Bexar County medical examiner's office has resisted issuing a supplemental autopsy report stating the new status in the manner of death. Changing a manner of death is not something that happens often, but when it does, it heralds that new professional evidence has been applied to the case. It is not an admission of wrongdoing or incompetence; it is simply a reflection that science is more than black-and-white, that there are shades of gray that make the discipline so very interesting. Shue and Davis's judicial victory was dampened when Justice James and Drs. DiMaio and Garavaglia ignored the court ruling, and I must confess, I can't understand that decision. As a coroner for many decades, I've had opportunities to amend a previous manner of death when new information surfaced to make it necessary, and my co-author, Dawna Kaufmann, tells me that her local Los Angeles County Coroner's Office is also amenable to issuing supplemental reports on occasion. The fact that Col. Shue doesn't merit this small act of kindness is sad. Shue and Davis vowed to continue their battle with the Texas state authorities.[48] Tracy Shue told me that DiMaio allegedly gave a taped interview to a reporter stating that the air force told him that the death was suicide, which is why he ruled it that way. In the same interview DiMaio acknowledged never having read Shue's psychiatric records or contacted Shue's psychiatrist.[49]

My dismay over the decision of the Bexar County experts was compounded when I learned about another case involving evidence and professionalism that should have set a better example.[50] In 1990, Larry Ytuarte, PhD, a chemistry professor with impeccable credits, was hired by the Bexar County Forensic Science Center to analyze cadaver fluids. He quickly learned that not only were some of his lab colleagues less than fastidious in their reports and didn't follow established protocols, but some employees even falsified readings on documents that would be presented in court for criminal cases. When Ytuarte complained to his supervisor, the chief toxicologist, he was told that the problem existed because there were too many cases and not enough staff, as if that were an appropriate excuse for slipshod work. Ytuarte contacted the commissioner's court and the district attorney and, failing to see changes implemented, wrote to the American Academy of Forensic Sciences—an organization of which I'm a past president, though I was not in the loop about Ytuarte's communications. Although he had earned commendations in his workplace, in 1994, Ytuarte was fired and escorted out of the building under the pretense that he had "knowingly issued incorrect toxicology reports"—the very conduct he was trying to expose. The doctor filed a civil suit that was eventually settled in 1997, with him awarded $350,000 and the right to discuss the case publicly. He was also reinstated in his job, but he resigned the same day.[51] He is now an assistant professor in chemistry and biochemistry at New Mexico State University, Las Cruces.[52] Besides Ytuarte's case, the county has paid more than $1.1 million to settle three separate lawsuits stemming from the medical examiner's office.[53] There's probably not a medical examiner's office in the country that doesn't have its share of lawsuits and settlements, but when they happen, it's time for the department heads to take stock and create a better environment, if need be. In egregious cases of laboratory contamination or careless procedures, all the similar cases that have led to convictions in court are at risk of being overturned.[54]

In March 2009, the CBS News program *48 Hours Mystery* aired an hour-long special on the case titled "The Curious Case of Col. Shue." The reporter, Troy Roberts, interviewed Tracy Shue, showed clips from Nancy's deposition where she cited the Fifth Amendment, and featured Dr. DiMaio defending his medical examiner's findings that Shue committed suicide. I also appeared on the program, in a separate interview, in which I expressed my dissatisfaction with the official results, spoke of my second autopsy, and maintained that Shue was murdered. You can never tell how much of what you say on videotape will actually appear on a television show, so I've learned to give concise quotes to deliver the maximum impact. I was pleased that they included my statement that there were no injection marks from anesthesia on the colonel's body, that the injuries on his chest were from his being tortured, that his fingerprints were not on the duct tape around his extremities, and that no rubber gloves were recovered. "I would place my bet that this was a homicide" was my final comment on the broadcast. CBS re-aired the *48 Hours Mystery* program in October 2009, adding a caption at the end that read: "In June 2009, the Texas Attorney General ruled Col. Philip Shue's death certificate does not have to be changed. The official cause of death remains suicide."[55]

There was one unforeseen benefit of the television special. Sometime after the program first aired, Tracy Shue was contacted by someone who had seen the show and realized he might have a powerful piece of new information. The man remembered driving on a side street near the Boerne Highway entrance Shue would have taken to go to work and seeing a car that resembled Phil's Mercury Tracer, pushed off the road and into a ditch, with a van nearby. Tracy's private investigator learned that the area had a natural deposit of caliche, a white clay substance. That could explain the white powder found on the bottoms of Shue's boots, which was never tested by the Bexar County forensic experts.

In the spring of 2005, Colonel Philip Shue was laid to rest at Arlington National Cemetery, with full military honors. I don't know who killed him, or why. I still have many questions, such as how the lidocaine and diphenhydramine, the active ingredient in Benadryl, came to be in Shue's system. Tracy had told me that Phil had no allergies, and she had no recollection of him ever using it as a sleep aid, a common usage for diphenhydramine.[56] It is worth noting, however, that lidocaine was used in 1985 on DEA special agent Enrique "Kiki" Camarena by drug cartel members who wanted to make sure his heart didn't fail as they tortured him, before finally killing him.[57]

The investigation into Colonel Philip Shue's death was performed in an abysmal manner and needs to be reopened at once. Tracy Shue could have gone away with her million-dollars-plus award and stopped trying to solve her husband's murder, but she hasn't done that. She is currently writing a book on the case with Cilla McCain, who authored the military-themed *Murder in Baker Company*, which inspired the film *In the Valley of Elah*. Thanks to Tracy's persistence, there is another piece of welcome news: The FBI has now decided to take over the case, and a meeting is planned between the San Antonio office and the witness who saw the parked vehicles. A fresh set of eyes willing to start at square one with new interviews of all the main players and a review of all the forensic evidence is what this case needs.[58]

CHAPTER THREE

BRIAN JONES
Death by "Misadventure"

A death by "misadventure" seems the perfect send-off for a world-renowned rock star, particularly one recognized as much for his decadent lifestyle as for his musical innovations. But the death certificate that categorized Rolling Stones guitarist Brian Jones's 1969 drowning death at the age of twenty-seven was far from the final declaration on the subject. In fact, it sparked fervent protests, multiple accusations of murder and cover-up, and demands for arrests and the exhumation of Jones's body. And the debate continues today.

In March 1994, I was brought into the case by author Geoffrey Giuliano, who provided me with Jones's official autopsy report and supporting information, and quoted me extensively in his book published that same year, *Paint It Black: The Murder of Brian Jones*. Giuliano is a New York–based author of several books about pop culture figures, including the Beatles and Rod Stewart, and his carefully researched work on Brian Jones is a fascinating read that showcases his commitment to finally "set the record straight," as he told me.

The exclusive details that Giuliano uncovered in his reportage were shocking and, if true, make a casual observer wonder why Jones's killer or killers escaped capture and justice. But as you will see here, the issue of crime and punishment is complex. In the passing years, more books and writings by critical witnesses have come out, as well as at least one deathbed confession, a feature film, and more controversy.

My commitment here is to use my background in science and law to clarify matters.

Lewis Brian Hopkins Jones was born on February 28, 1942, in Cheltenham, Gloucestershire, England, to parents Lewis, a Welsh aeronautical engineer, and Louisa, a piano teacher. Two sisters soon followed— Barbara and Pauline—although the latter would die of leukemia while still a baby. Brian, four years old at the time, would never get over her death; he even blamed her loss for making his parents push him away instead of embracing him closer.

Brian's near-genius IQ of 135 manifested itself during his grammar school years, largely because his bouts of chronic bronchitis and asthma caused him to spend time reading and excelling at art work, rather than team sports. He was an excellent swimmer though, which will be explored in more detail. But it was Brian's early aptitude with music that captured the attention of the small village. St. Mary's, the neighborhood evangelical church that dates back to medieval times, was the first venue for the lad's talent, cultivated by Louisa, who taught piano there, and Lewis, who was the organist and choir director. Brian was sight-reading by age six, then he taught himself to play the recorder and clarinet. Lewis had duel ambitions for his son—as either a classical musician or a dentist. Brian would soon have different ideas.

By thirteen, to the dismay of his parents, Brian discovered jazz. He bought a secondhand saxophone and soon after formed his first band, playing "skiffle" music, which was a salute to the American South, blending acoustic guitar and banjo with homemade instruments such as jugs, washboards, comb-and-paper kazoos, and cigar-box fiddles.

Growing more handsome by the day, with his tawny locks and blue eyes, Brian became a sought-after date among local girls, and was the envy of his buddies. At age sixteen, he impregnated a fourteen-year-old named Valerie, who put up the child—a boy—for adoption. For the conservative community one hundred miles west of London—but seemingly a world away—the scandal made Brian a pariah. He decided to leave Cheltenham and make his way in the world.

With a guitar on his back, Jones set off to hitchhike across Scandinavia, earning his keep as a busker and then bedding a succession of open-minded beauties. He referred to the period as "the most free and happy time of my life." Returning to Cheltenham in 1960, he honed his craft at every bar that played live music. He also impregnated another girl—this time, a twenty-three-year-old—who gave birth to a daughter she never told him about. Decades later, the Stones' bassist Bill Wyman explained in his book *Stone Alone* that he met the illegitimate child, and she told him she suffered from epilepsy, causing Wyman to wonder if Brian also had the malady. He wrote that Jones's oft-eccentric and ornery behavior in the band might have had a physical underpinning.

A serious romance with fifteen-year-old Pat Andrews was the impetus Brian needed to permanently move out of his parents' home and in with her kin and into a series of go-nowhere jobs to supplement his paltry music wages. Pat soon gave birth to Jones's third child, and at the hospital, Brian gave her roses that he bought by selling some of his favorite records. He then essentially abandoned her and the baby. Moreover, he had frequently been physically abusive to Pat.

Brian soon had a more profound passion—the blues. In a London club, he had seen the legendary Muddy Waters play electric guitar, and Brian finally envisioned a career path for himself. He moved to London's Notting Hill district and began playing blues on slide guitar and harmonica, writhing with a sensuous gusto that packed the houses and made the girls swoon. It was at the Ealing Club in April 1962 that Brian would perform in front of the two musicians whose appreciation for him would change all their lives.

Mick Jagger and Keith Richards had known each other since they were toddlers, having grown up in middle-class environs around Dartford, on the outskirts of London. The pair, both born in 1943, a year after Brian, idolized blues players, from Chuck Berry to Elmore James to Bo Diddley, so when they caught Jones onstage doing the white man's version of the black man's music, they were duly impressed. Jones left them spellbound with the way he held the audience's attention, using his body in almost effeminate spasms, a trick Jagger would later adopt himself as he became the Rolling Stones' lead singer. That Brian could read music and effortlessly play numerous instruments—including guitar, harmonica, keyboards, dulcimer, mellotron, sitar, tambura, recorder, saxophone, percussion, autoharp, marimba—as well as sing caused the trio to bond. Soon they began jamming together. Brian and Mick rented a flea-bitten Chelsea crash pad where Keith would often stay. They'd keep their bellies filled by stealing food and ripping off pals, while Jagger attended classes at the London School of Economics and fretted about whether he should become an accountant or turn to music full time. Brian's rhythm guitar playing was just the right boost for Richards's inventive lead guitar work; Keith would later call their blend "the whole secret behind the Stones."

In the trio's early days of gigging, Mick Jagger was fairly motionless onstage; it was Brian who was the showman, leaping into the air and snarling at the lip of the stage or dropping to his knees for a guitar solo. He was also the acknowledged founder of the band and the one who named the group, after a Muddy Waters song. By spring 1963, the trio had added Charlie Watts on drums and Bill Wyman on bass, as well as manager Andrew Loog Oldham, who had been a publicist for the other British musical sensation that was making waves, the Beatles. Keyboardist Ian Stewart, who frequently played with the Stones in those days and over the next decades, was bounced as a regular member by Oldham, who felt his dumpy appearance undermined the band's sex appeal.

There were other bumps in the road. Mick and Keith were furious when they found out that Brian was demanding and getting the biggest salary cut from club owners. Also, a lot of club and tour dates were missed because of Brian's health woes, which included back pain, ear infections,

Caylee Marie Anthony's "Missing" poster. *Photo is courtesy of Orange County, Florida.*

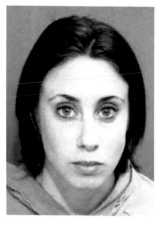

Casey Anthony's first mug shot. *Photo is courtesy of Orange County, Florida.*

A T-shirt similar to this one was found with Caylee's remains. *Photo is courtesy of Orange County, Florida.*

A blue tarp marks the area where searchers recovered evidence and Caylee's remains. *Photo is courtesy of Orange County, Florida.*

USAF Col. Philip Shue, American hero. *Photo is courtesy of Tracy Shue.*

Phil's first wife Nancy pleaded the Fifth Amendment more than twenty times. *Photo is courtesy of Tracy Shue.*

Tracy and Philip Shue's 1993 wedding. They had big plans for the future. *Photo is courtesy of Tracy Shue.*

The historic 1964 *T.A.M.I. Show* with the Rolling Stones' Brian Jones, Mick Jagger, and Keith Richards. *Photo is courtesy of Dick Clark Media Archives.*

Brian Jones's Cotchford Farm swimming pool where he drowned. *Photo is courtesy o Cindy Parkhurst.*

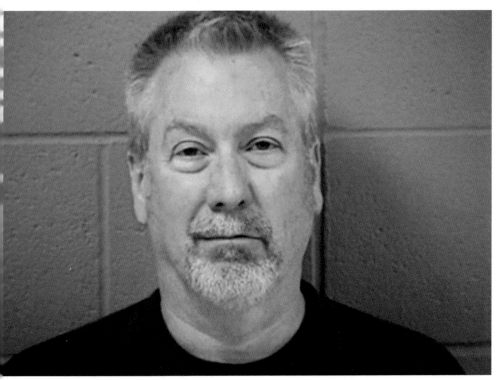

Ex-cop Drew Peterson's mug shot. *Photo is courtesy of Will County, Illinois.*

Was Kathleen Savio murdered or did she "slip and fall" in her bathtub? *Photo is courtesy of Dr. Cyril H. Wecht.*

Full-of-life Gabby Bechen, on her dad's ATV. *Photo is courtesy of the Bechen Family.*

Farmhand Jeffrey Martin was arrested for the twelve-year-old girl's death. *Photo is courtesy of Greene County, Pennsylvania.*

Mimi, Corey, Chris, and Gabby Bechen in happier times, at a local racing event. *Photo is courtesy of the Bechen Family.*

Carol Anne Gotbaum's last photo before she was put in the holding cell. *Surveillance camera photo is from Phoenix's Sky Harbor International Airport police.*

Airport police office; beyond the yellow tape is the holding cell. *Photo is courtesy of Dr. Cyril H. Wecht.*

The holding cell where Gotbaum died in custody. *Photo is courtesy of Dr. Cyril H. Wecht.*

Dr. Conrad Murray was charged with manslaughter for the death of the pop superstar. *Photo from AP/World Wide Photos. Photograph by Damian Dovarganes.*

Michael Jackson at the March 5, 2009, press conference where his London concerts were announced. *Photo from AP/World Wide Photos. Photograph by Joel Ryan.*

and his long-time respiratory problems—responsible for his raspy voice and for ruining his backup vocals. With so much time on their own while Brian was laid up, Jagger and Richards began writing songs and found the skill that would serve them well for the rest of their careers. Songwriters also make lucrative deals publishing their music, so even though Brian had wanted to participate in that money flow, he never had the confidence to bring the band any songs he might have written. Jones instead focused on becoming the "stylish" Stone, wearing ritzy Carnaby Street clothes and bohemian velvets, silks, and lamé. Dating a model named Linda Lawrence, who delivered his fourth illegitimate child—a son Brian named Julian—the budding pop star repeated the immature behavior he had shown in his relationship with Pat Andrews: physical disinterest and domestic violence. Not long after, Brian fathered another son, born to Dawn Molloy, a casual girlfriend. The Stones' management got Molloy to keep silent about the child in exchange for a total payment of about fifteen hundred dollars, again allowing Jones to slip away from any ongoing financial responsibilities. Brian also had nasty disputes with his bandmates and friends, pulling cruel jokes on them but whining like an infant if the same puerile behavior was returned.

With their singles topping the charts worldwide and new albums hitting every few months, the Stones were finally making decent money. They were in a friendly competition with the Beatles, who appeared to fans as the "good boys," while the Stones were the "bad boys." Some of this rivalry was cultivated early on by the Beatles wearing matching neat suits and ties, while the Stones wore more freeform outfits. The Stones also enjoyed flirting with the occult, including satanism, even naming one album *Their Satanic Majesties Request* and writing the popular song "Sympathy for the Devil." Still, these sorts of predilections were considered to be more artistic choice to show their edginess rather than revealing any religious or spiritual preference.[1] Of course, what most adults noticed about members in both groups were their shaggy hairstyles, which would lead to the hippie look that was revered and copied by teenagers and reviled by parents. As someone who lost his hair at an early age, I confess to having been envious, although a mop top probably wouldn't have been warmly welcomed in my conventional workplace as a young forensic pathologist.

My own awareness of the Stones, or of the Beatles, for that matter, was fairly low. I had heard their names and maybe some songs on the radio, but I wasn't a fan. The only music I heard in my home at that time was children's fare, since my wife, Sigrid, and I were raising four rambunctious offspring who were themselves too young to be rock aficionados. November 22, 1963—the date of the assassination of President John F. Kennedy—was a major turning point in my life and career, so every bit of my time not in my office or with my family was devoted to trying to ferret out the facts of that historic tragedy. (I'm still involved in that endeavor; I was the first independent forensic pathologist allowed to inspect the young president's remains and autopsy files at the National Archives, and I continue to write and lecture on the subject.) My co-author, Dawna Kaufmann, was very much influenced by the musical renaissance known as the British Invasion. As a schoolgirl in 1964, she was so excited to see the Beatles' first appearance on *The Ed Sullivan Show* on her family's television that she fainted in her living room. Much later, Dawna worked in the rock and roll television business and attended Rolling Stones concerts, once sitting front-row center, but that was long after Brian Jones had left the band.[2]

In 1964, following the Beatles' phenomenal groundbreaking tour of the United States, the Stones contributed in their own way to being England's ambassadors to America's youth by appearing on the *T.A.M.I. Show*, now considered to be one of the seminal rock concert experiences. An acronym for "Teenage Awards Music International," the event was shot live over two days in Santa Monica, California, and was designed to be an annual extravaganza of the most cutting-edge music makers in the business. The producers never got the chance to bring back the show in subsequent years, so the black-and-white concert film that played briefly in movie theaters was the only record of the remarkable achievement, until it was restored and released as a DVD in 2009 and broadcast on PBS. Recorded before an audience of wildly enthusiastic high school kids, the lineup consisted of Chuck Berry, Gerry and the Pacemakers, Marvin Gaye, the Barbarians, Lesley Gore, Jan and Dean, Smokey Robinson and the Miracles, Billy J. Kramer and the Dakotas, the Supremes, the Beach Boys, James Brown and the Famous Flames, and, topping the bill, the Rolling Stones. Steve Binder, a wunderkind of live television who directed the film, said that James Brown refused to rehearse his songs, warning Binder to just have the camera "follow" him. The soul singer gave such an outrageously theatrical performance that the Stones were intimidated to have to play after him. But they did, and the baby-faced quintet charmed America and solidified their popularity as they ripped through "Around and Around," "Off the Hook," "Time Is on My Side," and "It's All Over Now." The show ended with the Stones playing "I'm All Right," while all the other performers and assorted go-go dancers mixed it up onstage—a never-to-be-repeated triumph.[3]

His fame and fortune mounting, Brian became seduced by another mistress, one who took him to the edge of the earth, then dropped him on his head, and Jones was powerless to resist her. Always a robust drinker, Brian began experimenting with marijuana and cocaine, as well as uppers and downers from pharmaceutical prescriptions. His drug use wreaked havoc on his bronchial condition, and, feeling general malaise from burning both ends of the candle, he landed in a Milwaukee hospital for intravenous nourishment and bed rest. Jones had to issue a statement that, despite rumors to the contrary, he was not quitting the band for health reasons. "I fell ill during our American tour and I have to take it easy for a while," the statement read. "The thought of leaving the Stones has never entered my head." Popping pills, downing whiskey, and smoking three packs of cigarettes per day became Brian's norm, and after a Chicago hospitalization, he was warned by doctors that he'd be dead in a year if he didn't straighten up.

As Jones went into a downward spiral, the Stones' songs just kept getting bigger and better, including "Satisfaction," "Get Off of My Cloud," "Paint It Black," "Under My Thumb," "Lady Jane," "Ruby Tuesday," "Let's Spend the Night Together," "Street Fighting Man," "Sympathy for the Devil," and many others. Soon, many felt the Stones deserved the title "The World's Greatest Rock and Roll Band," an encomium they still enjoy today. According to Giuliano's book, Mick and Keith, under the pseudonym of "the Glimmer Twins," began producing their own music, adding to their wealth and status within the group. Fans thought of the band as "Mick Jagger and the Rolling Stones," which annoyed and depressed Jones, and soon the group not only appointed Mick to be their sole spokesman, but they wouldn't allow Brian to make public comments.

The Stones' organization hired a no-nonsense World War II paratrooper and combat vet named Tom Keylock to provide transportation services, first through a car-hire outfit he owned, and then full time as a chauffeur–aide-de-camp for the band. A Michael Caine lookalike, with the same Cockney accent, Keylock became a constant presence, touring the world with the group and marveling at how they would interact so well onstage, then have little to do with each other after a gig. Brian, he noted, was becoming more and more disenfranchised from the other Stones, partly because of his increasing drug addiction, but also due to his churlish nature. He began exhibiting paranoiac tendencies, once even trying to slit his wrists.

With the exception of Charlie Watts, who wed in 1964 and remains married to the same woman today, the Rolling Stones were notorious womanizers, enjoying relationships with famous women, as well as with the groupies who willingly paraded their wares in front of the boys. But Jones's treatment of women created special disharmony among his bandmates, who disapproved of how he doled out black eyes and bruises to friendly girls.[4]

In September 1965, backstage at one of their Munich concerts, Brian met a German model/actress named Anita Pallenberg. She homed in on him and was pleased to learn he could speak some German. Anita, the scion of wealthy aristocrats, grew up in Rome and was fluent in four languages. Her intellectual curiosity and trenchant wit matched Brian's own, and they shared a sexual chemistry that was off the map. Anita towered over him, but neither cared, and within weeks of meeting, the two moved in together. At a party in Los Angeles, Jones was given his first dose of lysergic acid diethylamide—better known as LSD, or acid—a hallucinogenic drug so new it had not yet been declared illegal. He brought some back to London and indulged in it with Anita; they would host acid parties at which friends, including Sonny and Cher, Jimi Hendrix, John Lennon, and George Harrison, would drop by to turn on. Jones's friendship with the two Beatles extended musically, too, after they invited him to attend recording sessions and contribute hand claps to their songs "Yellow Submarine" and "All You Need Is Love." Jones was pleased to feel wanted by the Beatles, since he wasn't getting much love from the Stones. His drug-taking activity with his bandmates mostly consisted of getting high with Keith Richards, who was always ready to try any and all drugs. Mick Jagger, however, wasn't interested in acid and disliked Brian's and Keith's joshing, which suggested that he was "afraid" of LSD.

In the studio, Brian would feign finger injuries to get out of playing guitar, forcing Keith to have to lay in his part in a song and killing the chemistry they once had when they played together. As one insider put it, "Once Brian put down the guitar, that was really the end." At home, Brian's jealous rages every time Anita would land a modeling job wreaked havoc with her career; he'd lob lamps, clocks, or anything handy at her, not stopping until she was bloody and bruised. Then he'd apologize. Geoffrey Giuliano's book describes the pair's trek to Tangier, Morocco, which for Brian was a fairyland of hookahs filled with hashish, open-air bazaars with handcrafted goods, and the haunting Berber folk songs with exotic instrumentation that he wanted to replicate in his own music. The idyllic trip was spoiled by screaming outbursts between the two lovers and by Brian fracturing his wrist in two places when he tried to hit her and missed. He came back to England with half a kilo of drugs he'd smuggled out of the country and his arm in a cast. In November 1966, Brian showed more poor judgment when he dressed in full Nazi regalia for the cover of the German magazine *Stern*. The negative feedback caused Brian to explain that he posed in the getup to prove he was anti-Nazi, and he blamed the caper on Anita, who was also in the photo, kneeling submissively. Shortly afterward, Anita was found unconscious from a drug overdose and was taken to a hospital.

The next year, Anita starred in a German avant-garde film, *Mord und Totschlag* (A Degree of Murder), for which Brian composed the soundtrack—the first time a rock star had ever done so. His tantalizing score wove together flute, jazz piano, autoharp, sitar, and banjo, and impressed experts who thought the hapless Stone might have a new career as a film composer.[5] His music was the best part of the movie.

News of the World, a salacious British tabloid, published a story that included quotes from Mick Jagger about his freewheeling drug use, allegedly told to a reporter at a nightclub. But the reporter mistook Brian, the actual source of the quotes, for Jagger. Jagger sued for libel, and the newspaper had to issue an apology. Less than a week after that, a major drug raid went down at Keith Richards's Sussex home, Redlands. Keith, Mick, and a few friends were arrested; the two Stones ended up serving a short jail stint. The Stones later stated that they believed the bust was payback from the newspaper, which worked with a drug dealer to set up the musicians.[6]

Another trip to Morocco followed, this time from Paris via Keith's new Rolls Royce, with Tom Keylock driving, Richards in the passenger seat, and the feuding lovebirds, Brian and Anita, in the backseat. Brian caught a bug in the south of France and was hospitalized; he told the others he'd catch up with them soon. Then, somehow, during the romantic drive through Spain, Keith and Anita fell into each other's arms.

To Keith, it was a fling, but to Anita, it seemed like an upgrade. When Brian rejoined his pals, he learned of the betrayal and pummeled Anita into near unconsciousness. When he did it again the next day, after Anita wouldn't participate in an orgy with two Marrakesh hookers, Richards had had enough, Giuliano reported. "I can't watch Brian do this shit to you anymore," he said. "Come on darlin', I'm taking you back to London." Brian was destroyed when his apology failed to win back his Teutonic temptress. That she had taken up with one of his best friends was especially bitter; he blamed Keith especially but also all the Stones. He spat out his frustration to a buddy: "They took my music; they took my band; now they've taken my love." A mental breakdown followed, with another hospitalization. Brian then had to face the shock of yet another tour, this time seeing his enemy Richards with his former girlfriend.[7]

Things were never the same with the band, who now considered Brian a liability. He would destroy hotel rooms, engage in sadomasochistic sex, anesthetize himself with the powerful barbiturates Tuinal® and Mandrax, strip off his clothes in public, shout that he was being harassed by police when he wasn't, repeatedly attempt suicide, and violently strike out at anyone in his line of vision. Another hospital stint followed, along with sessions with various psychiatrists. He spent a night in the Wormwood Scrubs prison in London after being busted for a small amount of pot, cocaine, and Methedrine (methamphetamine), then was busted again for a bit of cannabis that he swore was planted in his home. At a dinner party set up by Mick's girlfriend, Marianne Faithfull—intended to bring the warring Stones back together—Brian lunged at Jagger with a knife and missed stabbing him by inches. Then he ran outside and jumped into a moat that was filled with twenty feet of water. Jagger plunged in after him, grabbed his hair, and dunked his head into the grimy water again and again.

Alone, Brian went back to Morocco to record an album with local musicians. *Brian Jones Presents the Pipes of Pan at Joujouka* was released posthumously on Rolling Stones Records in October 1971 and is still heralded as a masterwork of ethnic rhythm and flavor.[8]

In November 1968, Jones bought a country estate called Cotchford Farm, once the home of British children's author A. A. Milne, and the setting of Milne's famous series of novels, *Winnie-the-Pooh*. The books, later made into numerous films, were Milne's tribute to his young son, Christopher Robin, and featured his boy's stuffed animals. The stories were among Jones's favorites from childhood, and he told friends he felt a magical connection to Milne's writing when he walked past the Pooh Bridge, the statue of Christopher Robin, and the sundial with its carved images of all the gentle characters. Jones paid about $47,000 for the rustic ten-acre property that was located in Hartfield, East Sussex, about fifty miles from London. The main brick house was L-shaped and had been built in the fifteenth century; also present were several smaller cottages that dated back to the early 1900s. In 1956, after Milne's death, Cotchford was sold to an American businessman who added a backyard garden and stone patio, along with a large, rectangular swimming pool—an unusual fixture in the damp and rainy community.

Mary Hallet was the farm's long-time housekeeper, and she lived with her family in one of the cottages two hundred yards up the drive. The first time she met Brian, he was dressed in a fur coat, and with his long golden hair, she mistook him for a woman. Mary's only son had been run over by a vehicle on the nearby road shortly before Jones moved in, and, as the guitarist was about the same age as the dead Hallet youth, Brian and Mary bonded deeply. She found Jones to be lonely but also full of life, especially when he would frequently play loud music, both alone and when his musician buddies would stop by. Hallet never saw Jones do drugs, but she sometimes witnessed his asthma attacks, as he struggled to breathe and gasped between words. Jones and Hallet often discussed the Bible; the rocker was able to quote long verses verbatim, despite his being an atheist. Although Brian complained of missing Anita Pallenberg, he had a new girlfriend named Suki Potier, who was very nurturing and loyal. In typical Jones fashion, he mistreated Suki too, once sending her to the hospital after a violent beating.

When the Cotchford farmhouse's roof began leaking, Jones turned to the Stones' minder, Tom Keylock, for help. Keylock had assigned an old school friend, builder Frank Thorogood, to supervise construction at Keith Richards' Redlands estate, and even though Keith was never very happy with the work done, Thorogood, forty-three, was brought to Cotchford. Thorogood and a trio of laborers moved into a guest flat on the property and became permanent fixtures, doing very little work but spending days and nights partying with gal-pals and mixing with Jones's fellow musicians. The construction crew's presence was so intimidating to Brian that he felt unable to give them orders or to fire them. And, according to Giuliano's *Paint It Black*, Jones was never certain how much money they were making since they were paid directly by the Stones' management, out of funds earmarked for Brian. Other than Keylock, nobody much cared for the builders or their work.

In early January of 1969, Brian and Suki jetted to the island of Ceylon, now called Sri Lanka. Giuliano wrote that they visited science fiction writer Arthur C. Clarke, and on a trek to a village met a man who claimed to have been Adolf Hitler's personal astrologer. Brian couldn't resist getting a reading and laughed when the old man warned him "not to go swimming without a friend" in the near future. The mystic also told Jones to beware of false friends. Returning to Cotchford, Brian found the house a disaster, with empty liquor bottles and dirty dishes everywhere. He was also disappointed to see that a wooden fence he had asked to be installed outside had not been touched. Brian ended up getting some friends from the local pub to put up the fence and told them his costly construction team would soon be handed their walking papers. Brian felt Thorogood and the laborers were ripping him off in other ways: furnishings would vanish from the home, along with stashes of cash that Jones kept in his bedroom. It wasn't just Brian's paranoia working overtime now; as he told several people, he was being systematically ripped off by these burly bullies whom he wanted out of his life.

News of another Rolling Stones tour to America surfaced, but Jones's last drug bust kept him from entering the United States. Mick and the management company knew that if there was ever a good time to ditch the guitarist, this was it. Brian had begun jamming with Jimi Hendrix and others, feeling that if he was fired, he would have another project to jump into. John Lennon, whose friendship with the other Beatles was strained, was also in the mix. Brian had become newly adamant in rejecting the lure of drugs, so much so that people entering his home would be searched for illegal narcotics before they'd be welcomed inside. But he still indulged in heavy alcohol use, mostly vodka or brandy. Frank Thorogood took such a commanding role in the household, it was as if Brian worked for him. Suki didn't like it, and neither did Mrs. Hallet. Both believed Thorogood was gaslighting the Stone with a campaign of terror, hiding his motorbike in the bushes, misplacing his items, flashing a strobe light into his bedroom while he slept, and disorienting him to the point that Brian would drink even more. Jones once found a dead pet cat with its eyes poked out in a kitchen cabinet and was certain it had been put there by Thorogood or one of his cohorts. By April, Suki had had enough and moved out. Brian had sessions with a psychiatrist and spoke of his overwhelming depression, but he didn't seem capable of making any positive life changes.

On the evening of June 9, 1969, things came to a head with the Stones when Mick Jagger, Keith Richards, and Charlie Watts made a surprise visit to Cotchford Farm. Brian poured them all drinks and brought everyone outside where they sat on deck chairs by the pool. Then the boys got down to business. As Charlie stayed mute, Mick and Keith informed Brian that he was out of the band. For the upcoming tour, they had replaced him with a blues guitarist named Mick Taylor. Brian put a game face on, saying that he didn't savor all the one-nighters anyway, and they all pretended that maybe things would change after the Stones returned to England. Meanwhile, Jagger mentioned that they would pay Jones a severance of about a hundred and fifty thousand dollars per year for as long as the Stones remained a band. And they all agreed that Brian could say publicly that he was resigning due to musical differences. Thirty minutes later, Brian, now an ex-Stone, was alone again and he sobbed nonstop for hours.[9]

Days later, Brian met a twenty-two-year-old Swedish student at a party and moved her into Cotchford; Anna Wohlin was her name. Mrs. Hallet and others would describe her as more of a companion than a girlfriend of Brian, since he was still pining over the loss of Suki Potier and Anita Pallenberg. Anna had purportedly griped to Brian that Thorogood had thrust his hand down her blouse, but Brian just shrugged, according to Giuliano's book. Brian wasn't prepared to help her if he couldn't help himself. On June 30, Brian asked his psychiatrist for a prescription of Durophet—or black bombers, as they were known colloquially. The pills were a form of amphetamine—a central nervous system stimulant—with the boost of a derivative, dextroamphetamine (Dexedrine®), which was usually prescribed in twenty-milligram dosages. The reactions are increased hyperactivity and depressed appetite, but as the effects of the pill wear off, the user is still able to fall into a restful sleep. The doctor wrote a modest prescription of ten capsules.

On the morning of July 2, Brian arose around eleven and, along with Anna, joined Mrs. Hallet in the dining room for tea and toast. There was a high pollen count in the air, which made Jones's asthma kick up. A tennis match was on television as Brian told the housekeeper he would be having a party that night. Later it was learned that Jones had told Suki the party was to provide safety in numbers, as he planned to fire Frank Thorogood and his workers after the attendees showed up. Frank invited a nurse friend—Janet Lawson, twenty-six, mistress of the Stones' aide-de-camp Tom Keylock—to stay at Cotchford for a few days. Mary Hallet left at 1 p.m., the last time she would ever see Brian Jones. Brian left a half-hour later to catch a bite and a pint at a local spot called the Haywaggon. There he ran into friends from London—Nicholas Fitzgerald and Richard Cadbury—who had been told by Suki Potier that Brian was in trouble at the farm. The two had planned to go to Cotchford anyway after their meal, but they were alarmed when Brian came over and told them his builders had been keeping him a prisoner at the estate. Giuliano's book detailed that Jones reiterated to the pair what he had told Suki—that the construction crew would be fired that night. Jones, Fitzgerald, and Cadbury all went to Cotchford where the two guests claim to have seen Thorogood's workers putting up floodlights around the pool. Keylock has given differing accounts about whether he was at Brian's home on July 2.

In the early evening, Brian played demos of his songs with Hendrix and Lennon, then confided that some tapes had gone missing and that Anna Wohlin had seen Thorogood going through the tapes on more than one occasion. More of Brian's friends arrived for the party, and he revealed to several that he was planning to fire his construction crew that night. Meanwhile, the booze flowed, and Brian was in his element, smiling broadly while serenading the partygoers on his guitar. Fitzgerald and Cadbury went back into town to pick up a female friend who had no way to get to the party; they would hang out for hours, waiting for her, but she never hooked up with them.

Accounts vary about what happened next, but there seems to be a consensus that after watching the American comedy program *Rowan and Martin's Laugh-In*, Brian suggested they go for a swim. At this point, around 10 p.m., the only people who claim to have still been present were Brian, Frank Thorogood, Janet Lawson, and Anna Wohlin. Janet's version of events, as per her police statement, is that Brian had been drinking but was still lucid enough to discuss a drainage problem with Frank, and that Jones had somewhat garbled speech, giggling to her about having taken his "sleepers," which she took to mean sleeping tablets. Janet alleges that she declined their invitation to go in the water herself and told both men they were too inebriated to swim; Brian even needed to be held up on the diving board before he "flopped" into the water. She said that Anna was in the water and Brian's dogs were nearby. Thorogood's statement to police also mentions how unsteady Jones had been on the diving board, but he found nothing unusual in Brian's demeanor and said he was as strong a swimmer as he usually was. Both ladies eventually went inside the home, leaving the men in the pool.

Frank Thorogood told police that he went inside the house to find a cigarette, then passed Anna who was heading outside toward the pool. Moments later, she would yell at Frank that Brian was lying on the bottom of the pool. He claimed he ran outside, got into the water, and, with Anna, tried to pull out a now-limp Jones. Janet, he said, helped them set the musician on the ground. Janet's statement was that she had been inside the music room, doodling around on a guitar, when she looked outside and saw Brian floating motionless, face down near the bottom of the pool's deep end. She said she screamed at Anna, who was inside on the phone, and ran out with Anna and Frank to rescue Jones. While the two women tried to revive Brian, Thorogood went into the home and dialed 999, the British equivalent of our 911 system. Janet stated that while she knew Brian was already dead, she still put him on his side and furiously tried to pump water from his system. Then she performed cardiac massage while Anna gave mouth-to-mouth resuscitation. After about fifteen minutes, she said there was still no pulse or sign of life in the young man. Anna's version conforms to Janet's, except that Anna was certain Brian's hand gripped her own. Emergency medical personnel and a doctor soon arrived, with the latter declaring Jones deceased.

Unanswered questions abound, including whether Brian ever, in fact, fired Thorogood and his team that night—and what bearing, if any, that might have had on the tragedy. Clearly no one forced Brian to go swimming with Frank; indeed, it was Jones's own idea.

The big scoop of Geoffrey Giuliano's book—and what he conveyed to me in our interview—comes into play here. It provides the rationale behind his subtitle, *Paint It Black: The Murder of Brian Jones.* (The primary title refers to one of the Stones' most notable songs, recorded during Jones's time with the group.) Giuliano insisted that while on a book tour for his 1992 biography on Paul McCartney, he was approached in a hotel lobby by a man who stated that he had read all the author's books and had some urgent information regarding the death of Brian Jones. They went to Giuliano's room, where the large man with shoulder-length graying hair gave the writer permission to audiotape the conversation but refused to tell his name. *Paint It Black* includes a transcript of the purported interview with the man Giuliano named "Joe," just to give the speaker a name. The man said he had been burdened by his secret since he was a twenty-year-old hippie, back in 1969, but had never breathed a word of it to anyone; now he wanted it off his conscience. Joe claimed he had run into someone who was helping a builder at Cotchford Farm and offered Joe some cement work there too. It would be easy money, he'd get to meet an idol, and there'd be plenty of booze and girls.

On the night of Brian's death, Joe and his friend were liquored up and had taken some Mandrax sleeping pills. Joe got into the pool with his friend Frank (not Frank Thorogood, but another crew member named Frank). Brian came over and was in an arrogant mood. He began bragging about what a good swimmer he was, jumping off the diving board and swimming the length of the pool several times. A bit of horseplay followed, with Joe deciding to teach the Stone some humility by holding Brian under the water, then laughing as he flailed and panicked. Brian got loose and hurled some obscenities, which angered Frank, so he joined Joe and started seriously dunking Brian. They pushed down on his shoulders and head, then pulled him up by the hair—at least seven or eight times over about a fifteen-minute period. Eventually Jones went limp, and the two bullies realized they had a problem. "We didn't mean to kill him," Joe told Giuliano, "it just happened." They leapt out of the pool, ran for their car, and drove straight to London where they immediately shaved off all their hair in case the police were to look for them. Off the record, Joe also hinted at others being in the pool and holding down Jones, but he wouldn't elaborate. Joe told the author he kept his eyes on the news for weeks, and was astonished that there seemed to be no investigation. Brian died due to an asthma attack, drugs and alcohol, he had heard. End of story. While adamantly denying to Giuliano that he was paid to kill the Stone, Joe admitted that Frank later told him to keep his mouth shut and paid him a couple hundred pounds, which Joe considered back pay. He lost touch with Frank for a while, then was surprised to see him the next time, dressed to the nines and driving a fancy car. Frank would later die of a heroin overdose, Joe said. Giuliano added that Joe turned off the tape recorder to tell him one last thing—that Frank Thorogood had told Joe and his friend Frank to "take care of this matter," indicating he didn't want to see Brian come out of the water. That seems to contradict what he had said on tape, that the death was from accidental horseplay.

Giuliano also interviewed Tom Keylock, the Stones' senior employee who had hired Thorogood to do the repairs at Cotchford. Keylock defended his lifelong pal's work at the farm and said that the night of the drowning only four people were present—Brian, his girlfriend Anna Wohlin, Thorogood, and the nurse Janet Lawson. It was an unfortunate accident, Keylock stated. All the other workers had gone home, and there was no party, he maintained. Mrs. Hallet, the housekeeper, told Giuliano she heard a lot of shouting that night and seemed spooked even years later, but she couldn't offer any real opinions because she was up the road in her home that night.[10]

A. E. Hotchner is another credible author with years of experience writing important biographies, including the life stories of Sophia Loren and Doris Day. In his 1990 book on the Rolling Stones, *Blown Away:*

The Rolling Stones and the Death of the Sixties, he reported that Nicholas Fitzgerald and Richard Cadbury gave up waiting for the girl they were supposed to meet and drove back to Cotchford around 11 p.m. They were blinded by a car's headlights in the road outside the property and saw a car with its door wide open and engine running. Peering through the trees that encircled the pool area, they could see three men standing on the lip of the pool, although the bright floodlights washed out their faces. One of the trio knelt and pushed down on the head of someone in the pool, holding it under the water's surface. Then they noticed two other people, a man and a woman, standing at the other end of the pool, watching. The man next to the person who was dunking the swimmer jumped into the water, landing on the victim's back. Just then, a different man—burly and wearing glasses—stepped behind the observers and said in a Cockney accent, "Get out of here, Fitzgerald, or you'll be next." Fitzgerald and Cadbury raced to their car and drove off without stopping to glance back.

In researching his book, Hotchner went to England to find anyone who might have information about Jones's death. In exchange for a few hundred dollars, a man in London agreed to talk but would not allow his name to be used. Hotchner called him "Marty" in his book. Marty, who was described as short with long sideburns, claimed he was an apprentice on the construction crew and that two of his coworkers "had it in" for Brian. Marty watched as the two men, both inebriated, began to taunt Brian, who was swimming in the pool. They would grab the musician by the leg and pull him down, interfering with the laps he was trying to swim. When Jones tried to get out of the pool, the two men would pull him back in, again and again. The rough and tumble turned ominous as Brian kept getting pushed under the water and would gasp for air as he surfaced. Marty then heard someone say, "He's drowned," and the men let go of Brian and jumped from the pool. That is all that Hotchner writes about his secret source or the death scene.[11]

From the brief physical descriptions given, it's unclear whether Giuliano's source, "Joe," and Hotchner's source, "Marty," are one and the same, although their stories seem to match. But if either or both exist, and their accounts are accurate, it puts a major crimp in the testimony given by Frank Thorogood, Janet Lawson, and Anna Wohlin who all told police and the coroner's inquest that they were the only people present with Brian when he went into the pool.[12]

Wohlin returned to Sweden where stories would surface that she had committed suicide. But in 2000, she proved that she was still alive when her book *The Murder of Brian Jones: The Secret Story of My Love Affair with the Murdered Rolling Stone* was published. And in 2004, rock journalist Terry Rawlings wrote *Who Killed Christopher Robin?: The Truth behind the Murder of a Rolling Stone*. Both books make claims that Frank Thorogood killed Jones but offer little in the way of proof.[13]

In 2008, shortly before she died of cancer, Janet Lawson met with a freelance journalist named Scott Jones (no relation to Brian), whose article appeared in London's *Daily Mail*. Lawson told the reporter that she had never shared her story with anyone else before but felt it should be told. She categorized her statement to the police as "a pack of lies" and claimed that a detective had told her what to say, and she went along with it because she was tired and frightened. The true story, she said, was that she was at the estate because her boyfriend, Keylock, had asked her to keep an eye on Brian, whose health he was concerned about and because he knew there was tension between the musician and Frank Thorogood, who was going to be fired that night. The foursome had dinner together, then retired to the garden where Brian began swimming. Brian's friend Anna went inside to talk on the phone, and Jones asked Janet to find his asthma inhaler. She went in the house to look for it and was soon joined by Thorogood who was "shaking" and in a "terrible state." Lawson had a bad feeling and went outside to find Brian floating in the pool. She called for help, then ran toward the house, still shouting. Thorogood burst from the house, ran past her and dived into the pool, which surprised Lawson because she had not said what was wrong and wondered how Frank knew to go there. Janet believed Thorogood caused Jones's death, probably by roughhousing that went wrong, rather than an act of premeditated murder.

Scott Jones's article stated that he perused six hundred documents on the case, then made a formal request of Sussex authorities to reopen the investigation; the request was denied. He was dismayed to find out there are still files in the British National Archive that must remain sealed until the year 2044. The official reason for the "75 years rule" the government cites in sensitive cases is to "protect living persons from any embarrassment because the files contained details of their sex lives," which is an absurd notion here.[14]

In February 2011, Scott Jones turned up another exclusive for the *Daily Mail*. He located a forty-five-year-old man named John Maynard, the son Brian Jones fathered with Dawn Molloy in 1965, and whom Molloy—then only nineteen—gave up for adoption. Maynard told the reporter that he had contacted his birth mother after marrying and having his own children. Molloy informed him that his father was Brian Jones and showed him photos of the musician that resembled Maynard's own appearance as a young man. Scott Jones explained about his failure to get police to reopen the drowning investigation, and Maynard chimed in with his own demand for the truth. "I defy anyone to read the evidence and think my father drowned in his swimming pool," he said, adding: "I want to know exactly what this police review made of all the evidence that points towards Frank Thorogood killing my father. I want to know why Sussex Police today are relying on witness statements that we now know were written by the police and not by the witnesses. And I want to know what role the Home Office played in making sure Thorogood walked away a free man, so drink and drugs could take the blame."[15]

Every few years, a new batch of articles appears, calling for a new probe and, in some instances, an exhumation of Jones's body. Still, there are curious twists. Most people who believe Brian Jones was murdered point to Frank Thorogood as the killer. But if police felt he was a viable suspect, they never developed enough evidence to charge him—or anyone—with the crime.

As does the United States, England has strict laws against libel and slander. But those protections apply only to living people, not their estates. So if someone wants to write a book saying that Brian Jones was murdered by Elvis Presley, John Lennon, or my great-grandmother, no lawsuit for libel can proceed. It may be no coincidence that the strongest movement to suggest Brian was slain came after Frank Thorogood died in November 1993. And the person doing the talking was his decades-long friend, Tom Keylock.[16]

In an interview on the BBC's *Crimewatch* TV program, a clip of which is available online, Keylock describes visiting Thorogood as the construction chief was dying of cancer. "Tom, there's something I've got to tell you. I've got to put my house in order," Thorogood supposedly told Keylock, adding that he would tell him only if he promised not to repeat anything until after his death. Given that assurance, Keylock said Thorogood confessed: "It was me that done Brian." Keylock gave his theory: "Maybe Brian provoked him. He was a very strong man. Maybe Frank's mind snapped. I don't think he tried to kill him. I think it was an argument, maybe they had an argument. Maybe he tried to frighten him, scare him, dunked him under, and it all went wrong."[17]

The plot thickens with a 2009 Internet blog posting by former Rolling Stones' tour manager, Sam Cutler, who wrote a memoir, *You Can't Always Get What You Want*, named for the well-known Stones' song. Cutler, who was working for the band when Jones died, called Brian "an arsehole and a total nightmare to be around" and referred to the police investigation into his death as a "farce." But his most pointed comment is this one: "Brian Jones was murdered. Of this there is little doubt. He was not murdered by the man who was in charge of the building work at Brian's farm, a gentleman by the name of Thorogood who is popularly credited by conspiracy theorists with doing the deed. He was almost certainly murdered by the very man whose role it was to protect him, Tom Keylock. The man who less than forty-eight hours after the murder, emptied the house of its valuable contents, and burnt substantial amounts of papers and personal items of Brian Jones on a bonfire in the front garden."

Cutler's blog cited an investigation funded by the Stones' co-manager, Allen Klein, whose private detectives purportedly interviewed people around the globe and determined that Tom Keylock was not only at the home when Jones died; he was in the pool with him and was "directly responsible" for the death. Cutler wrote that the witnesses who targeted Keylock had been threatened into silence, but he doesn't mention who made the threats. He ended his online accusation by pointing out that Keylock died on July 2, 2009, exactly forty years to the day after Brian died. In one confusing paragraph, Cutler wrote: "It is believed that the police in the United Kingdom now have copies of the Klein report" and "it is unknown whether the Klein report ever was given to the British police, but it is known that the police made no attempt to contact any of the witnesses named in the report." Cutler also stated that no autopsy was performed on Brian, which is untrue, and he repeatedly misspells Klein's first name.[18] Ergo, if his research is faulty in these areas, one might wonder how solid it is overall. None of the information can be verified by Allen Klein, who died in 2009 from conditions related to Alzheimer's disease.[19]

Brian Jones's autopsy took place on July 3, 1969, at the mortuary of St. Victoria's Hospital in East Grinstead, Sussex County, and was performed by forensic pathologist Dr. Albert Sachs. As was standard at that time, the subsequent documentation was prepared on a manual typewriter. The entire report, including the toxicology, inquest results, and death certificate, totals seven pages, which was atypically brief, even for back then.[20] (By contrast, the 1962 autopsy report of Marilyn Monroe, on which I consulted, was eighteen pages in length.[21]) The date of Jones's death was registered as July 2, between 11:30 p.m. and midnight. The report lists Brian's age wrongly as twenty-six, instead of twenty-seven, and gives his height as five foot nine. His weight was not given, but he was described as "powerfully built with a tendency to obesity."

There is no manner of death listed—something we now include in modern autopsy reports—so there is no statement as to whether the death was an accident, homicide, suicide, or something else. The cause of death stated was drowning: immersion in fresh water. (Swimming pool water is considered fresh water.) Other significant conditions that contributed to his death, but were not directly related, were severe liver dysfunction due to fatty degeneration and the ingestion of alcohol and drugs. There were no anomalies listed in his external examination, except that he had pallor of face and frothy fluid around his nostrils.

His internal examination showed a brain weight of 1,553 grams and noted that there was congestion and edema, or swelling, with "punctuate hemorrhages in white matter," or pinpoint blood spotting in the colorless nerve tissue that makes up most of one's brain. Jones's brain membranes and blood vessels were also congested. The thoracic cavity—mouth, tongue, tonsils, and esophagus—was lightly stained with blood, possibly from the artificial respiration activity. The respiratory tract—larynx, trachea, bronchi, thyroid, and thymus glands—was congested. The bronchi contained a few flakes of "glairy mucus," but not the kind of "viscid adherent mucus associated with death due to an asthmatic attack."

Jones's lungs were described as "voluminous"; the left weighed 632 grams, and the right weighed 643 grams. Some areas of collapse were noted, mainly that the lungs "pit on pressure," or show a depression when touched. Frothy blood-stained fluid exuded from the lungs at sectioning, with few subpleural petechial hemorrhages, or pinpoint blood spots beneath the outer lung membranes. His heart weighed 411 grams and was noted to have "general hypertrophy," or mild enlargement, with both sides dilated. The myocardium, or heart sac, was "fatty and flabby," but there was no evidence of vascular or valvular disease, so the damage was not immediately life-threatening. A blood alcohol level of 140 milligrams was listed. There was about one ounce of undigested food in his stomach, with the mucosa, or lining, congested.

His liver weight was 3,000 grams, with congestion noted and "architecture lost." Upon sectioning, excessive fatty degeneration was found. His gall bladder was empty. His spleen was congested and weighted 247 grams, while his left kidney weighed 190 grams, the right one weighed 181 grams, and both were congested. A little urine was present in the bladder, but the toxicology lab noted 1,720 micrograms of a "basic amphetamine-like substance." His pancreas, breasts, and prostate were normal for his age and unremarkable. In the section for further remarks, there was this unclear note: "In death from an asthmatic attack lungs are light and bulky." Liver and lung specimens were sent to a pathologist named Dr. Angus Christopher Sommerville, whose microscopic examination noted that the lungs were dilated and showed bullous, or green, areas due to breakdown of the septa, or linings. Albuminoid material, or blood plasma, was present in the alveolar spaces, or lung sacs, and there was some hemorrhaging, he wrote.

The report also includes a summary from the coroner's inquest, which took place on July 7. Drs. Sachs and Sommerville testified to the circumstances of Jones's drowning and the anatomical findings, and revealed the conclusion of the consulting biochemist, whose name was listed only as "Mr. Cook" of the Royal Sussex Hospital in Brighton. Cook's report noted that Jones's blood alcohol reading was 140 milligrams, which would be the approximate equivalent of seven whiskeys or three and a half pints of beer. The urine reading was 1,720 micrograms of an amphetamine-like substance, with a notation that in normal urine, this level never exceeds 200 micrograms. Cook also reported that a thin-layer chromatography—a sophisticated piece of equipment to determine toxicological readings—failed to reveal the presence of the following: amphetamine, Methedrine, morphine, methadone, and iso-prenaline, the ingredient in asthma drugs that dilates the bronchial tubes. But the report noted the presence of "two dense spots, one yellow orange which has not been identified and the other a purple spot. This could be due to diphenhydramine, which is present together with methaqualone in Mandrax, which the deceased is known to have taken." Although the report doesn't list their having participated, Anna Wohlin, Frank Thorogood, and Janet Lawson all gave testimony at the coroner's inquest.

Finally, an investigator with the coroner's office interviewed Brian's psychiatrist, Dr. A. L. Greenburgh. The doctor stated that he had worked with Jones to lessen his dependency on prescription medicines, with "considerable improvement of late." His regular medicines included Mandrax, or sleeping tablets, which combine methaqualone (Quaaludes) with diphenhydramine; Valium® tranquilizers; a Medihaler for breathing; Durophet, or "black bombers," which combine amphetamine and dextroamphetamine; and Piriton for hay fever.[22]

The official death certificate was issued on July 9, 1969, in East Grinstead, County of East Sussex, and signed by registrar M. P. Lacey. The handwritten document rehashes what Dr. Sommerville had written in his report and ends with the cause of death as "Drowning: Swimming whilst under the influence of alcohol and drugs. Misadventure."[23]

My analysis of this autopsy report—and what I discussed with author Geoffrey Giuliano—is that the findings are consistent with a death by drowning. The heavy, wet lungs, frothy fluid around the nostrils, and blood-stained fluid in the mouth all point to drowning. Whether that means an accidental drowning or a fatal dunking at the hands of another cannot be determined based on the medical evidence provided.

The fatty liver is from degeneration due to alcoholism. Jones was a bit overweight, which can fatten the liver, but we wouldn't see this extensive damage to someone so young if alcohol had not been a factor. And his fatty liver would not have caused a sudden death, as we see in chronic alcoholics who have poor nutrition. His blood alcohol level of 0.14 is not particularly high for someone who is an experienced drinker, as he was. A nondrinker who imbibed that much alcohol might be falling over or drowsy, but not someone whose intake was as chronic as Brian's. There is no scientific basis for blaming his fatty liver for his drowning death.

As to whether he was impaired by the drugs in his system, I can answer an emphatic no. The amphetamine-like substance found was in his urine, which means it was on its way out of his body. It would have had zero effect on his brain, so he did not die of a drug overdose, nor did drugs play a role in his death. The lab seems to have done a fairly thorough job of eliminating the presence of drugs in his system, although today's toxicological testing would also include marijuana. But even if he had marijuana in his system, it would be an unlikely factor to cause his death by drowning. Marijuana is pharmacologically classified as a relatively mild hallucinogen; it is not a central nervous system depressant that might cause someone's loss of consciousness.

What role Brian's asthma played in causing him to drown is another subject of debate. Giuliano showed me a letter from Dr. Sommerville that read: "In an asthmatic attack, the bronchi are in spasm: this would tend to seal the lining of the tissue and prevent the entry of water while the spasm lasted." I must disagree with that statement. While an asthma attack will cause *some* broncho-spasm, it doesn't create a hermetic seal that water can't seep through. Plus, we know that Jones's lungs were heavy and wet. Still, an acute asthma attack leading to death is a difficult diagnosis to make at autopsy. A spasm of the bronchi does not remain in place postmortem like a spasm of arteries. A tube structure like the bronchus or the larynx will loosen after death. And while there is some mucus, there is not the kind of inflammation one might see if there was an asthma attack. I would have liked to review the slides microscopically, but they were not offered to me. For the sake of argument, let's say Jones had a massive asthma attack while in the middle of the pool. He was an accomplished swimmer, and he was in his own pool, which had a width of about ten feet, or three or four strokes to the side. He wasn't in the middle of the ocean, and he didn't suffer a heart attack that would have disabled him. Even if he was hit by asthma and had trouble breathing, he'd be able to swim to the edge and climb out. So that eliminates asthma as a direct factor in his death.

Official witness statements indicate that Brian was only underwater for about three minutes before one of the other people found him and pulled him from the pool. That can't be accurate because it takes a minimum of about five or six minutes underwater for a brain to be deprived of oxygen, causing someone to become unresponsive to resuscitative measures. I should think the nurse would have known that three minutes would not have been long enough for him to be beyond some form of recovery. A person with a bad heart might not last five minutes if submerged and totally without oxygen, but Brian didn't have a bad heart.

The biggest problem with the autopsy is its lack of detail. I was surprised at the limited amount of commentary, especially since they knew they were dealing with a celebrity and there would be great public interest. I can only surmise that had there been something outstanding—for instance, bruising on Jones's limbs or shoulders that could be signs of force, perhaps from someone holding him underwater as he struggled—it would have shown up in the external examination and been noted in the report. There was no bruising mentioned. And the internal reflection of the scalp could reveal blood clots where the hair might have been pulled as his head was lifted in and out of the water. I say "could" because it's also possible that the right amount of force, under the right circumstances, might leave no collateral signs. So then it becomes a question of whether a dedicated killer would take the risk of possibly leaving physical signs of force during a struggle. I can't rule out the possibility that one or more people may have brought about his drowning by playing games with him, continuing to dunk him, pulling him under, and making him swallow water. After a while, even though you may be a good swimmer, as Brian Jones was, if you were not permitted to breathe and you begin to swallow water, then you may tire, stop struggling, and drown.

On its own, the autopsy report would not cause me to see this case as a homicide. The interviews Giuliano and Hotchner conducted would cause suspicions if their secret sources—Joe and Marty—had told authorities their stories and given detectives more to work with. Officers might have suggested the two take polygraph exams and share the names of others who could corroborate their accounts, then turned the duo over to prosecutors who would put them under oath. If Joe and Marty were truly interested in clearing their consciences and giving closure to Jones's family, they would have acquiesced. But two sources—assuming they're real people at all—who choose to tell their extraordinary observations to journalists rather than to law enforcement leaves an unsettling feeling. What does this say about the moral character of such people who won't help authorities solve what they claim is a homicide?

There might have been a sincere attempt by the authors and others to crack this case, and I can understand how a journalist getting such a scoop would be exhilarated. But in the real world of crime and punishment, these off-the-record sources and death-bed confessions are not enough to run with. And what of the fans who cry that the case should be reopened, or that Jones's body should be exhumed? To what end? Taxpayers should not be expected to squander funds on cases that cannot be prosecuted and, hopefully, won. If all the evidence is what we have been discussing here, it's not enough to merit action because the main suspects are dead. And not only are dead people insulated from being libeled, they're also insulated from being charged criminally.

The fact is, the mystery of Brian's death has created a cottage industry of people who have written books and made movies, including a 2005 feature film titled *Stoned*, which is largely based on Giuliano's book. To such people, the concept of Jones dying as a result of homicide is more intriguing than learning that he died from a simple accident.[24]

Another example of that goes back to 2006, when I was contacted by Trevor Hobley, the founder of the Brian Jones Fan Club. Hobley, an affable British fellow, had spent considerable time compiling documents about Jones's death and was convinced there had been a sloppy police investigation. He wanted the coroner's inquest verdict to be overturned and the case re-examined—and because he called Jones "the silent witness" who could reveal the truth, he wanted the body exhumed and re-autopsied. He made the rounds of media expressing his views.[25]

According to my notes, I discussed the case with Mr. Hobley and gave him the same information I have stated here. But I believe he heard only what he wanted to hear. The following year, I was contacted by a Hollywood television producer who was preparing a documentary titled *TV Land Myths & Legends*, based on Hobley's research on Jones. He had suggested they interview me on camera to bolster his theories. The producer was ready to send a camera crew to my office in Pittsburgh within hours but first wanted to ensure that my comments matched what Hobley had told her—and that caused a problem. Hobley said that Jones's autopsy proved he died of injuries similar to those found in "shaken baby cases," or "contrecoup" damage. Such injuries occur when there is a particularly violent impact and the brain accelerates forward into the skull, then reverses course and hits the other side of the skull with equal force. There was no indication of that in Brian Jones's autopsy report, I explained. But what *is* in the report are classical findings of drowning; namely, the congestion, edema, and punctuate hemorrhages that indicate a brain deprived of oxygen.

The producer also had an "informant" who told her that Jones's body was buried deeper than usual and in an airtight coffin, indicating that "the murderer" wanted to preserve the body so that it could be exhumed and re-autopsied someday. I pointed out that that would be the opposite of what a murderer who wanted to stay out of jail would want; such a murderer would want that body and its secrets to remain undisturbed forever. A killer would most want a body to be cremated, so there could never be an exhumation, but if he or she didn't control that and the body was buried, the least desirable circumstance would be an exhumation, which could produce a new interpretation and, possibly, an arrest for homicide.

I went through the scientific evidence once again, stating that even if there had been a half-baked investigation, the chance of the case being reopened at this late date was nil since there are no viable suspects still alive and no one to arrest and prosecute. She wrote down everything I said and promised to get back to me about when I would be interviewed by the TV crew. I never heard back from her and did not participate in any taping. I don't know whether the program aired without my contribution.

The death of Brian Jones will continue to garner public attention, and every few years there'll be a new batch of media outcries calling for a new probe and/or exhumation of Jones's body. It's human nature, I suppose. I only wish there was as much fascination with science as there is with science fiction.[26] While researching this chapter, my co-author Dawna Kaufmann made a status request of the Sussex police department, as well as the New Scotland Yard, and learned the Brian Jones case is as it ever was—a closed file.[27]

The Saturday after Brian's death, the Rolling Stones were scheduled to give a free concert in London's Hyde Park. There was debate in the press as to whether it should be canceled, but Mick Jagger announced it would go on, as Brian would have wanted. Two hundred and fifty thousand fans showed up for the event, which included Jagger reading a poem in tribute to their lost colleague. It was also Mick Taylor's first public outing as Brian's replacement.[28]

Keith Richards was mystified by his former bandmate's death and was unable to get a clear picture of what had happened that night.

"There's a crowd of people, then suddenly there's nobody there," he said. Richards believed that Jones had surrounded himself with people who didn't take care of him, but no one, he felt, who would want to murder him. He had witnessed Brian swim off the coast of Fiji, through menacing waves, without a problem, so he didn't understand how Brian could drown in a swimming pool. "It's the same feeling with who killed Kennedy," Keith added. "You can't get to the bottom of it."[29]

Author Terry Rawlings said that in eight years of research and countless interviews with people who knew Brian Jones, he never found one person who had anything good to say about him. Rawlings felt that Brian was his own worst enemy, one who overindulged in alcohol, drugs, women, and spending money. And since he was no good at mixing with the lower-class people who worked for him, Rawlings stated his drowning death was inevitable—presumably because he believed the musician lorded his wealth and fame over those who coveted the same.[30]

Perhaps Rawlings should have spoken to Cindy Parkhurst, an autoworker from a suburb near Detroit, Michigan, who has run a website for fans of the Stones since 1998, and who took photos of Cotchford Farm, including the one found in this book. "Brian Jones had a complicated life, and an even more complicated death," Parkhurst said to Kaufmann. "But his musical vision was keen and the band that he created has made its mark on the world in ways that I'm sure would have made Brian proud."[31]

Indeed, the Stones have endured like no other rock band in history. Mick Jagger and Keith Richards are the only two band members who continue to record and tour; many other musicians have come and gone from the group over the years, along with various wives and girlfriends. At last count, the Stones have recorded ninety-two singles, twenty-nine studio albums, and ten live albums[32]—and of bands that are still touring, they remain the world's top-earners of all time.[33]

———

As for Brian, on July 10, 1969, his memorial took place in the St. Mary's church in Cheltenham where his family worshipped, the sermon delivered by canon Hugh Evan Hopkins. Outside, news cameras captured the proceedings, and thousands of fans mourned the fallen star. Charlie Watts and Bill Wyman were the only Stones in attendance. Jones was buried in the church cemetery, in a hole dug twelve feet deep to thwart souvenir seekers who might want to exhume their idol. His headstone lists his death date as July 3, rather than July 2, and its epitaph cites a phrase he once sent in a telegram to his parents following a drug bust: "Please don't judge me too harshly."[34]

CHAPTER FOUR

DREW PETERSON

Ladykiller or Misunderstood Clown?

C riminal investigations are delicate matters. Police and prosecu-tors, on one side, and defense attorneys, on the other, hope that nothing torpedoes their efforts on the road to courtroom justice. But when the very target of the investigation makes a public display that increases suspicion, it's the prosecution's best gift and the defense's worst nightmare. Welcome to the case of Drew Peterson, the former Boling-broke, Illinois, police sergeant and SWAT team member who is now in jail, awaiting trial for the murder of his third wife, Kathleen Savio. There never would have been an exhumation of Savio's body and reopening of her case had it not been for Peterson's outrageous and insensitive behavior following the disappearance of Stacy Peterson, his fourth wife. Open mouth, insert foot, and lose freedom.

My co-author, reporter Dawna Kaufmann, began covering this case shortly after Stacy Peterson vanished without a trace on October 28, 2007. For more than two years, Drew was front-page news in the crime media circuits, and Dawna would apprise me of updates that I felt were more in line with something a Hollywood screenwriter might dream up. I answered her queries about various death scenarios for her print news stories and radio shows, then began to get calls from television and other national media asking for help in understanding various "what if?" situ-ations. As the evidence and intrigue mounted, it became clear that most folks had negative opinions about Drew Peterson. If Peterson were to be arrested, I had to wonder just where in this solar system his attorney would find a venue in which his client could get a fair trial.[1]

Drew Walter Peterson was born on January 6, 1954, in Oak Park, Illinois, the eldest of three children. At twenty, he married a woman named Carol, with whom he had two sons. He was stationed with the US Army in Virginia, and his duties included guarding President Gerald Ford. A licensed pilot and expert at the Korean martial art tae kwon do, in 1976, Peterson moved his family back to Illinois, where he joined the police department for the Chicago suburb of Bolingbroke. He was working on the Metro Area Narcotics Squad as an undercover agent when his wife discovered he was cheating on her; they divorced in 1980.[2] According to acandyrose.com, one of the most comprehensive online sources for all high-profile crime cases, Drew, after four months of dating, proposed marriage to Kyle Piry, but she found him too controlling and thought that, at twenty, she was too young to be a stepmother to his boys. She also learned he had been unfaithful when she found long black hairs in his bed. In 1983, after Drew married his second wife, Victoria, he and another officer arrested Kyle for having unpaid parking tickets. She was put into his cruiser and fingerprinted, but the charges were eventually dropped. The marriage to Vicky was also doomed when he allegedly told her he could kill her and make it look like an accident.[3] Vicky's daughter, Lisa, lived with her mother and Drew from the time she was eight until she turned seventeen. She alleged that he "physically, mentally and emotionally abused" her, a point disputed by Peterson's attorney, Joel A. Brodsky.[4] Still, Drew and Vicky bought a beer bar called Suds, which Vicky ran. During this time, Drew was demoted to police sergeant after getting involved with a loan shark and being indicted for the felony of not reporting a bribe. While still wed, he began an affair with an accountant named Kathleen "Kathy" Savio. Vicky filed for divorce but continued to work at the bar. Driving on a country road one day, she found her brakes had failed. The car rolled three times, pushing her nose backward and leaving her in a coma for ten weeks. She couldn't prove that Drew was behind the accident, but that, and the fact that he would break into her home, spooked her enough to get out of the marriage and let him buy her share of the bar.

All the women in Drew's life were at first attracted by the seemingly affable guy who had a steady job and was, by all accounts, a decent father to his children. But, according to *Drew Peterson: Under Suspicion*, a documentary that aired on the Biography Channel, his incessant womanizing tore apart each relationship. In 1992, he married Kathy Savio, and they soon had two sons. Drew blamed her hormone levels for making her too emotional, but others allege that he taunted her to drop the baby weight and brutalized her physically, sometimes dragging her out of the house by her hair. According to her relatives, Drew isolated Kathy from her family and friends. In 2002, a still-married Drew began dating seventeen-year-old Stacy Ann Cales, whom he met in a hotel where she worked as a desk clerk.[5] Stacy, the third of five children, had a troubled background. While eight months pregnant with Stacy, her mother crawled barefoot out of the family home when it became engulfed in flames; an older daughter died of burns and smoke inhalation. Another of Stacy's older sisters died of sudden infant death syndrome. Stacy's younger brother would later go to jail for aggravated sexual abuse of a minor. And in 1998, Stacy's mother ditched her family and was never heard from again. Her father moved the family dozens of times and was prone to alcohol-induced rages. For Stacy, finding Drew, who seemed stable and wooed her with compliments and expensive gifts, must have seemed like a life jacket to a drowning victim—despite the fact that he was thirty years her senior.

Stacy soon became pregnant and would eventually have a son and a daughter with Drew. They couldn't marry until his divorce from Kathy was finalized, and there were a number of issues standing in the way, such as the dividing of their assets, that would deprive Drew of one-half of his holdings. For her part, Kathy was furious that Drew had taken up with someone she felt was "a child" and was even angrier when he and his young girlfriend moved into a house down the street from where Savio, now in nursing school, and the two boys lived. This gave Drew and Stacy plenty of opportunity to wage war on Kathy; the two would drive by Savio's home yelling obscenities. Some of the encounters between the two women even turned violent, with Drew watching in rapt amusement as they clawed and punched each other. According to an excellent book by former policewoman Stacy Dittrich, *Murder behind the Badge*, Kathleen called police on eighteen occasions with various complaints, from not bringing the kids back from parental visits in a timely fashion, to what she felt were serious threats against her life.[6] In a November 14, 2002, letter Savio wrote to Illinois assistant state's attorney Elizabeth Fragale, Kathleen referenced "several visits" to the emergency room, protective orders she had sought, and specific acts of domestic violence against her. She also said repeated calls she had made to police were ignored. She claimed Drew had reprogrammed her garage door so that he could open it, and described finding him inside her living room one day, dressed in his SWAT gear. He told her he didn't want to pay child support and said that she needed to die. He allegedly pulled out a knife, held it to her neck, and asked if she was afraid. She recounted another time when she caught Stacy videotaping her with a camcorder stolen from Savio's home. When she tried to grab it back, Drew—who was not on duty—arrested her, pushing her face in the grass and spraining her wrist. Her plea ended with: "He knows how to manipulate the system, and his next step is to take my children away. Or kill me instead." Kathleen also told her sister that Drew was going to kill her and make it look like an accident.[7]

Drew and Kathleen's divorce came through on October 10, 2003. One week later, he married a pregnant Stacy. Over the next few years together, he would mold Stacy into his version of a Barbie doll, according to domestic violence expert Susan Murphy Milano, who was interviewed for the documentary. He bought his young wife braces, breast implants, a tummy tuck, and liposuction, and then claimed the procedures were her idea.[8]

On February 28, 2004, Drew claimed he tried to return his two sons to Kathleen after a visitation, but she didn't answer her door or phone. He brought the boys back to his home and tried again the next day—February 29 (2004 was a leap year), and again on March 1—to no avail. He called for a locksmith to open the door and went to a neighbor's home and asked the residents to go inside, saying he didn't want to go inside alone in case there was a problem. Kathy was found in an upstairs bathroom, dead in the bathtub. Steve Carcerano, one of the neighbors who found the body, told Fox News' Greta Van Susteren that Drew was steps behind him, and when he saw the body, he began screaming, "Oh my God, what am I gonna tell my kids?"[9]

Drew's colleagues from the Bolingbroke police force, knowing about the turbulence between the parties, questioned Drew and Stacy about their whereabouts over the last couple of days. But the pair was not separated; Drew sat next to Stacy while she supported his alibi that they were together during the key hours. It would later be learned that Savio left a one-million-dollar life insurance policy for her nine- and eleven-year-old sons, as well as her home that was valued at $600,000.[10]

Illinois's Will County coroner is an elected position, with a four-year term. Patrick K. O'Neil has been in the slot for four terms. According to his campaign website, O'Neil is a board-certified medicolegal death investigator who has supervised over twenty-two thousand death investigations and performed over fifteen hundred inquests. While he holds a master's certificate from the St. Louis School of Medicine Forensic Science, he is not a medical doctor or forensic pathologist.[11] When those services are required, there are a number of qualified medical examiners who can actually conduct the autopsy.[12]

The official autopsy of Kathleen Savio, age forty, was performed on

March 2, 2004, by Brian Mitchell, MD, a board-certified forensic pathologist who received his medical degree in 1991 from Loyola Chicago University. Observing the procedure were deputy coroner Kevin Stevenson, two interns, and Illinois state police officers Brian Falat, Bob Diehl, and Bill Belcher Jr. In his report, Mitchell described Savio as having brown eyes and hair, weighing one hundred and fifty-four pounds and measuring five feet five inches. He established the cause of her death to be drowning—but did not make a ruling as to whether the manner of death was homicide, suicide, accident, natural, or undetermined. As is general practice in that jurisdiction, that call is made by a coroner's inquest.

The fiberglass bathtub in which Savio was recovered was oval shaped and cream colored. Around the surface of the tub were numerous bottles of shampoo, conditioner, a brush, bubble bath and salts, a rubber duck, soaps, and towels—none of which seemed disturbed, as one might expect them to be if there had been a struggle. A bottle of what seemed to be shampoo was in the tub with her, and her body was covering a water-logged bar of soap. Her position in the tub would invoke much debate as to whether she drowned after a "slip and fall" in the tub, or whether she was dunked while outside the tub and later placed inside by someone else. Her feet were pushed up against the part of the tub near the faucet, while her naked body was twisted, the left side of her body and face near the tub floor. All the water had drained out, leaving only a substantial amount of bloody purge—a natural by-product of decomposition—under Savio's body. Because there was no ring of bloody purge around the tub, we can presume that the water drained prior to the purge being released.

Mitchell's ruling of drowning was due to finding water present in Savio's lungs and sinuses inside the skull cavity. He also found some swelling of the brain and other organs, signifying a lack of oxygen that caused the bodily functions to halt. And he found mild thickening of the mitral valve, which is between the heart's third and fourth chambers. This was likely an age-related change that limited some cardiac blood flow but would not be life-threatening. Findings were negative for tumors, chronic disease, or infection. He also observed white foam coming from her nostrils, a distinctive sign of drowning caused by air and fluids in the lungs ascending from the trachea. Importantly, while pill bottles for medications including Celebrex® (celecoxib, for pain relief or arthritis), Niafol (nicomide, for acne treatment), Lipitor® (atorvastatin, for lowering cholesterol), Zoloft® (sertraline HCI, an antidepressant), Nicosyn (sulfacetamide sulfur, an antibiotic), Yasmin® (drospirenone and ethinyl estradiol, for birth control), hydrocodone (for pain relief), and Xanax® (alprazolam, for anxiety relief), were collected from Savio's home, her toxicology report came back negative for any drugs or alcohol in her system.

Mitchell noted numerous bruises and contusions on Savio's body, including a one-inch laceration on the back of her scalp.[13] This defect was not noticed by the investigators who collected her body, likely because her thick, dark hair covered the injury. And since her face was pointing downward, there was no blood in her hair, which was still wet from the tub water. Only when she was laid faceup in the body bag did blood exit from the wound and coat her hair. This happened because once a heart stops pumping and death occurs, bleeding also ceases, although blood might seep from an open wound as a response to gravity. How Savio acquired that head laceration is unknown, since the crime scene technicians failed to spray the tub and fixtures with luminol spray to find blood, nor did they apparently even look for hair or skin cells that might have been left by her head coming into contact with a hard surface.[14] Mitchell reported that under the laceration was a "little bit of bruising" on the surface of the scalp, but there was no hemorrhage to the brain or defect to the scalp.[15]

This is a critical finding that suggests the blow might not have been enough to render her unconscious but merely could have stunned her. There's no way of knowing when the blow was administered prior to her death, but if it occurred while she was still dressed, one might see blood drips or spray on her clothing. To my knowledge, that clothing was neither collected nor tested. If the injury happened while she was naked and upright, one might see blood residue on her back or in her hair, which was not the case.

I wish that Mitchell's description of the wounds had been more detailed. If the injuries were excised and submitted for microscopic study, there is no record of it—and that's a crucial omission. When a living body suffers any injury, white blood cells—the body's natural defenders—rush to the scene to initiate the healing process within about an hour. This vital reaction is not detectable to the naked eye but shows up under a high-powered microscope. Had slides been taken of these wounds, the presence of white blood cells would have been a helpful tool in determining the amount of time between the head blow and the drowning.

So the mystery remains. Savio's last known contact—a phone call with her boyfriend—occurred about thirty-six hours prior to her death, leaving a pretty large time span in which she either died accidentally or was killed. If the latter, the murderer could have used the water temperature as another tool to thwart identifying the time of death, since there is less decomposition in a cool environment than in a heated one. Another component for estimating time of death is rigor mortis, the stiffness of the body's muscles that sets in after a person dies. Rigor becomes fixed in about eight to twelve hours and remains so for another twelve to twenty-four hours, then begins to leave the body. Within forty-eight hours, it's come and gone. Savio's body had no signs of rigor mortis, meaning she was found many hours after she died. The body also showed some minor skin greening, an indicator that decomposition was setting in, something that is typically not seen in the first twenty-four hours after death.[16]

Mitchell chronicled a series of other external changes, including substantial livor mortis, or pooling of blood due to the pull of gravity. Lividity typically becomes fixed between eight and twelve hours after death. If a body is moved or repositioned before livor becomes fixed, there is a corresponding break in the livor mortis pattern, which leaves a blanched area where the purplish color is replaced by whitish streaking. If a body is folded over, those fold marks will show blanching while the areas above and below will show lividity, producing almost a candy cane pattern. There were areas of blanching on various parts of Savio's body but most particularly on her right breast, which had an imprint suggestive of several fingers coming into contact with the tissue, sometime after Savio's death. Similar, though less distinctive marks were on the left breast, as well as on her right knee.[17] If you grasp your own arm and apply pressure, you will see momentary signs of blanching. But these fingerprint-type marks could be viewed as an example of authorities dropping the ball. There are a number of relatively new processes to pull up possible latent fingerprints from a dead body, including cyanoacrylate— or superglue—testing. The body is put into a chamber, and the cyanoacrylate is warmed until it becomes gaseous, then it is introduced into the chamber. The fumes react with organic compounds, such as oils or fats on the skin, and if there are fingerprints, they will surface as brown or black marks that can be digitally photographed. Such prints can then be analyzed to point to or eliminate a suspect. The marks on Savio's breasts were certainly not from the paramedics fishing Savio out of the tub since that is not how they would grab the body for transport.

Another error could be ascribed to Bob Diehl, the crime scene investigator at the site. Following Will County protocol, the deputy coroner put paper bags over Savio's hands to protect any forensic evidence that might be under her fingernails. But Diehl, for reasons unstated, declined to test the trace evidence. Diehl also took the photographs at the scene, but I found the images very underwhelming.

Coloration is a major hint for freshness of injury, with red and purple meaning most fresh, and green and yellow indicating most healed.[18] Savio's left buttock showed a blood-red scrape, meaning it was a relatively fresh wound with no scabbing. It's impossible to know at what point before her death that scrape occurred, though if she were wearing clothing at the time, there might be an imprint from the clothing or fiber evidence, but there wasn't. The same would be true if the scrape came from a rug burn—but there was no visible trace evidence to suggest the area had come into contact with a rug. Bruises and abrasions dotted her right shin, left knee, left thigh, right wrist, left elbow, and back of her right index finger, with a large one on the lower left quadrant of her abdomen. That last bruise didn't show a clothing-type pattern when it was attained, which indicates that Savio was not wearing underwear or clothing at the time.[19] One possible scenario might be that she was draped over the edge of the bathtub, with her head in the water and her abdomen against the tub's edge. On the other hand, she was a mother of two active young boys who could easily and innocently injure a parent—but the bruise coloration was so fresh, and the children had been with their father for days. What I do know is that if a person showed up on my autopsy table with these kinds of injuries, I would speak to the detectives in charge and ask them to gather more information. Were I to learn they had a professional relationship or friendship with the deceased or any possible suspect, I would recommend that they seek independent review from an outside law enforcement agency. In all my years of seeing drowning victims in bathtubs, none were positioned as Kathleen Savio was. However, science is full of variables, and if there's one thing that can be stated with authority, it is "never say never."[20]

Coroner O'Neil convened an inquest, and Savio's sisters testified about Kathleen's fears of Drew. But state police officers assured the panel there was no physical evidence suggesting foul play. O'Neil ruled Savio's death as "accidental," and Bolingbroke police chief Raymond McGury issued a statement that each complaint of domestic violence was investigated fully and no cover-up had taken place. Savio's sisters were beside themselves with frustration, especially when they learned that the inquest jury was given no option but to rule the death as "accidental." One of the six members on the panel would later speak out that he would have voted for "undetermined," but he was not allowed to. The case was closed—for the next three years.[21]

Over the next couple of years, Stacy, who was still in her early twenties, found herself saddled with four young children: the two children she'd had with Drew and Kathleen's two boys. She saw other girls her age in college or having fun, while her life centered around cooking, cleaning, and tending kids. Drew seemed to change toward her. He was now limiting the amount of money she could spend, and he would check the mileage on her car, harass her if he thought she was seeing friends or relatives, and monitor her phone calls. She was sick of the total control he had over her and told her sister, Cassandra Cales, that she planned to leave him.

On October 27, 2007, Stacy was supposed to go to her sister's residence to help with a painting project, but she never showed up. Cassandra was the one who notified Bolingbroke police that Stacy was missing. Drew told investigators that Stacy had called him to say she had met someone else and was going to the Caribbean with her new love. She had parked her car at the airport, Drew claimed, and had cleaned $25,000 out of the home safe and taken her passport and bikini. Police soon learned there was no activity on her credit cards or cell phone. Stacy's family was indignant: They knew the whole premise was bogus, as Stacy would have never left her children.[22]

Two months before she went missing, Stacy had requested a meeting with Neil Schori, the former pastor of Westbrook Christian Church, and told him that she "feared for her life." Then—according to what Schori told Fox News' Greta Van Susteren—Stacy hit him with a bombshell, blurting out, "He did it, he killed Kathleen." The pastor said there were more details of the conversation that he would not disclose, but that the information fit with Savio's death timeline. As soon as the meeting ended, Schori said, he got a voice mail from Drew, letting him know he was aware that Stacy was speaking with him. Drew also requested a meeting, but Schori turned him down.[23] Later, Drew would scoff about his wife's friendship with the young preacher, saying that Stacy would get "all dolled up every time she went to see him." When asked why the church representatives didn't report the Savio information to police rather than the media, senior pastor Rob Daniels said: "The church's clergy are only legally mandated to alert authorities of allegations of child abuse or if someone threatens to harm themselves or others." Joel Brodsky, Drew's lawyer, told reporters that Schori testified before a grand jury that, on the night of Savio's death, Stacy repeatedly tried to reach Drew by phone and claimed she saw him wearing a black ninja outfit. But Brodsky ridiculed the comments as "leaks."[24]

On October 29, Bolingbroke resident Walter Martinek Jr. told the *Chicago Tribune* that the day before he had received a panicky phone call from an acquaintance, Thomas Morphey, who was Peterson's stepbrother. Morphey told him that he had earlier been at the Peterson home when Drew asked for his help in moving a large blue plastic container from the Peterson bedroom into the back of Drew's SUV. Morphey claimed he never looked inside the container, but he believed it felt warm to the touch and feared that Stacy's body had been inside. Peterson adamantly denied the account, stating that Morphey had substance abuse problems. Morphey was soon hospitalized in what was described as a suicide attempt, but he survived.[25]

On November 9, the Bolingbroke police department stated that Stacy was likely dead and that Drew was the prime suspect. But the media went further, anointing him as culpable for the murder of not one, but two wives. News footage showed cadaver dogs searching Drew's home and yard and evidence technicians seizing his car, guns, and other items from his property. Playing to the cameras, Drew wore an American flag bandanna, while cursing reporters and claiming there was no proof against him. As he left the courtroom of the court that was seeking to indict him for Savio's death and learned that other women in his life would be testifying against him, he joked, "Let's have a party! I didn't know it was going to be a reunion!" He told his children that Stacy had run off on a vacation, and he would later tell reporters that she was in the Philippines with her boyfriend, not wanting to be found. He also shrugged off her behavior as copying what Stacy's own mother did when she abandoned her family. Through it all, searches for Stacy's body continued. There would be many alleged sightings that would turn out to be mistakes or hoaxes, and they all got their moment in the media sun.[26]

The rampant media interest caused Bolingbroke authorities to decide to take another look at Kathleen Savio's case. In early November 2007, Will County state's attorney James Glasgow announced there were "strong indications" that Savio's death was a homicide. "I read the autopsy protocol," Glasgow said. "I read the inquest, I looked at the crime-scene photographs, and I looked at the photographs from the autopsy—and with twenty-nine years of experience, there's no doubt in my mind it wasn't an accident." He filed a petition to have her body exhumed, which was granted by Judge Daniel J. Rozak. That same day Peterson was suspended without pay from the Bolingbroke police department.[27]

On November 11, Geraldo Rivera, one of America's most diligent reporters and host of *Geraldo at Large* on Fox News, traveled to Bolingbroke for an exclusive interview with Peterson. Drew would not go on camera, but he gave Rivera this statement: "I feel I've been misquoted by the press and the media has done nothing but harass my family and terrorize my children. This entire ordeal has been the most traumatic experience of my life. As a result of this nightmare, I've lost over 25 pounds." Rivera also interviewed Stacy's two sisters, Cassandra Cales and Debbie Forgue. Both said they were not surprised when Drew was named a suspect in Stacy's disappearance. Cales reemphasized that Stacy "wouldn't leave her kids."[28]

On November 13, Savio's white coffin was exhumed from Queen of Heaven Catholic Cemetery in Hillside, Illinois, and brought to the Will County Coroner's Office for a second autopsy. Three days later, the postmortem was conducted by Lawrence "Larry" W. Blum, MD, a board-certified forensic pathologist who works freelance for several of the surrounding counties. In his report, he classified the Savio case as a "homicide." A third autopsy, at the behest of Savio's family and Fox News, was performed by nationally renowned forensic pathologist Michael M. Baden, MD, the former New York City chief medical examiner and a Fox commentator. Though I have not spoken to either doctor about the case (which is standard operating procedure), the media have reported some of their statements—they both believed Savio had been beaten before she was drowned.[29] Baden was quoted as saying there were indications "of multiple blunt force traumas, of being beaten up. Those bruises were still there and could be seen from the naked eye. They were still fresh."[30] At the completion of Savio's exhumation, her body was reinterred in the same grave.

In the days after the exhumation, I made a flurry of media appearances to answer basic questions about supplemental autopsies and what the Savio autopsies might produce. I said that I doubted there would be any new anatomical findings that were not already noted in the first report. Blum and Baden were not going to suddenly find a bullet hole or skull fracture that the original doctor missed. Due to a faulty seal in the burial vault, there was advanced deterioration of the corpse's hands and forearms, leaving them skeletal, and other parts of the flesh were turned to adipocere, a waxy component of decomposition. The scalp was very dehydrated, which changed the wound. This time the fingernails, which were still present, were collected and sent for testing. Blum had visited Savio's former home and, with an Illinois state police crime scene investigator, Patrick Phillips, took measurements of the tub and clocked the amount of time water would take to drain from it. Blum actually sat in the tub, as did a female trooper who was approximately Savio's height. They were unable to duplicate anything that would come close to an accidental fall. That's not surprising. Since we can't be certain of the exact motion, equilibrium, and physics of how Savio might have fallen, it is not possible to replicate the fall experimentally.

As we would later learn, the new reports mostly echoed the findings of Dr. Mitchell's initial examination, listing the same bruises and abrasions, either from direct observation of the corpse or review of the original autopsy photographs. While Mitchell would comment that the breasts showed blanching that could suggest marks from someone's fingers, Blum admitted he couldn't be sure what caused the marks. He considered that it might be some sort of lettering, perhaps from the bar of soap that had become mushy and was discovered under Savio's body. At trial, those two competing viewpoints might confound jurors.

Recall that, while Dr. Mitchell declared the cause of death to be drowning, he never made a conclusion as to manner of death—by law, he had to let the grand jury make that declaration, and they were given no option other than "accident." I'm sure Mitchell must have felt frustrated by the people who think he was the reason the case wasn't tried in 2004. It was the grand jury's decision, and those panelists, as always, are at the mercy of prosecutors who decide what evidence or witnesses will be produced. The defense case is never presented to a grand jury. With media reports being broadcast around the clock and around the world, the presumption was that a new inquest would likely indict Peterson, and it did. Coroner O'Neil issued a press release defending his office's conclusions as to manner of death for the 2004 autopsy, as well as for the 2007 one, citing a 2007 change in state law that now gave coroners the option of bypassing the grand jury process and ruling on the manner of death independently. Had this option been available in 2004, he wrote, the ruling in the case would have been different.

There's nothing wrong with revisiting a case by getting a second, or third, autopsy opinion. Besides being able to review the body and all sundry reports from the first team, the new physicians can send tissue or fluid samples to an independent laboratory for fresh analysis. The initial screening found no drugs or alcohol in Savio's system. Blum and Baden wanted to confirm that, and so they ordered additional testing for heavy-metal poisons, such as arsenic, strychnine, thallium, cyanide, and sodium fluoroacetate, as well as for chloroform and ether, none of which are part of a boiler-plate toxicology screen. They wanted to eliminate the chance that Savio was incapacitated by poison, and the results confirmed that no toxins were in her body at death. If she wasn't debilitated by drugs or alcohol, and there was no sudden cardiac arrest or stroke—as noted in the autopsies—the idea of a bathtub "slip and fall" becomes a less plausible way to drown. Another vital difference between the old and new autopsies is that Blum and Baden took tissue samples for microscopic testing, the results of which fortified their views that Savio was killed. Police, prosecutors, and Drew's defense team were all looking ahead, so the exhumation was a strategic procedure in terms of the investigation and, ultimately, with an eye toward the trial.

The families also wanted clarification and more resources allotted for their investigations. In life Stacy and Kathleen were bitter enemies, but in death their families were working together against the man who made them so unhappy. If Savio's case is proven to be murder, and a grand jury indicts Drew for her death, Stacy Peterson's family will argue that Drew killed her too, and he can be prosecuted for that even if her body is never recovered. Poking the hornet's nest of these cases might also turn up new evidence, from re-interpretation of police and deposition reports, to key witnesses who come forward.[31]

Drew's next-door neighbor, Sharon Bychowski, began waging a war against Drew, posting "Where's Stacy?" signs in the community and working with Internet organizers to keep the heat on the ex-cop.[32] In January 2008—the very week that Stacy would have turned twenty-four—Drew surprised Chicago morning radio listeners when he called into host Steve Dahl's WJMK-FM program. Perhaps the booking was to counter some of the negative press Drew had been getting, but it turned out to be a colossal example of bad taste. Peterson offered to come on the show for a "Win a Date with Drew Peterson" contest. Peterson later appeared on Fox News' *Studio B with Shepard Smith* to describe the game as a "good-natured" "comedy bit" but complained that it got cancelled when "the radio station chickened out." Smith asked how Drew was handling Stacy's disappearance, and Peterson replied, "You do what you can. I'm not going to go in the corner and cry about it." He grieved about it on his own, he said, and added that his younger two children believed their mom was on vacation, but the older two—Savio's sons—realized that Stacy "ran off." Smith pressed for comments about the Morphey reports, but Drew sighed and said their agreement was that Drew would not answer those questions. With that, he took off his microphone and walked away from the camera. Smith responded with: "He'll talk about the dating game, but he won't talk about the neighbors who say they saw him with a large, fifty-five gallon blue barrel, carrying it out with someone else, shortly after his wife went missing."[33] Drew and his attorney, Joel Brodsky, next sat with the *Today* show's Matt Lauer to defend Peterson's reputation. "Drew Peterson has said from day one, and he believes and he knows, that Stacy has run off with another man," the mouthpiece roared. "He's a single man. He's raising his children the best he can. And he's entitled to get on with his life. Stacy's run off with another man, so she's moved on with her life. Why should Drew be sitting in a dark room?"[34]

In the latter part of 2008, Drew filed for divorce from Stacy, claiming abandonment. He also moved a twenty-three-year-old mother of two, Christina Raines, into his home and announced their engagement, but she soon moved out, telling CBS News the matter had been orchestrated for publicity by attorney Brodsky.[35] Peterson also briefly took part in a public relations stunt involving a Nevada brothel.[36]

In March 2009, a grand jury began convening weekly meetings in which prosecutors called sworn witnesses to prove that Drew Peterson killed Kathleen Savio. And this time, these six jurors would be allowed to vote whether the death was due to an accident, homicide, suicide, natural causes, or of undetermined origin. As the weeks went by, media attention stayed focused on all things Peterson.[37] On April 29, Drew was doing a radio interview on WLS-AM with Matthew Erich "Mancow" Muller when Stacy's sister Cassandra called in and confronted Peterson. "You murdered my sister," she snarled. "You killed her after she got off the phone between 10:15 and 10:59. The state police know where you were and what you did and you will pay." As Peterson sought to minimize the impact of her accusations, she added: "Drew, just keep talking, 'cause you're just digging yourself a deeper hole." Attorney Brodsky assured the audience that there would not be an indictment. After more angry words from Cassandra, the phone call ended.[38]

On May 7, the grand jury voted to indict, and Peterson was arrested while driving his car. Police waited for him to leave his home so as not to have to detain him at gunpoint in front of his minor-age children. He has been in jail since, on bail of $2,007,500.[39]

And when it was announced that Chicago radio station WGN-AM's *Legally Speaking* program would feature a mock trial—closing arguments only—of his client, Brodsky warned that he'd be sitting in the gallery, taking notes. *The People v. Drew Peterson* aired in two parts, on June 14 and 21. A professional jury expert had been consulted to choose the twelve jurors, but the panel failed to arrive at a unanimous verdict.[40]

After the exhumation, and occasionally over the next two years, Joel Brodsky would contact me for my views on the case, and he even visited me once in Pittsburgh. He told me he earned his Juris Doctor at DePaul University's College of Law and was admitted to the Illinois bar in 1982. His typical cases involved drug offenses or civil matters; this would be his first murder case. He planned to beef up his team with experienced co-counsel, but he would call the shots. After seeing an early appearance of Peterson on the *Today* show, Joel said that he contacted NBC and asked that his contact information be given to Drew, in case he needed representation. He ended up vying for the job along with a dozen other attorneys, some of whom wanted $250,000 up front. His first meeting with Drew was in Joel's car, so they could get privacy from the media hordes outside the Peterson residence. Although Brodsky brought paperwork to lay out his credentials, Drew didn't read it. "He said, 'You're it,' Brodsky explained, adding that Drew either trusts someone or he doesn't. I understood why Brodsky took on such a major and controversial case and told him that if he keeps his client off of death row, he'll have achieved a victory. I don't know whether he plans to call me as a witness during trial, but I suspect he won't, since I did not conduct my own examination of Savio's body. Besides, in this circumstantial case, testimony from people who knew Kathleen and Drew will be more germane than hearing yet another doctor comment on the injuries.[41]

Judge Stephen White began deciding how much, if any, of the outcry or second-party witness testimony would be deemed admissible, and in May 2010 he disallowed eight of the fourteen "second-hand" statements. State's attorney James Glasgow filed for appellate relief, citing legislation he helped write known as "Drew's Law," which was implemented to make it easier for prosecutors to use hearsay evidence in criminal trials.[42] White ruled that Dr. Baden can testify, despite the defense's claim that his procedure had been "irretrievably compromised."[43] Through discovery it was learned that Fox News had paid a sum of $100,000 for the chance to videotape the autopsy.[44] Fox producer Steph Watts, who shot the footage, swore in court that he only took notes and never moved or touched Savio's body. He also stated that the footage only showed Baden in and outside the operating room, and did not include shots of the body.[45] Whether that footage will one day be shown on Fox, or on Baden's own occasional HBO special called *Autopsy*, is unknown.

Serious questions remain in this case, however: How did this otherwise healthy forty-year-old woman fall in the tub and land on her left side and face, yet get a laceration to the left, top side of her head? Why did she have a large, fresh mark on her left buttock, along with all the other marks? And how did she wind up drowning in her own bathtub? Consider that all of Savio's doors and windows were closed, and there was no sign of a break-in. No evidence, such as footprints, showed that Drew was in the home, and the police probe was so insufficient, any trace evidence that could have led back to Drew was not collected. To my knowledge, he was never even photographed after Savio's body was found to see if he had injuries on his body that could have been from a fight.

Savio's medical history shows doctor visits in 1999 at which she complained of dizziness and weakness. While I feel those visits are too remote from the time of her death to suggest she fainted and drowned, the defense may try to get those medical records presented in court. It's also well documented that middle-age women bruise more easily than do men of the same age, so there are arguments that could give reasonable doubt to jurors who might believe she died accidentally. They may think that she bumped her head on something, went to take a bath to relax, became light-headed from the heat or steam, and fell over in the water and drowned. All it takes is one juror to refuse to find guilt, causing a mistrial, and Peterson could walk free—at least unless or until he is re-tried. Or he could be acquitted outright and be immune from retrial due to the law against double jeopardy. Normally, most people sit in the tub with their back against the end farthest from the faucet, but that's the opposite of how Savio was positioned—if she died accidentally. An accidental death might make more sense had there been evidence of a heart attack or a reaction from drugs or alcohol, but none of those were a factor. So we're left with only speculation and many competing theories.[46]

In an eerie coincidence, a Manhattan mother of two named Shele Danishefsky Covlin was discovered dead in her bathtub with a head injury thought to have been sustained from a slip-and-fall accident. Her husband, Rod Covlin, from whom she was estranged and who was to be removed as the beneficiary of her will on the next day, would not allow an autopsy to be performed, invoking their orthodox Jewish faith, which frowns on postmortems. Danishefsky Covlin was buried almost immediately. But her family protested to the district attorney's office, citing threats the husband had made against his wife's life and, months later, her body was exhumed. An autopsy was performed, with the conclusion that she was murdered by strangulation. While police will admit that Rod Covlin is a "person of interest," no arrests have been made, and the case is still being investigated.[47]

While Drew Peterson, now fifty-seven, continues to proclaim his innocence of any crime against his two wives, he sits in the Will County Adult Detention Facility in Joliet, Illinois, awaiting trial.[48] No court date has been set. Illinois currently has a moratorium against the death penalty, although prosecutors could still try Peterson for a capital offense, and a jury could sentence him to execution. If there is a conviction, there will be many areas ripe for appeal, so we will probably not see the last of Drew Peterson for a long time. Neither Drew nor anyone else has been charged in the disappearance of Stacy Peterson. That case remains under investigation.[49]

A cable TV movie titled *Ladykiller: The Drew Peterson Story* has begun filming, starring Rob Lowe—co-star of the sitcom *Parks and Recreation* and, previously, the drama *The West Wing*—in the title role. The film is scheduled to air on the Lifetime Movie Network in 2012.[50]

Drew Peterson's attorney, Joel Brodsky, was asked what his client thought about Casey Anthony's acquittal of murder charges for the death of her daughter. "He said it was good to see a jury not act emotionally," Brodsky replied.

"In the Casey Anthony case, they had a pathologist say there was a homicide, an odor from the trunk, chloroform, fibers, the Internet search for chloroform, the duct tape [and] a body disposed of in a swamp," Brodsky explained. "In Drew's case, they do not have one single piece of hard evidence, not one."

Brodsky continued: "They have a pathologist that said it is a homicide, [but] we have got three pathologists that say it is an accident.

When it comes to hard evidence, they had some in Casey Anthony's case [but] in Drew Peterson's case they have zip."[51]

In July 2011, the Third District Appellate Court upheld the lower court's decision to bar eight second-party statements that purport to link Peterson to Kathleen Savio's death—which include some of what Stacy Peterson alleged to her pastor, some of Savio's written statements, and testimony by Peterson's second wife and oldest son about his proclivity for domestic violence. In a two-to-one vote, the appellate jurists didn't consider the reliability of the comments, but based their ruling on the fact that the Will County State Attorney's Office missed its filing deadline by two weeks. State's attorney James Glasgow said his prosecutors had been waiting to hear back from the Illinois Supreme Court on the lower court's decision; he is now considering asking the higher court to overturn the appellate decision, as well.[52]

Let's be realistic: If the preponderance of the second-hand statements and outcry witnesses has been tossed, leaving only the debatable autopsy evidence, the case against Drew Peterson may have evaporated, unless there's strong evidence we haven't heard about yet. Prosecutors may hope to have the case salvaged by the state supreme court, but that's a long shot. In the meantime, Peterson should be allowed to leave jail with a reasonable bond. It's even possible the state's attorney may drop the case entirely, or at least until detectives develop more evidence. Glasgow is a savvy politician who is up for re-election in 2012. The Casey Anthony acquittal shocked the nation, but an attempt and failure to win a prosecution against the nation's other most loathsome defendant—Drew Peterson—might spell career suicide for the prosecutor calling the shots. Still, a notorious person like Peterson, who has inflamed the public with his antics, may be someone the citizens will want to see put on trial. If he's tried and convicted in the Savio case, you can expect he'll also be charged for the death of Stacy Peterson, even if her body is never recovered. Stay tuned.[53]

CHAPTER FIVE

GABRIELLE MIRANDA BECHEN
Death of the "Tomboy Princess"

The death of any young person is tragic. But when I'm called upon to perform an autopsy on the child victim of a violent crime, it's an especially somber process. Gabrielle Bechen was just starting her life when it was cut short by a monster. As I looked down at her broken body and reflected on all the harm that had come her way, I knew I would be the first person to understand what had happened to this girl. And I hoped I would be able to help her family find justice for her loss.[1]

It was Tuesday, June 13, 2006, a gorgeous spring morning in southwest Pennsylvania. In her deep slumber, Mimi Bechen could hear her daughter whispering, "Mom, Mom!" Mimi had gotten home from work after midnight and, after doing chores, collapsed into bed. She was used to going to sleep next to her husband, Chris, then waking up to find him replaced by their two children after he left for work. Gabby, twelve, was on her right side, and four-year-old Corey was on her left. She never really thought about how that tag-team switch came about, but it was a sweet thing to wake up to each morning.

"Mom, I'm going out to ride my quad, okay?" Mimi wasn't ready to be awakened, so her subconscious kept her from answering. Without her mother's permission, Gabby would not be able to go outside. Maybe her daughter would just go back to sleep for awhile, Mimi wished, even as she could sense the girl getting up and walking around the room. Then the other side of the bed began moving. "Mom, wake up! Gabby wants you." Now it was Corey's voice she heard, and it was accompanied by his little fingers gently poking her face. Whatever dream Mimi might have been having was dissipating quickly, and when Corey squeezed her nose and said "Honk, honk," it was impossible to ignore. She cracked one eye open and saw Gabby getting dressed and both kids giggling at Corey's mischievous reveille. "Ouch," Mimi said. "What's up?" "I want to go outside and ride my quad," said Gabby. "I have to give Miss Tracy the card I drew for her, so I'm going, okay?" Glancing at the alarm clock, Mimi could see it was 8:12 a.m. "Can't we lay down for another hour? Mommy's pooped." "You guys sleep in," said Gabby, now dressed and putting on her helmet. "I'm gonna go now, all right?" "Okay, but you be back here by eleven for lunch." "I will," Gabby promised, grabbing her purse, then bending down to kiss Mimi's forehead. "I love you." "I love you too, honey."

Then with a tousle of her brother's hair, Gabby left their mobile home, got on her all-terrain vehicle, and puttered off to her destiny. She would never be seen alive by her family again. Mimi and Corey spooned and fell back into the Land of Nod, unaware of the nightmare to come that would change their lives forever.

Gabrielle "Gabby" Miranda Bechen was born on February 27, 1994, in Morgantown, West Virginia, the firstborn child of Christopher and Blanche, or, as they were better known, Chris and Mimi. The family relocated just across the Pennsylvania border to Greensboro, a city so small, the joke goes, the New Year's Baby is born in midsummer. Everyone knows everyone else's business there, yet they don't hold anything against one another. Family roots run deep, with whole communities sharing last names and businesses founded by ancestors who go back to the Civil War. Mimi, thirty-eight, was a merchandise sorter at the local Gabriel Brothers department store, and Chris, forty-three, held a welding job just a couple of towns away. Each had been married and divorced before, and there were several step-siblings in the extended family, providing Gabby and Corey with plenty of older kids to play with.

When Gabby didn't return home by eleven-thirty, Mimi became annoyed. The girl knew their afternoon was chock-full of errands, including a trip to the pet store for food for Tweety, her bunny, and Cookie, the Bechens's St. Bernard. Gabby had a cell phone, but it wasn't activated; she used it only for taking photos. Mimi slapped peanut butter and jelly on some bread, handed it to Corey, and bundled him into the car. "We've got to go find your sister," she told the pre-schooler, fastening their seat belts and taking off down the road. Perhaps if they lived in the city, a half-hour delay wouldn't be a big deal, especially for a young girl who had just finished the school year and had boys to flirt with, malls to hang out at, and endless movies to entertain her. But that wasn't even close to the summer vacation Gabby had in store. Hers was to be filled with pond diving, teaching Corey to catch frogs, riding her quad, learning new songs on the guitar, and grooming every horse within a ten-mile radius. The last three items were career builders, reasoned Gabby, whose goal was to grow up to be a NASCAR-winning rock star who owned a horse ranch. Voted "Shortest in Sixth Grade" at Bobtown Elementary, she was small in stature but had a giant personality.

Horses were Gabby's special passion, and her favorite place to visit them was at the nearby farm on Mount Joy Road in Dunkard, where Tracy Hammond, a dog breeder, lived with her attorney husband Jack Montgomery. The two families didn't really know each other, but Gabby would drop by to feed and brush the horses, in hopes that one day Tracy would let her ride one of them. Gabby had a magic way with all animals—for a time, she even had a pet butterfly that followed her everywhere.

The farm, a half-mile from the Bechens's mobile home, was the farthest distance Gabby was allowed to ride her ATV. On the short drive there, Mimi kept her eyes open for Gabby, who she feared might have run out of gas or had her battery conk out, as had happened before. But there was no sign of her on the main road or on any of the brushy paths she passed that led into the forest. Driving up the dusty driveway to the farmhouse, she remembered that Gabby had said she was going to deliver a drawing to "Miss Tracy." Probably they're inside having snacks that will ruin the child's appetite for lunch, Mimi thought. But Gabby's ATV was nowhere in sight, and the trucks that Tracy and Jack drove were both gone. A knock on the door brought no response. Mimi was puzzled. From the porch she could scan much of the three-hundred-acre farm, and there seemed to be little activity, just the usual whinnies of the horses and the quacks from the black puddle ducks. She got back in the car, tooting her horn so that Gabby could hear her, and rolled past a big gravel pile on her way to the end of the driveway. Then she and Corey headed home, hoping Gabby would be there so they could get their day started. No such luck.

Question: Where could a youngster go on an ATV? Answer: Anywhere he or she wanted to go. That's why they're called ATVs—all-terrain vehicles, also known as quads for their four oversized tires. ATVs can travel across paved roads, dirt fields and sand dunes, up and down hills, and through creeks and forests, and are often used for hauling farm equipment. They're limited only by how much gas is in the three-gallon tank. Mimi Bechen couldn't be certain when Gabby's quad was last filled up, but at thirty miles per gallon, Gabby could cover a lot of ground, even if she had only a bit of fuel.[2] In Pennsylvania, there are 230,633 ATVs registered with the State Department of Conservation and Natural Resources, and an untold number that are unregistered. Nearly two thousand ATVs are registered in Greene County.[3] In the rolling hills around Greensboro, kids begin riding ATVs shortly after they learn how to ride a bicycle. It's family fun, with parents and kids racing their quads down the country roads or into town. Gabby must have been five the first time Chris let her steer his ATV. And once she got a feel for it, she was relentless about asking for her own. When she turned twelve, in February, Chris and Mimi surprised her with a SunL® 90cc quad, a child-sized model that was painted black with flame decals on the fenders. Gabby was fearless on it, but never reckless.

While Corey watched cartoons, Mimi started calling family members and Gabby's friends to see if anyone had seen the girl, but no one had. She racked her brain about whether there were any horses in the vicinity that might be ready to foal—that would be something that could distract Gabby into losing track of time. But she came up empty on that, too. Finally, she called Chris at work. "You'd better come home," she said. "Gabby was supposed to be here an hour ago and she isn't. You need to get on your quad and hit the trails." When Chris arrived, Mimi caught him up on the news of their daughter, or lack thereof. Could Gabby have said she was going to a friend's house, and then gone into town? he wondered. No. Even though Mimi had been half-asleep when she last spoke to Gabby, she had a clear recollection of what the girl had said: She was going for a ride over to Miss Tracy's to drop off a card, and she'd be back by eleven. No room for error there. As Chris walked to the kitchen counter to grab a banana, he spotted the card Gabby had drawn for her neighbor. It was a colorful sketch of three trees from the Hammond farm under a sunny sky, with the handwritten caption "To Miss Tracy, hope to ride horses with you someday" and dated June 2. "Looks like she forgot to bring this," Chris said to Mimi. Could it be Gabrielle never went to the farm after all?

Chris spent the next two hours going over every trail and dirt road on his ATV within a five-mile radius, including the Hammond farm, but Gabby was nowhere to be found. His concern increased with every mile. If she'd had an accident, she could be lying on the ground somewhere, bleeding. She might be unconscious or too disoriented to find her way home. The woodsy environment made for a nice place to live but also provided a number of unforgiving places where one could fall and not be seen. He headed back to Tracy's farm again. In the distance he spied a farmhand baling hay and trekked over to the man. Chris introduced himself to the worker, who asked what he wanted. "I can't find my daughter," Chris said. "Any chance you saw a young girl on an ATV?" Nope, the man said, but he'd been out in the fields all morning, so he couldn't be sure. The owners, Tracy and Jack, would be back in a while, he offered. Maybe she's with them. Chris thought it unlikely that Gabby would go off with anyone without checking with her mom first, and even if she did, where was her ATV? But the man didn't care to talk; he "had a fire to attend to," he told Chris before they parted company.

Back at the Bechen home, Chris and Mimi glumly compared notes and agreed that if they wanted to find their daughter, more manpower was needed. By 2 p.m., Mimi placed a call to 911, the Waynesburg County state police, and shortly after, Trooper Thomas W. Shuster came to the home. As he was brought up to date, he told the Bechens there were three avenues he would pursue: that Gabby had an accident, that she ran away, or that she had been kidnapped. All three possibilities required swift action from his skilled teams and cooperation from Chris and Mimi. They assured him that there were no arguments or unpleasantness that could have motivated Gabby to run away; in fact, the last thing she told her mother was that she loved her. Still they appreciated that the trooper needed to look at all the angles.

Over the next several hours, state troopers went all out to find the missing girl, bringing in bloodhounds as well as firefighters from four Greene County departments. While the Bechens were instructed to stay at home in case Gabby phoned, searchers—made up of professionals and friends and family—set up a tented command post and organized grid searches of the rugged terrain. At police headquarters, residents with ATVs were phoned and asked to be on the lookout for Gabby's vehicle, and the state sexual offender registry was consulted to see if any pedophiles resided in the community—the answer to that was no, thankfully. As dusk set in, and into the night, a police helicopter with a thermal imaging device took to the skies.

For a community whose police log consisted mostly of stolen bicycles and dog fights, this was major news. Soon there were news trucks parked outside the Bechen home, with TV reporters asking the same numbing questions to slot onto their local broadcasts. Mimi described her daughter as four-foot-nine-inches tall, about seventy-seven pounds, with hazel eyes and shoulder-length brown hair with blonde highlights. She had both ears pierced, with one extra piercing through the left ear's cartilage—and when last seen she was wearing khaki shorts, a black top, sneakers, and a black helmet. Chris appealed for help and offered a five hundred dollar reward for Gabby's safe return, monies pledged by searchers. To each reporter who held a microphone to his face, he said clearly, "If she wandered off, she's in no trouble. We want her to call home and please let us know she's all right."[4]

It was on one of those news broadcasts that I first heard the name "Gabrielle Bechen." My wife Sigrid and I try to catch the local 6 p.m. news while we prepare dinner. Usually it's just running in the background, while we chat about our respective days, but the mention of a missing twelve-year-old caught our full attention. We live in Pittsburgh, about seventy miles due north of Greensboro. But for those throughout our state, this was certainly an urgent story. As we learned the details of the disappearance and search, I couldn't help but wonder if the child was dead and if I might be performing her autopsy in the near future. Greene County is one of several districts where I assist law enforcement with postmortems. Sigrid's eyes met mine. We couldn't help but think of our own family—four adult children and eleven grandchildren, with two girls the same age as Gabby. What a dreadful day for this poor family to have not seen Gabby for ten hours now. The Bechens seemed so unpretentious, not the type of people who would gravitate to a television camera, yet there they were, showing their pain to millions of viewers and answering incessant questions with grace, as if they couldn't bear to stop talking about their girl. While Sigrid and I hoped the situation might have a happy ending, we both understood that matters could turn much worse, with either a death or with no resolution at all. After dinner, we had a meeting out of the house, and when we came back we turned on the TV for a Gabby news update, only to learn nothing had advanced. By now the Bechen case was headline news on every channel, and it would stay that way for days.[5]

At the Bechen home that evening, little Corey picked up on the frantic reactions of his parents and began whimpering, so the Bechens took turns cradling him until he finally fell asleep and could be put to bed. Chris and Mimi didn't eat or sleep much that night. Such a thing couldn't be contemplated when their young daughter was out in the world somewhere, certainly terrified and desperate to come home. Tracy Hammond told officers most emphatically that Gabby had not been on her property that day. They had an agreement that Gabby needed to call for permission before she could come over, and while Hammond had received a voice mail from the girl asking to come and ride horses, she had not returned the call. The next day, Tessa R. Cooper, an FBI agent from West Virginia, joined the task force. Mimi Bechen would later say that Cooper's presence was both welcome and daunting. She appreciated the extra help the feds could provide the locals, but it also heralded doom. When one of the investigators mentioned needing a copy of Gabby's dental X-rays just in case they had to make an identification, Mimi knew her baby probably wasn't coming home safe. She kept envisioning her alarm clock, frozen at 8:12 a.m., the time when Mimi failed to stop her little girl from marching off to what could have been her death. To this day, seeing a clock hit that time of day still makes Mimi wince.

Two rescue agencies organized quickly and efficiently: the Shenandoah Mountain Rescue Group and the Mountaineer Area Rescue Group, out of Kingwood, West Virginia, sending off volunteers on foot, on horseback, and on ATVs. There was a great outpouring of people who knew Gabby and her family from school, church, or community activities, as well as good-hearted strangers who heard about the search on TV and wanted to help. The hunt for Gabby covered hundreds of square miles of woods and fields around Greene County. In targeted areas, grid searches were assigned, with people linking arms and looking at the ground for clues. Bloodhounds were given a whiff of an outfit Gabby had worn the night before, as well as her pillowcase, hairbrush, and toothbrush, and were sent off to follow their noses to a hopefully living girl. The Red Cross set up an outpost, giving out free refreshments and drinking water, and handling first aid for searchers who got blisters or scrapes. The FBI printed top-quality, full-color, high-resolution flyers that were widely disseminated, going to all homes in the area and dotting store windows with Gabby's smiling face and pertinent data. The Bechens were shown a helmet collected by searchers, but it wasn't Gabby's. However, when Mimi saw a blue-ink light-up pen recovered by one of the volunteers, she recognized it as coming from Gabby's purse, which was missing. The reporters stayed onsite, interviewing whomever they could catch. It was explained that no Amber Alert was issued because law enforcement requires a confirmed abduction with details of a suspect and his or her vehicle. Here, none of that information was apt.

By day three, the esprit de corps began to fade as the mission changed from rescue of a live individual to recovery of a corpse. The bloodhounds were replaced by cadaver dogs who only "hit" on the smell of death. As the hours rolled by, searchers got tired feet, red eyes, and a profound disappointment in their fellow man as they realized someone —perhaps even someone in their midst—had committed an atrocity. And they were right. The man who murdered Gabrielle Miranda Bechen was one of the searchers. Although neither of the Bechens saw him at the searches, other people did and remembered him enjoying the snacks, bragging that he had daughters himself, and, in retrospect, acting keenly interested in what the cops might know.

On Sunday, June 18, the search for Gabby ended. It was Father's Day, and that morning Mimi told Chris what Gabby had planned for him: his favorite breakfast, a handmade card, and some of those orange wild-flowers he liked that she would pick from a nearby roadside. Instead, what Chris got was the news that his daughter's body had been found.[6]

The case had been cracked Saturday afternoon, when two searchers near a creek at the Hammond farm caught a glint of light coming from the ground, and when they kicked at the dirt, they found the handlebars of Gabby's ATV, buried deep in a horse manure dump. All four tires had been flattened and its lights smashed to compress it. Authorities zeroed in on the farmhand—Jeffrey Robert Martin, the same man Chris had questioned. Deputies grilled Martin in the field, then handcuffed and pushed him into a police cruiser for several hours, in ninety-degree weather. He was driven downtown, given a polygraph exam, and harshly questioned at the station until he broke down in tears and made an audiotaped confession. By four the next morning, his hand-drawn map led cops to Gabby's body, which he had buried under a mound of gravel—the very gravel pile that Mimi passed when she was looking for Gabby—in a five-foot-deep grave on the other side of the property. He also showed them the child's helmet and shoes, which were buried elsewhere. And he pointed out where he burned the purse, in which she kept her pencils, ponytail holders, and hair clips, in the fire he told Chris he had to attend to. He was arrested for homicide, aggravated assault, and tampering with evidence.[7]

Jeffrey Robert Martin, forty-eight, grew up in Greene County and was one of ten children in a home fraught with alcoholism and neglect.[8] A high school dropout in his junior year, he jumped into a life of petty crimes, drug dealing, and deplorable behavior toward women. His first arrest was in 1975 when he was seventeen and charged with molesting two children. The records were expunged because he was a minor.[9] An early marriage produced two daughters—Heather and Jennifer—but he did little to support his family and often beat his wife. When she caught him fondling six-year-old Jennifer, she pressed charges, but he eluded punishment. The couple divorced, and his daughters didn't see much of him after that.[10] Though he never served time in state prison, he was in and out of county jails, including stints in Greene County for receiving stolen property, passing bad checks, and making sexually explicit phone calls to three young females. The calls were so vile, the women reported him to police, and he was caught via wiretaps. In a statement to authorities, a twenty-two-year-old victim said Martin's calls were "sexually perverted" and that she feared "whether he was capable of something much more violent than phone calls." He was busted in Fayette County for drunk driving, for driving with a suspended license, and for attempting to elude an officer, and was sentenced to a year in lockup. Despite all his crimes, he was let out of jail early, given court-ordered probation, and allowed to walk away from the thousands of dollars he owed in fines or restitution.[11] The perverted phone calls were not considered serious enough to land Martin on the state sexual offender registry, and the one sex crime that might have qualified—when he molested his own daughter—occurred long before the state kept such lists.[12]

At the time of Gabby's murder, Martin had been married for six years to a woman named Linda L. Deak Martin. Since the 1990s, he had sporadically worked at the Hammond farm, tending the fields, cleaning the horse stalls and dog kennels, and feeding the animals. As long as the work got done, he was free to come and go, although he was not permitted to go into the home if the owners were not there. Tracy Hammond and Jack Montgomery offered condolences to the Bechens after Gabby's body was found, saying they didn't think their farmhand was capable of such a thing. The couple had paid for Martin's wedding reception, and Jack had represented Martin after the drunk driving arrest. When Mimi told Tracy how much Gabby "adored her," Tracy wept, while Montgomery remained stoic. Still, there seemed to have been warnings the farm owners could have heeded. Rumors abounded that two housekeepers had quit when Martin harassed them and that he invited teen girls to swim naked in the Hammond pool. Jack had once fired him but rehired him a week later.[13]

Martin told officers he hadn't meant to hurt Gabby, whom he barely knew. But, according to him, she had ridden her quad onto the farm that morning with a dark purpose—she planned to falsely accuse him of molesting her. First she would tell the farm owners, then she would tell her parents, and finally she would tell the cops. His job and liberty threatened, he panicked and grabbed her arm. She broke away and jumped off her ATV, and he chased her. When she slipped on the gravel, he jumped on top of her, and throttled her neck for "a good while." He insisted that he did not molest or sexually abuse her in any way. When he realized she was dead, he had to hide her and her belongings. He used a backhoe to dig the grave for her and the holes for her ATV, helmet, and shoes. Then he covered her body with two fifty-pound bags of calcium oxide, better known as lime, a caustic crystalline powder used to speed decomposition. It was so effective, the search dogs running across the area never picked up her scent.[14]

Sometime on Father's Day, before the reporters broke the news, I got a call from the Greene County coroner and local funeral director Gregory P. Rohanna, informing me that Gabrielle Bechen's body was being recovered from a farm where she had been buried. Mary Lewis, the deputy coroner; Linda Chambers, a Greene County first assistant district attorney; and the victim's advocate and witness coordinator for that office, Cherie Rumskey, were all present as the body was carefully unearthed. I instructed them to have the body transported to Carlow University in Pittsburgh, where I conduct my autopsies for Greene and neighboring counties. I would do the postmortem the next day, and later in the week I would visit the crime scene and review all forensic evidence.[15]

The post-mortem examination began Monday morning at nine-thirty and lasted a couple of hours. In attendance were Rohanna, Lewis, Chambers, Raymond Thomas of McCormic Removal, and three representatives of the Pennsylvania state police: Corporal Beverly J. Ashton, and troopers Tom Schuster—the lead investigator—and Richard D. Hunter. Trooper Hunter took extensive photos of the procedure and collected multiple samples of various materials on the body, as well as swabs of the oral, vaginal, and rectal canals that were later submitted to the state police forensic science laboratory for analyses.

Gabrielle Miranda Bechen's manner of death was homicide; the cause of death was asphyxiation due to manual strangulation. She was a well-nourished, pre-pubescent female of twelve years old, who was four-foot-nine-inches and weighed approximately seventy-five pounds. When her body was removed from her makeshift grave, her clothing was in disarray—her blue denim pants with red embroidered flowers were pulled down to her ankles; her pink and white polka dot underpants were rolled down to expose her genitalia; her matching halter-style bra was pulled up to expose her breasts; and a white, pink, and green knitted sweater was inverted and tossed over her body. As she was laid out on the morgue table, those items of clothing were noted, then removed. The clothing, as well as her body, from her brown hair to her feet, contained multiple particles of white clumps that were identified as lime, along with dirt and debris. The clothing description differed from what Gabby's mother had told searchers her daughter was wearing when she vanished and from what appeared on the "Missing" posters; in my view, that was simple confusion from a sleepy parent and not indicative of mysterious changing of outfits.

Rigor mortis—temporary stiffening of the body—had passed, and while there was a pattern of reddish-purple livor mortis—the discoloration that occurs on a dead body—on some posterior areas, it was somewhat obfuscated by the lime, debris, and decomposition. Hair samples were collected, but her fingernails—which had been carefully bagged at the crime scene—were extremely short, so no clippings or materials from beneath the nails could be obtained. There was some post-mortem discoloration and skin slippage on the body and a superficial, older abrasion on the left lower calf that measured about 4½ inches in length by ⅛ inch in width. Otherwise, there were no bite marks, lacerations, fractures, dislocations, tumors, cysts, fibrosis, disease, necrosis, abnormalities, hemorrhages, abscesses, free fluid, adhesions, obstructions, evidence of pregnancy, or life-threatening issues—other than those that directly factored into the child's assault and strangulation.

Gabby's left eye was hemorrhaged, as if her assailant struck her there with a hand or blunt object, and there was a red abrasion just inside the upper right lip. Both sides of her skull showed bleeding, suggesting she had been struck by or against a solid object. The signs of vaginal rape were apparent, from the bright red coloring, bruising, and inflammation, to the hymen not being intact. She was penetrated by a blunt object, possibly a penis. No semen or foreign bodily fluids could be identified; time, bacteria, moisture, soil, and lime all conspired to eliminate any trace evidence that could link back to Jeffrey Martin. The sexual assault occurred directly prior to Gabby's death because there were no white blood cells present in her vagina. Typically those cells are an injured area's natural response to promote healing; Gabby died before this vital reaction could occur. The external neck region showed extensive, dark bruising, the result of manual strangulation, leaving no identifiable fingernail abrasions or imprints. The hyoid bone and thyroid cartilage in the neck were fractured, a common phenomenon in manual strangulations. The neck compression caused Gabby to lose consciousness after about thirty seconds, but it took another four to six minutes of constant pressure before she died from asphyxiation.[16]

I finished my written report and had a series of meetings with Greene County district attorney Marjorie Fox and her team. Based on my assertion that Gabby was sexually assaulted, they would add rape to the charges Martin faced. The prosecutors told me some interesting developments: Gabby's father, Chris Bechen, had said that on the night before Gabby's death, he and the kids had arrived home from shopping just after nine o'clock. The summer night was warm, so he let Gabby ride her quad for about ten minutes. It's possible she went over to the Hammond farm and had some kind of encounter with Jeffrey Martin. He might have exposed himself to her, or made an untoward gesture or suggestion, and it could have festered in her mind all night. It would have been in character for her to handle her own problems, rather than telling her parents or tattling on someone, according to her mother. The next day Gabby might have gone back to confront him, without knowing how dangerous that would prove to be. It's also possible that he told her to come back the next day because Tracy would be there and would let her ride a horse, even though he might have known Tracy and her husband would both be away that day. We'll never know the full story unless Martin elaborates, and he seems disinclined to do so.

Martin now had legal representation, Greene County's chief public defender, Harry J. Cancelmi Jr., who wanted to ensure that the jury respected his client's presumption of innocence. Martin had recanted his taped confession, and Cancelmi was determined it should not be played in court, saying it was a result of cops brutally depriving Martin of water while making him wait in a hot car for hours until he was in such an agitated state he falsely confessed just to please the officers. In fact, Martin had a whole new explanation for what happened that morning—the SODDI defense, which trial watchers know is an acronym for "Some Other Dude Did It." A good criminal defense attorney knows never to ask a client too many details about the crime the client is charged with. If a client lies, and the attorney—an officer of the court—knows it's a lie, the information cannot be used in court as a defense strategy. But if a client swears to something's truthfulness—even a cockamamie story—and the attorney doesn't know otherwise, the defense attorney is supposed to embrace it wholeheartedly and let jurors assess its merit.[17]

Martin's latest version of events was that while he was working the farm, a man he had never seen before ran out of gas at the end of the Hammond driveway. Martin, being helpful, walked down to the man's older-model white Ford truck, which had an ATV in the back. The man said he wanted to pull an insurance scam and offered Martin a hundred dollars cash if he would help him bury the ATV. He and the stranger dug a hole and put the ATV in it; the man then told him to cover the quad with dirt, as he had shoes and a helmet to bury elsewhere. Alone at the truck, Martin claimed that he had looked into the passenger seat, had seen a hand sticking out of a coat and some hair, and had realized it was a dead body, but he had not seen the person's face. When the man returned, he assured Martin that there had been an accident and they needed to bury the person, as well. Martin was too scared to protest, he said. When cops asked him about the money, Martin claimed he spent it the next day but couldn't remember what he bought and had no receipt. When he learned of Gabby's disappearance, he thought that was the person the man buried. He never got the man's name because he never asked. When told to describe the phantom man, Martin was vague on details but said with assurance that the guy was completely bald.[18] Later, as his trial began taking shape, he claimed the man had long brown hair.[19] Of course, there was no other man—Martin did everything himself. But what would the jury say? It only takes one person to find reasonable doubt and let a defendant off the hook.

The judge would decide down the road whether to admit the taped confession, but the DA's office was already preparing for every possibility. As an expert witness for the prosecution, I'd be asked about Gabby's autopsy. But I was confident in my scientific findings, and I would bring color slides of her injuries to make my points to the jury and counter any suggestion that Gabby's genital injuries existed earlier than the day she died or that they could be otherwise explained away. At autopsy, I had sent a sample of Gabby's blood to Pittsburgh Criminalistic Laboratory for toxicological analysis. The report, signed by the director, Charles L. Winek, PhD, came back negative for any licit or illicit substances, but there was a positive reading for alcohol—a level of 0.019 milligrams per liter. For a person of Gabby's weight, that reading could mean she had consumed up to four alcoholic beverages, but it also is a by-product of the decomposition process. I wanted the jury to understand it was a natural occurrence and not because, say, she went over to the Hammond farm to drink a few beers with the farmhand before they had consensual sex.

Because of the tender age of the victim, and the fact that the homicide followed a rape, Jeffrey Martin qualified for the death penalty in Pennsylvania. The DA's office decided to prosecute the case that way, giving them the extra duty to find jurors willing to consider execution, if Martin was convicted. First assistant DA Linda Chambers would be the lead prosecutor, with DA Fox taking over for any penalty phase.[20]

The preliminary hearing before district judge Lee Watson on June 21, 2006, featured the playback of Martin's audiotaped police confession, while Chris and Mimi Bechen and other family members held hands and quietly sobbed. I was not available to testify that day, so deputy coroner Mary Lewis described Gabby's injuries. Martin's public defender tried to exclude her testimony since I, and not Lewis, had performed the autopsy; the judge disagreed, and Lewis testified. Mimi Bechen brought the house to tears when she testified about the last morning she saw her daughter and how the injuries were so severe, the family had to have a closed-casket funeral. The Bechens and others in the courtroom wore black T-shirts showing photographs of Gabby. Judge Watson ruled to hold Martin over for trial without bail. In September, I would testify before the same judge as the rape charge was added to Martin's roster.

On May 1, 2008, the trial of the *People vs. Jeffrey Robert Martin* began at the Greene County Courthouse in Waynesburg, with president judge H. Terry Grimes presiding and a jury of twelve citizens and four alternates hearing evidence. Chambers's opening statement consisted of her showing the courtroom a large poster-sized photo of a smiling Gabby, making the point that the case was about her. She gave brief information on the timeline, apologized for graphic images that would be shown during the trial, and promised jurors they'd hear the killer's voice confess to the crime and see me go through the evidence that supported the rape charge. She also warned of the "CSI effect," which occurs when some jurors watch TV procedural shows and expect that all loose ends will be tied up at the end of one hour. She cautioned that in real life, some homicide cases do not need DNA evidence for a slam-dunk conviction. DNA would not be a factor in the Bechen case. Harry Cancelmi's opening statement was hamstrung by the judge's decision to allow in the taped confession, so the attorney told jurors his client had been deprived of water in a hot police car and traded the statement for something to drink. He also said the agitated state troopers pressured his client to stop wasting their time and confess.[21]

Chris and Mimi Bechen were among the first witnesses to testify, telling jurors first of the horror of discovering Gabby's disappearance, then learning of her death. They also gave a colorful view of the sweet young child she was and how much she meant to them and to her brother, Corey. Mimi even mentioned the amethyst birthstone earrings that Gabby never took off, but that were never recovered with the body. Chris had returned to the site with a metal detector but failed to find the earrings; Mimi is convinced that Martin stole them to keep as a demented trophy.

State troopers and FBI agents who participated in the search and recovery also spoke, illustrating their points with maps and other images. Witness coordinator Cherie Rumskey wisely ushered the Bechens out of the courtroom when she knew photos of Gabby's body in the grave or at autopsy would be shown; otherwise, the girl's parents sat through all the testimony.[22]

I testified on Friday, May 2, for about two hours, spending the first portion of my time on the stand answering the typical questions about my training and expertise, while the Bechens listened raptly. I had met them for the first time in the hallway and found them to be a lovely couple. As my testimony moved into the more sensitive aspects of Gabby's process of dying and my post-mortem exam, Rumskey led them from the courtroom. That appearance was my first opportunity to see Jeffrey Martin, who was apparently cleaned up by his counsel and looked like an accountant instead of a farmhand. Knowing that in Martin's confession he had insisted he didn't rape the child, Linda Chambers questioned me in detail about the telltale signs I saw of Gabby's sexual assault. On cross-examination, Cancelmi asked me about an article written by another forensic scientist that suggested it could take as long as four hours for a bodily injury to produce white blood cells, but I strongly asserted that such information was wrong.[23]

After I left the stand, Tracy Hammond testified about Martin's work duties and history at her farm, and spoke of receiving a jailhouse letter from him, demanding that Hammond pay him for the week he allegedly killed Gabby or else he would report her to the Internal Revenue Service. Other witnesses who were part of the search teams testified about seeing Martin on the site but said that he was not doing much and that he left when cops looked his way. The defense cross-examinations of some troopers zeroed in on whether any officer "poked" or in any way abused Martin during questioning and how the defendant had spoken of a mysterious "bald, fat guy" who offered him money to bury the body and ATV. The prosecution's case ended with the playing of the taped confession, letting jurors hear Martin's own words about how he killed—but didn't rape—Gabrielle.[24]

The defense presentation consisted of only one surprising witness—Jeffrey Martin took the stand for five and a half hours over Monday and Tuesday, something his public defender said was Martin's own idea. In a flat monotone, Martin denied the confession and weaved an elaborate encounter with the "mystery man," described now as young, with long brown hair. During Chambers's cross-examination, she asked with incredulity why he had not contacted authorities about the alleged stranger and pointed out that he had more than a year behind bars to craft his testimony. If he was telling the truth, she stated, every other witness was lying. The Bechens told my co-author, Dawna Kaufmann, that having to sit through Martin's testimony was "painful" and that Chris wanted to leap up and pummel him more than once, especially when he looked at them with a cocky expression, but they held their emotions in check. They also said that Cancelmi was "just doing his job," and that Chambers "kicked butt."[25]

By Wednesday morning, the case went to the jury for deliberation. Would they find Martin guilty of first-degree murder and sentence him to execution? It took six hours over two days for the jury to come back with a guilty verdict on all charges. As the session ended, reporters tried to get a reaction from the Bechens, but they were too spent to do more than give small smiles, probably their first since the trial began. When asked for a comment, Martin—who wore loafers with pennies in them for good luck—only snapped, "Go get it off someone else!" Martin's wife, Linda, made her first appearance in the courtroom for the verdict and was in a wheelchair for reasons unknown; she wept and was allowed to give her husband a brief hug.[26]

The penalty phase began the next day with an astonishing visitor to the proceedings. Jennifer Martin, the daughter Jeffrey had molested, now twenty-four, entered the courtroom and sat next to the Bechens, holding Mimi's hand during the testimony. Jennifer had only seen her father twice after her parents divorced: briefly when she was thirteen, and once again in 2005. A mother of two sons, she had followed local media reports about the search for Gabby and was struck that the missing girl was a doppelganger for what she looked like at age twelve. When Martin was arrested, Jennifer, her mother, and her sister kept track of the investigation and trial, disgusted but not shocked.

She hadn't met the Bechens before she showed up in court to support them, but her bold statement was much appreciated. Martin didn't recognize her when she entered the courtroom, but since she was a new face and pretty, he eyed her flirtatiously. Jennifer whispered her identity to his attorney, who told Martin, and from then on, he glowered at her. She would say it was a face of pure evil, probably just like the last thing Gabby saw as he raped and strangled her to death. While behind bars,

Martin sent her two handwritten notes, swearing his innocence, but Jennifer tossed them in the garbage.[27]

Gabby's cousin, Shannon Presock, testified about the girl she called a "Tomboy Princess" who had a love for all creatures and was deprived of a bright future. "She didn't deserve this," Shannon said, sobbing. "No one deserves this."

Dr. Mark J. Tabackman of Townsend, Maryland, appeared for the defense. He testified that Martin should not be put to death because of his dysfunctional childhood and a traumatic brain injury from being hit by a car as a child, which stunted his IQ to between seventy and seventy-nine (one hundred is average). Tabackman also stated that Martin had been molested several times as a child, and that as an adult he was alcohol dependent, depressed, and suicidal. Martin's mother and wife were scheduled to give testimony about why his life should be spared, but despite being subpoenaed, neither woman showed up in court. Two of his brothers testified, telling chilling accounts of his hellish life growing up.[28]

The jury was out for only sixty-five minutes before they came back with a death verdict. Jeffrey Robert Martin is the first inmate from Greene County to get that sentence since 1894. He now resides at the State Correctional Institution at Graterford, with forty other death row inmates. Pennsylvania currently has two hundred and twelve inmates awaiting execution, including four females; the last execution was in 1999. Under state law, lethal injection is the method for execution and there is an automatic appeal.[29]

District attorney Marjorie Fox, who handled the penalty phase, agreed with the jury's decision, stating: "This is not something we look to do but justice was served for Gabby. We don't take any joy in having a death sentence imposed, but this is the law and this is the appropriate sentence for the crime that was committed. I believe it was pretty clear from the evidence that this was the appropriate sentence to impose." Public defender Harry Cancelmi said of the sentence: "Life is life and death is death and I don't have much comment other than that."[30]

It's not the first time, and I doubt it will be the last, that my testimony has helped send a killer to death row. I don't take any particular pride in that, but I consider it the will of the citizens of the state. I'd probably be satisfied if there was no death penalty, for two reasons—one, I don't think it's an effective means of stopping would-be criminals from committing horrendous acts, and two, with the cost of appeals and special housing to keep death row inmates isolated from the general prison population, our money might be better spent on proactive methods to identify and punish high-risk offenders. By legal definition, premeditation—a hallmark of an executable offense—can exist in a moment's notice, such as the time it takes to cock a gun, or, in Martin's case, to react in a fit of fatal fury. Also, his victim was a child, and the unconscionable rape and murder of an innocent girl elicits a strong reaction from the public, as it should. Chris and Mimi Bechen feel satisfied with the death verdict, as does Jennifer Martin, and their suffering outweighs other opinions.[31]

According to FBI statistics, 80 percent of stranger abductions occur within a quarter-mile of a child's home, and over seven hundred thousand children are reported missing each year in this country, more than two thousand per day. Approximately 25 percent of those are family custody disputes, but almost sixty thousand children are taken by a non-family member. Of those, about one hundred and fifteen fall victim to a complete or partial stranger who kidnaps them for a period of time and/or kills them. Sexual offenders often fall into this last category; their crimes are not given wide media attention due to privacy standards affecting children. However, it's precisely these kinds of cases that deserve to be discussed openly if we ever hope to get ahead of this national crisis and give kids and parents the tools to keep families safer. But sometimes, no matter how cautious a family is, disaster strikes.[32]

The Bechens did everything right in raising their daughter Gabby to be sensitive and independent. As parents of a murdered child, they've been inducted into the awful club of which no one wants to be a member. It's an agony that never ebbs, yet they have to stay strong for each other and, especially, for young Corey, who, now ten years old, has to redirect his anger over losing the big sister he loved so much. He gets in fights when rude kids tease him about his sister's death, but when he sees a shooting star in the sky, he feels it's a sign that Gabby is looking down at him. The family finds solace in these kinds of signs, like the 1994 penny they found under the television set when they moved to a new location. They had started a penny collection for Gabby when she was alive, and her birth year was 1994, so they believe that finding that penny was her letting them know she was thinking of them. Then there was the black and blue butterfly that landed on Mimi's hand not long ago, a reminder of how, the year before Gabby died, she told her mom that when she was reincarnated, she'd come back as a butterfly. When Mimi asked why a butterfly, Gabby said with startling prescience, "Butterflies don't have predators." The Bechens's new home has bookshelves full of photos and mementos of their missing girl near the urn in which her remains are kept. Even though she died on June 12, her death date is officially recorded as the day her body was found, and the Bechens think of June 18 as "Gabby's Angel Day."[33]

One other thing that is helping the family mend is the Gabrielle Miranda Bechen website that Chris built and keeps updated. It includes family photos, MP3s of Gabby's favorite songs and videos—from Kenny Chesney to Hannah Montana to the Pussycat Dolls, remembrances of her from people who loved her, and kind words from strangers around the world who heard about her death. People light virtual candles and write poems in her memory, or just pop in to say hello. They do it to ease their own minds but mostly to let the Bechens know that Gabby will never be forgotten. Five years after Gabby's death, people still visit the website and leave their thoughts and prayers.[34]

CHAPTER SIX

CAROL ANNE GOTBAUM

Terminal Tragedy

A s a forensic pathologist, I see numerous cases of individuals who have died at the hands of law enforcement personnel. Certainly our men and women in uniform face daily challenges requiring life-and-death decisions, and society benefits from their willingness to take on those duties. But citizens expect peace officers to possess more than just a gun and badge when they're out in the field—they also expect good judgment and proper training.

The death of a citizen involving officers merits special attention from the media. Such involvement can catapult the death into a high-profile matter that can polarize a community and lead to violent unrest. And the legal implications of a wrongful death are enormous: The slightest exposure on the part of a peace officer can result in the decedent's next of kin filing a lawsuit, with taxpayers writing a multimillion-dollar check to settle the matter.

For decades now, I've traveled the country, giving speeches to police and sheriff's department employees about how they can implement changes that will protect them as they protect the public. Since 2007, I have added the facts of this chapter to my lectures, because what happened to Carol Anne Gotbaum is a worst-case scenario of what can occur to someone in police custody.[1] And recently, I have included this kind of a case in a textbook I wrote with my colleagues Henry C. Lee, PhD; D. P. Van Blaricom; and Mel Tucker called *Investigation and Prevention of Officer-Involved Deaths.*[2]

219

Carol Anne Stiger Gotbaum was a native of Cape Town, South Africa, where she earned a master of business administration at the University of Witwatersrand in Johannesburg. The blue-eyed beauty with reddish-brown hair moved to London and worked at two prestigious department stores, Harrods and the House of Fraser, where she became a senior buyer. A divorcée who loved tennis, yoga, and entertaining, she met and fell in love with Noah Gotbaum, an American businessman living in London. (Some details herein were supplied by Noah Gotbaum to my co-author, Dawna Kaufmann.) Noah was an Amherst College graduate who received a master's degree in public policy management from Yale University. He would later take a position as director of the Central Europe Trust Company, a consulting and investment firm. Public policy was a mainstay in his socially prominent family, and, after college, Noah founded one of New York's leading nonprofits, an international model for volunteer organizations called New York Cares. Noah's mother, Sarah Gotbaum, PhD, is a public affairs and health policy consultant in Washington, DC, and his father, Victor, is a retired labor leader who served for twenty-two years as president of New York's largest public employee union. His stepmother is Betsy Gotbaum, the former executive director of the New York Historical Society, and the city's former public advocate, who influenced city planning, budgets, and the management of retirement funds.[3] The Gotbaum name was one I certainly recognized from years of reading the *New York Times* and other publications.[4]

Carol and Noah married in June 1995, when she was thirty-three and he was thirty-five. The lavish ceremony at Manhattan's Central Park Loeb Boathouse ended with a display of fireworks in the night sky—they were actually from a nearby Disney film premiere, but it was still a perfect touch to their nuptials. Their two eldest children were born in London, and in 2003, the family moved to New York City's Upper West Side, where Noah served on the board for a cellular technology company and started his own investment management company.[5] By September 2007, the couple had a trio of active youngsters: Ella, eight; Nathaniel, six; and Tobias, three. The last birth had left Carol with severe postpartum depression. The accomplished businesswoman whom Noah described as "a super mother and the pillar of strength of the family" was dissembling. Noah's work required him to travel, sometimes more than half the week, so Carol carried most of the homefront burden—an exhausting routine. She missed working in the retail world and felt distanced from her friends in London and her family in South Africa. To add to her angst, her father, a retired commander of the South African Navy Diving School, had just died after a seven-year battle with cancer. Carol spent time in a psychiatric institution, where she received therapy. Once home, she took prescription medication, when she remembered, but mostly she drank alcohol. Noah had reportedly found her passed out drunk in their home on at least one occasion. An extremely private person, Carol only drank at home, by herself, and kept up a brave face, even with her closest friends, most of whom knew nothing about her problem.[6]

While visiting a well-known substance abuse expert—and after a year of urging by Noah—Carol finally agreed to enter a thirty-day alcohol rehabilitation program at Cottonwood de Tucson, in Arizona. She was looking forward to ending her dependency and wrote in her diary: "I want to do this for Noah and our children." The day she made that entry would be her last.

On Friday, September 28, 2007, after insisting that Noah stay home with their young children, Carol Gotbaum flew from New York to Phoenix, where she was to change planes for the remainder of the trip to Tuscon.[7] The flight to Phoenix was an emotional one for Carol, according to Jodi Hall, a wheelchair-bound passenger who sat next to her. Carol broke down several times, telling Hall that she was going to rehab and was upset about leaving her kids. Gotbaum told Hall that it was her decision to travel by herself. Hall never saw Gotbaum order an alcoholic drink, but a flight attendant recalled serving her a Bloody Mary near the plane's galley.[8] After arriving at Phoenix's Sky Harbor International Airport, Carol was to meet friends who would accompany her to Tucson, but they had been rushing there from out of town and didn't make the rendezvous in time. Carol helped Jodi get on her way, then she sent some e-mails and called Noah to discuss the flight and their children. At 1:06 p.m., she went to the check-in desk for US Airways' 1:30 flight to Tucson. Because the flight was overbooked, Carol was bumped to the next Tucson flight an hour and a half later. She called Noah to tell him about the change in flights and said she was getting something to eat. While there's no direct evidence that Gotbaum drank during that unplanned layover, it's believed she ordered drinks at the bar in Terminal 4.[9] Carol sent Noah two lucid e-mails at 2:27 and at 2:35, then called him at 2:40. Shortly afterward, she went to the check-in desk for US Airways for the 2:58 flight to Tucson but was again told the plane was filled to capacity. Gotbaum didn't take the news well, becoming irate and running around the waiting area.[10] Gate agent Rikki Greiner offered to book her onto the next flight and promised her a free round-trip ticket. Carol persuaded another passenger to accept the freebie in exchange for his boarding pass. However, Greiner vetoed that idea, saying it was a security breach. Some of the other waiting passengers tried to calm Carol down, but they couldn't assuage her. When Carol tossed her BlackBerry at Greiner, police were called. That call was logged in at 2:49 p.m. Carol Gotbaum had less than one hour to live.[11]

Three surveillance video cameras captured the scene in the airport corridor. There are no close-ups or sound in one clip posted online that is almost four minutes in length. The first camera shows Carol Anne in the distance, by herself, wearing blue jeans and a white buttoned shirt. She does not seem to be wearing shoes and is not carrying a purse or luggage. (Her shoes were left at the security gate, and her purse and British passport were found in the waiting area; the only medications she had been carrying were Motrin® and birth control pills.) The video shows Carol to be in a state of distress, running down the hallway, then stopping and bending from the waist, as if crying or having some sort of attack. Other passengers turn to look at her; some would later state that Gotbaum was using foul language and slapping people.[12] Several heard her yell, "I'm a depressed, pathetic housewife" and "I'm not a terrorist."[13] An airline worker in a white shirt approaches and Carol appears to jump up and down. More personnel surround her as she waves her arms and seems combative. An airport police officer in black shorts approaches, followed closely by two more officers in long black slacks. Carol waves her arms again, then tries to back away as one of the officers grabs her. She fights him off, then goes limp and falls to the ground. For the next minute and a quarter, the officers are also on the ground with her, attempting to restrain her with handcuffs. The officers do not use pepper spray or a Taser®. Passersby watch the commotion intensely but don't interfere. With an officer on each side of her, holding her up as she appears stiff-legged and still shouting, they walk her out of frame. A second and third camera briefly catch the trio from the rear as they continue walking; her wrists are behind her back.[14]

Carol Gotbaum was taken to the Phoenix police station in the airport, a tiny office equipped with a wall clock, computer, fax machine, and communication devices. Two chairs are behind a desk where officers can field calls and dispatch help to any area in the facility. At the end of the desk is a solid-black door with a silver numeric lock—and through that door is the holding cell where Carol Anne Gotbaum died. The cell is a windowless closet-sized space, with white tiled walls and a black-and-white tiled floor. The only seating is a white cement bench with three bolts connected to handcuffs and a two-foot-long chain, which can attach to the handcuffs or leg iron a detainee might be wearing. There is enough room for three people to sit, side-by-side, shackled. The cell was empty when Carol was brought in, and she was placed on the spot to the far right, as one looks into the room. When I visited the location and snapped some photos, I imagined that Carol, in her frenzied state, must have felt claustrophobic when the door closed, leaving her alone and in custody.[15]

Arresting officers were never able to read Gotbaum her Miranda warning because she was too hysterical to listen. Spokesman Sgt. Andy Hill told reporters that Phoenix police encounter three to five irate passengers a day, but of the 265 arrests at Sky Harbor in 2007, only fourteen were for disorderly conduct.[16] In a response to CNN, which is posted online, the Gotbaum family's attorney, Michael C. Manning, cast a question mark on everything that might have happened after Gotbaum reached the holding cell: "Unfortunately, there's no video in that portion of the airport, so that we can tell. And more unfortunately, Carol's not here to tell us one way or the other," he stated.

This fact would loom large. A Phoenix police department manual bans audio or video equipment inside the cell so as not to invade the detainee's "personal privacy."[17] But why would any privacy concern outweigh a person's potential safety? The detainee is going to be in that cell for only a very short time, and since he or she is shackled, there's little that can occur of a "private" nature. Perhaps the premise needs to be reconsidered. Another solution might be to have an unbreakable glass door, rather than a solid one. Being able to keep eyes on the arrestee could help the officers and give the detainee less of a feeling of abandonment.[18]

In a press conference after Gotbaum's death, police spokesman Hill stated: "The officers were not able to calm Ms. Gotbaum and eventually arrested her for disorderly conduct." He said that officers could hear her screaming inside the cell. They were checking on her every fifteen minutes, but between six to eight minutes after one check-in, they noticed she had gone silent. Officers opened the door to find she was slumped over and unresponsive. Carol was found in a near-seated position with her legs out toward the doorway area. Her hands, still cuffed behind her, were to the left of her face, which pointed toward the wall. The long chain was pulled across her neck. "It appeared as though Ms. Gotbaum had possibly tried to manipulate the handcuffs from behind her to the front, got tangled up in the process possibly and they ended up around her neck area," Hill explained.[19]

Hill told reporters that the standard used to determine whether a detainee should be under constant watch is whether that person is a danger to herself or to others. It was felt that Gotbaum posed no such danger, which is why she was left alone while officers waited to process her for the misdemeanor arrest. Officers were unaware of Gotbaum's alcoholism or personal issues, Hill said. They only knew that she had missed a connecting flight and had become volatile. When they discovered she was not breathing, police made desperate efforts to revive her. Hill added that at one point, an officer began mouth-to-mouth resuscitation and CPR, and Gotbaum vomited into the officer's mouth. The policeman spit up himself but continued the mouth-to-mouth procedure, to no avail. At 3:15 p.m., police called for a defibrillator, and at 3:29, a fire department official pronounced the forty-five-year-old Gotbaum dead.[20]

It would be discovered later that Noah Gotbaum, perhaps after having gotten a frantic message from Carol, began a flurry of phone calls from New York to officials at Sky Harbor airport. According to transcripts, Noah told one dispatcher that his wife was "suicidal" and "alcohol abusive." Noah warned that Carol was in a deep depression and that "police have to understand that they're not dealing with someone who's been just drinking on [a] flight and . . . acting rowdy." The dispatcher said he believed another dispatcher had already heard that and had passed along the information. With increasing urgency, Noah called back repeatedly and also placed calls to representatives at US Airways. Insisting that his wife had a medical condition, he begged the employees to treat her with "kid gloves." Noah's first call was logged in seventy minutes after Carol was declared dead, but for reasons unclear, he wasn't given that information. It's also unknown at what point airport police figured out the identity of the woman they had in lockup.[21]

The official autopsy of case #07-05669—Carol Anne Gotbaum—was performed on October 2, 2007, by Ann L. Bucholtz, MD, the Maricopa County medical examiner. Also present were Lieutenant Eric Edwards, legal adviser for the Phoenix police department, and his coworkers Sergeant Jim Gallagher and Detective Joe Petrosino; the private investigator for Michael Manning's law office, Judd Slivka; and some of Bucholtz's staff. It took weeks for the toxicology and other lab results to be returned and for the autopsy report to be completed, but when it was, the cause of death was determined to be asphyxia due to hanging, with a contributing factor of acute ethanol and prescription medication intoxication. The manner of death of the five-foot-seven, one-hundred-twenty-three-pound female was listed as an accident.

Bucholtz's pathological diagnoses of the asphyxia by hanging included ligature abrasion of the right neck, patterned livor mortis—the discoloration that naturally occurs on a dead body—over the front of the neck, and hemorrhaging of the right neck strap muscles. No petechiae were noted, and there was no deep neck organ trauma or injury. Abrasions, or scrapes, were cited on the left scapula, or shoulder blade, and around the wrists, from the handcuffs. There were also contusions, or bruises, of the right arm and elbow. Her internal organs were of normal size and weight, with only her lungs slightly heavy under microscopic inspection. There was no fracture to the bones or cartilages of the throat. The doctor reported Gotbaum's history of alcohol abuse and depression, and that she used antidepressant medications. The toxicological report showed a blood alcohol content of .24 percent, which is three times the legal limit for driving in Arizona, and there was a positive reading for citalopram (an antidepressant sold under the brand name Celexa®) and duloxetine (an antidepressant sold under the name Cymbalta®). She also had ibuprofen, an over-the-counter pain reliever; diphenhydramine (also known as Benadryl®, an allergy medication that can make one sleepy); chlorpheniramine (another antihistamine sold under a variety of brand names); and dextromethorphan (a cough suppressant sold under various names). These cold medications were of therapeutic doses and unrelated to Gotbaum's death.

Dr. Bucholtz, to her credit, conducted an experiment on the day of the autopsy, visiting the Sky Harbor detention area, along with Detective Joe Petrosino and forensic photographer Barbara Powell. The doctor, who was the same basic height and weight as the decedent, sought to re-create Gotbaum's situation with the handcuffs and leg iron and compare it to the observations from the arresting officer who found Carol unresponsive in the cell. According to the report, the officer explained that as he walked Gotbaum to the holding area, she did not complain of any medical condition and did not seem to be overheated or hallucinatory—but she was agitated and noncompliant with instructions. He called for a female officer to search her and place her in the holding cell. From outside the room, with the door closed, the police could hear her making noise in the cell. After a few minutes of quiet, he opened the door and looked inside, seeing her in what he thought was a sleeping position. When he saw that she was unconscious, he called for assistance and uncuffed her hands. He could not recall how the leg iron chain was positioned in relation to the decedent. He laid her on the floor and began the futile attempts to revive her. Bucholtz spent more than an hour gathering her information.[22]

Soon after Carol Gotbaum's death, I got a phone call from high-profile Phoenix attorney Michael Manning, saying that he represented Noah Gotbaum and inquiring whether I could come to Phoenix to perform a second autopsy on the decedent. I said I could. I didn't know Manning or any of the Gotbaums, but it's not unusual for me to get urgent calls of this nature, and I try to accommodate them when I'm able.

On October 2, I was scheduled to fly to Phoenix and attend the autopsy conducted by Dr. Bucholtz, but my flight from Pittsburgh was delayed. By the time I arrived, in the afternoon, Bucholtz's work was finished. I was met at the airport by attorney Leslie O'Hara, who showed me the holding cell and explained the facts of the case. I was impressed by the two lawyers, both of whom were convinced that Gotbaum was "manhandled" by police and that her death should not have happened. The team was considering filing a wrongful death claim against the city police on behalf of Noah Gotbaum and his children. As I always tell people who seek a second autopsy, I can't promise whether my assessment will help them, but it will be an honest review, and they can then make their plans accordingly. If there is a lawsuit and trial, I will be available to testify regarding my findings.

The Maricopa medical examiner's office had delivered Carol Gotbaum's body to the Sinai Funeral Home, where I conducted my procedure. I opened the Y-incision and removed sutures on sundry parts of the body, taking specific notes on the various abrasions and bruises. I counted a total of thirty-five marks, all of them arguably fresh. It was important to chronicle each defect's size, shape, and color, so that if I testified, I could point to portions of the surveillance video where some of the specific injuries were likely sustained.

As I worked, I noticed three critical items were missing: Carol Gotbaum's brain, heart, and neck structure. They had been sent to the forensic lab for neuropathological and other anatomical study. I would have to make a return visit to see these items, and I did so on November 2. This time, I went to the medical examiner's office and met with Dr. Bucholtz and her two assistants. The three items were in separate containers, and the two organs had been extensively sectioned for microscopic study. The neck showed one area of acute hemorrhage, as noted in Bucholtz's report, and we discussed the elements of the neck structure. I later reviewed the slides, autopsy photos, Bucholtz's report, and the toxicology results before I wrote my own report for the attorneys. In general, I agreed with Bucholtz's professional opinion, although I described the death as "positional asphyxia," which I felt was more precise than her "asphyxia by hanging."

In my ensuing conversations with the Gotbaum legal counsel, I stated that the official autopsy was suitably proficient, and that the weight of all the findings showed that there were questionable actions on the part of the Phoenix police department in their handling of this woman who died in their custody. Another thing to consider was the unfortunate fact that Carol was not wearing shoes in the holding cell. Her nylon socks might have slipped on the tile floor, causing her to lose her footing as she flailed around. The existence in her system of the two antidepressants was something any opposing counsel would focus on, and I couldn't argue against that. The lawyers would have to delve into her medical history and determine whether the Celexa and Cymbalta were prescribed by separate doctors, each of whom might have been unaware of what the other was doing—or by one doctor who should have known better than to prescribe two competing pharmaceuticals. Then again, maybe Carol was not following any doctor's instructions about her dosages. Many people feel if one pill has a positive effect, two would be even better, not realizing that such dosing could put their well-being in jeopardy. Drugs can have counter effects, and when mixed with alcohol, the results can be deadly. As for the high blood alcohol content, a person of Gotbaum's weight would have to consume about eight to ten mixed drinks within a two-hour span to get the .24 percent reading. The lawyers' investigators would have to trace Carol Ann's behavior at the New York airport, on the plane, and at the Sky Harbor airport bar to create a precise timeline of her alcohol intake. And, of course, the investigators would need to talk to all possible witnesses. The police were already saturating these same avenues in their investigation—possibly with the view that they might be sued—so the Gotbaum team had to get the same, or better, information.[23]

Michael Manning knew his way around this territory. He was on the winning side of two lawsuits involving clients who died in a Maricopa County jail and, in those cases, testimony suggested that medical examiners had mishandled evidence. "They destroyed evidence, lost evidence, changed evidence and created evidence (in those cases). We were not going to take the chance that something like that would happen again," Manning told a local reporter. "There is a very tight relationship between law enforcement and medical examiner offices everywhere in the country, including Phoenix."[24] I can't deny that such clannishness exists in certain jurisdictions. It's always a disappointment when any medical examiner lacks the confidence or community support to remain a separate entity from its police department.[25]

In the first week in October that the intrastate rivalry went national, a new scandal hit Arizona. A forty-one-year-old man had died after Phoenix police struggled to get him into custody. The man had been seen parked in front of two separate known drug houses before cops decided to stop him for a traffic offense. The driver kept going for a few blocks, stopped abruptly, then got out of the vehicle. As officers approached, the man jumped back into his car and sped off. A chase followed, with the suspect driving erratically, then leaving the car and running through a park. Officers won the footrace and fought with the man as they attempted to take him into custody. Physical force was used, but no pepper spray or Taser. The man became unresponsive and was pronounced dead at the hospital. Neither officer was injured, but the department took a black eye when all attendant media reports reminded the potential jury pool of Carol Anne Gotbaum's death.[26]

Noah Gotbaum brought his wife's body back to New York City, and on October 7, she was memorialized by senior rabbi Robert Levine at the Congregation Rodeph Shalom synagogue. In the hour-long ceremony, Carol's loved ones spoke of her gentle nature. Tears were shed when Noah told the crowd, "If the airline or the police authorities had treated Carol with some modicum of dignity and grace, or if one single person at that airport had put an arm around her shoulders, sat her down and given her some attention, she might still be with us today." He also spoke directly to his three youngsters, who were in the audience. To Ella, who had been born prematurely, he recalled how her mother had cradled her "from morning until night." He told Nathaniel that his "Mommy was so proud of you, her little man," and reminded little Tobias that he had inherited "Mommy's incredible ability to light up a room with her smile." The news media shot touching footage of a bare-foot Tobias sitting on his Daddy's shoulders, as Noah and his children left the ceremony behind the lily-covered coffin.[27]

On May 8, 2008, Gotbaum family attorneys filed an $8 million civil claim against the city of Phoenix and others, stating that police officers used excessive force, violated Gotbaum's civil rights, and improperly shackled her. With a 2010 trial date in mind, the two sides went about lining up witnesses and evidence. It didn't take long for a public-opinion war to be stirred up between New York and Arizona. Manhattanites supported this tragic yet innocent woman and her well-regarded family.[28] Quoting from the lawsuit, the *New York Post* published the family's allegation that police "used excessive and unreasonable force on Carol, as if she was a dangerous criminal, rather than as the sick, intoxi-cated, and vulnerable person she was."[29] Meanwhile, Phoenix mayor Phil Gordon told the *Arizona Republic*: "I have reviewed the facts and read the reports. Mrs. Gotbaum's death was tragic, but this was not a tragedy at the city's making. She was traveling alone, yet people she never met tried to help her. Our police officers acted correctly and pro-fessionally."[30] The debate exploded in the blogosphere, where unbridled remarks ran wild: angry Arizonans didn't want to write a fat check to a family that didn't need the money and would use its fortune to buy jus-tice, and New Yorkers claimed that poorly trained cops killed a troubled woman. There was such animosity toward the Gotbaums in Phoenix that the family attorneys felt it might be necessary to seek a change of venue for a trial.[31]

The case was transferred to federal court, but it later ended up back in state court after Gotbaum's lawyers dropped the civil rights aspect and reduced the amount of requested damages to $5.5 million. Federal cases take longer to wend their way into a courtroom, and attorney Manning wanted the fastest possible resolution for his clients. Also, federal juries have to unanimously agree on allegations in a civil case, whereas in state court lawsuits, only a majority of the jury has to agree.[32]

That August, the officers who detained Gotbaum caught a break when local prosecutors said no charges would be filed against them. Said Maricopa County attorney Andrew Thomas: "Mrs. Gotbaum's death, while tragic, does not warrant criminal charges against police officers who were simply trying to carry out their duties."[33]

Ending its two-year battle, in October 19, 2009, the insurance company that represented the City of Phoenix settled the case for a sum of $250,000, to be paid to the Gotbaum children. The city had already spent half a million dollars on the case, with a projected cost of a trial adding another $750,000, so it was just smart business to settle. Because it was covered as an insurance matter, no taxpayer monies were used to pay the settlement. Noah Gotbaum issued a statement quoted in the *Arizona Republic*: "For many personal reasons . . . I have concluded that continuing to pursue litigation is not in my children's best interests, nor of Carol's memory." He added that the family's agreement "does not represent an end to our deep concern about how the law enforcement community and we as a society treat people who suffer from issues of alcoholism, mental illness and emotional distress." The Phoenix police department's statement included extending condolences to the Gotbaum family for their tragic loss but stood by their position that their officers "acted appropriately and within policy." They added: "Ms. Gotbaum's death had and continues to have a profound effect upon all the officers who were involved."[34] I don't doubt that one bit. Those officers did not go to work that day to end the life of an inebriated, depressed individual. They were just caught up in a perfect storm of terrible events with the worst possible outcome.

I believe both parties were wise to have settled this case—even though I would have wanted to address the jury—and by extension, law enforcement—regarding areas where I maintain errors were made. Having a defibrillator on hand and personnel trained to use it would have saved time once Carol was discovered unconscious—but it was the officers' crude, brutal, and aggressive insensitivity that was directly responsible for her demise. This death could have been prevented if police had taken her to a hospital instead of into custody, or if they had simply watched her more closely.

But Carol's drug intake presented a problem for her legal team. While the drugs were not directly responsible for her death, the two competing antidepressants made her more vulnerable to oxygen deprivation when she got tangled up in the shackles. And her oxygen was already somewhat depleted by her high-adrenaline outbursts in the airport corridor and from fighting with officers.

And while casual observers may claim that a woman in her fragile condition should never have traveled without a companion, they don't understand that this was Carol's own decision. Alcoholics can be sneaky, and she may have planned to drink on the plane or while waiting for her connecting flight—a kind of last blowout before rehab.

In the end, a lovely woman is dead, and her husband and children will never get her back. Alcoholism can affect both genders and any racial or economic group. We can't make it go away, but we can recognize its victims and treat them with greater compassion.[35]

CHAPTER SEVEN

MICHAEL JACKSON

Gone Too Soon

On March 5, 2009, Michael Jackson stood before the world press and two thousand screaming fans and announced that he would be doing a series of live concerts at London's O2 Grand Concourse stadium, beginning in July. The show would be called "This Is It," and he referred to the concerts as his "final curtain call." After Jackson left the dais, the promoter explained there would be ten shows, beginning July 8, and together they would be "the event of the decade."[1] Within weeks, the concerts would be expanded to fifty shows, all at that venue, with hopes of going worldwide to Paris, New York City, and Mumbai, and employing hundreds of workers. But Michael would never make any of the dates. On June 25, the "King of Pop" died at his Los Angeles home.

I was at my Pittsburgh, Pennsylvania, office, finishing some paperwork when I got a call from my co-author, Dawna Kaufmann. "Michael Jackson is dead," she told me. The singer? I asked. As she confirmed it, I turned on my television. CNN, MSNBC, and Fox News were all reporting the story, but each news report said that Jackson was in the hospital, possibly due to a heart attack. I mentioned that to Dawna, but she said they were all wrong. Jackson was dead, period. Knowing Dawna for more than a decade, and realizing how plugged in she is as an investigative journalist, I knew better than to argue. Michael Jackson, who sold 750 million albums and won thirteen Grammys, was dead, and the entertainment world was about to get jolted.

Just after midnight on Thursday, June 25, 2009, Michael Jackson, fifty years old, had returned home from one of his last rehearsals before leaving for England. A lot was riding on his slender shoulders; not only were these concerts a jumpstart to his dormant career, but at stake was a huge contract with the promoter, Anschutz Entertainment Group Live (AEG), which would bring him the kind of money he had not made in a long while. It was important that he be in good shape for the shows, which would be a challenge for any performer, but for the reclusive and weakly Jackson, the task was Herculean. He had already taken steps to improve his diet and build his strength and endurance with daily exercise. Sleep, however, was elusive. He couldn't seem to ever get a good night's rest—at least not without the help of prescription medication.[2]

From the upper-floor bedroom of his rented mansion, Jackson called his primary physician, a cardiologist named Dr. Conrad Murray, who had been in Jackson's exclusive employ for the past several weeks. Murray traveled the short distance from his Santa Monica apartment and joined Jackson a bit after 1 a.m. Michael couldn't sleep and was dehydrated, he told Murray, so the doctor gave him some medication and sat at the star's bedside for the next eleven hours, according to Murray's statement to Los Angeles police detectives. Around noon, Murray discovered that Jackson was not breathing, so he pulled him onto the floor where he began cardiopulmonary resuscitation and called for someone to notify 911. Soon paramedics were at the home and found Jackson "asystolic." That means there was no respiration or cardiac electrical activity. He had flatlined; his pupils were fixed and dilated. But Murray was not willing to declare his patient dead, and since he was the doctor, he set the rules. Murray insisted that the emergency technicians continue with CPR and advanced cardiac life support to clear Jackson's airway, initiate an IV, and apply a defibrillator, in hopes of reigniting a heart rhythm. Jackson was also given two rounds of lifesaving drugs: epinephrine, or adrenaline, which increases the heart rate, contracts blood vessels, and dilates air passages; and atropine, which is made from the poisonous belladonna plant and increases firing of the heart's right atrium while opposing the actions of the vagus nerve that helps regulate cardiac rhythm. All this occurred as Jackson and Murray were rushed by ambulance to the nearest hospital, the Ronald Reagan UCLA Medical Center.

Dr. Richelle Jody Cooper was the attending physician in the hospital's emergency room when the Jackson group entered. Michael was checked into the facility under the pseudonym "Soule Shaun." Cooper's team placed central lines and an intra-aortic balloon pump into Jackson. But when there were no vital signs, Cooper pronounced him dead. It was 2:26 p.m., Pacific Standard Time, around the time that Dawna phoned me. The announcement to the public would not be made for quite some time, until all the family members could be notified. Behind the scenes, a Los Angeles Police Department (LAPD) detective at the hospital reported the case as an "accidental vs. natural" death to the county office of the medical examiner. Coroner's investigator Elissa Fleak was assigned the case and arrived at the hospital at 5:20 p.m., along with assistant chief Ed Winter and forensic attendant Alexander Perez. Fleak conducted a body examination of Jackson, who was then transported by the Los Angeles Sheriff's Department Aero Bureau to the coroner's Forensic Science Center downtown. Fleak and Winter then went to Jackson's residence in the tony suburb of Holmby Hills. They went upstairs to his bedroom and also to another bedroom, where he had been sleeping when he had gone into cardiac arrest. This room featured a queen-sized bed, numerous tables and chairs, a dresser, and a television; a large walk-in closet was on one side. The bedding was disheveled and appeared as if Jackson had been lying on the bed's left side. On the bed were a blue plastic pad lined with cotton, a string of wooden beads, a tube of toothpaste, a book, a laptop computer, and eyeglasses. Near the foot of the bed was a closed bottle of urine on top of a chair. To the left of the bed was a tan-colored sofa chair where Dr. Murray had sat. A green oxygen tank was nearby. On a table were several empty orange juice bottles, a telephone, a lamp, Jackson's prescription medication bottles, a box of IV catheters, a broken syringe, disposable needles, and alcohol pads. On the floor lay latex gloves and an ambu-bag, which is a handheld mask and pump used for ventilation purposes; it's unknown whether this was left behind by paramedics or was in Murray's medical bag. Workers from the Los Angeles County Coroner's Office (LACCO) took photographs every step of the way: at UCLA, during transport, at Jackson's residence, and before and during the autopsy.

Fleak collected numerous prescription pill bottles and containers from the site, including two forms of depigmentation liquid, used to lighten skin color: hydroquinone, which is banned in Europe, and Benoquin®; neither container displayed a doctor's name. Dr. Murray had prescribed these medications: diazepam (an antianxiety drug sold under the brand name Valium®); lorazepam (Ativan®, a sedative); temazepam (Restoril®, a sleeping aid); tamsulosin hydrochloride (Flomax®, for help with male urination); and the anesthetic lidocaine, which was prescribed for Dr. Murray. Two medications were prescribed by West Hollywood internist Dr. Allan L. Metzger: clonazepam (Klonopin®, a muscle relaxant), and trazodone (Desyrel®, an antidepressant); and two prescriptions were written by Beverly Hills dermatologist and cosmetic surgeon Dr. Arnold W. Klein, one for tizanidine (Zanaflex®, a muscle relaxant), which was written for an "Omar Arnold," and one for prednisone (for treating inflammation). Two antibiotics showed the doctor names of Dwight James/Cherilyn Lee: the one for amoxicillin had the patient's name blacked out, and the other, for azithromycin (Zithromax®), had the patient name of "Kathlyn Hursey." Also collected were an open bottle of Bayer® aspirin, an over-the-counter skin ointment, sunscreen, eyedrops, a blue rubber strip, an IV clamp, a blood pressure cuff, one pulse finger monitor, an empty glass vial of flumazenil (Anexate, which counters sedation), and an empty glass vial of propofol

(Diprivan®, a hypnotic agent)—the latter two medications had no doctor or patient information on their packaging. On a return visit to the site three days later, Fleak collected more vials of injectible medications, none of which had doctor or patient names: propofol, lidocaine, and midazolam (Versed, a sedative).[3] It's important to note that clonazepam, diazepam, lorazepam, temazepam, and midazolam are all benzodiazepines—psychoactive drugs that can produce sedation and should not be used in concert with other, similar drugs.

Of course, it would take weeks to learn which, if any, of these prescription medications would show up in Jackson's bloodstream at autopsy; simply having bottles or vials of the medications does not mean he had been ingesting the contents. But the fact that there were numerous medications without labels giving the prescribing doctor's name or that of the patient—or labels giving what might be a patient's pseudonym—should serve as an alert to any experienced eye. State medical boards and federal agencies do not permit medications to be written to patients using aliases, a common problem among doctors who treat celebrities, as I recounted in the chapter on Anna Nicole Smith in my previous book, *A Question of Murder*. Smith's two doctors and lawyer were arrested and tried for a number of charges relating to her being overmedicated; a jury acquitted one doctor of all charges, but Dr. Khristine Eroshevich, Smith's psychiatrist, and her attorney, Howard K. Stern, were found guilty on two counts each of conspiring to obtain controlled substances by fraud and by providing false names (a judge later reduced or dismissed their convictions).[4]

Michael Joseph Jackson might have been the most influential and best-loved performer of our time. He was a singer, multi-instrumentalist, composer, record producer, dancer, choreographer, movie actor, television star, businessman, art collector, philanthropist, son, brother, two-time ex-husband, and father of three. But he was also a controversial figure who seemed to enjoy giving both his fans and critics much to talk about.

Michael's parents are Joe, a divorced, former steel-worker who played early rock and roll with a group called the Falcons in working-class Gary, Indiana, and Katherine Scruse, a country music lover, polio survivor, and devout Jehovah's Witness from Alabama, who moved to Indiana in her youth. Joe and Katherine married in 1949, when he was twenty and she was nineteen, and by the next year, their first daughter, Maureen (better known as Rebbie), was born. Sigmund (Jackie) followed in 1951, then Tariano (Tito) in 1953, Jermaine in 1954, La Toya in 1956, and Marlon—a premature twin whose brother Brandon died almost immediately—in 1957. Michael was born on August 29, 1958, Randy in 1961, and last born, Janet, in 1966. As Joe gave up his own plans for a music career, he transferred his ambitions onto his three older sons. Joe controlled every aspect of his boys' lives, not only to keep them safe from gangs and trouble but to perfect his vision of a new kind of musical act, one in which the siblings would travel far and wide singing, playing instruments, and dancing to fresh songs, and wearing hip, matching costumes.[5] In 1964, Michael and Marlon first stepped onstage with the Jackson Brothers, initially on congas and tambourine, but they soon contributed to the vocals and dancing. It didn't take long for audiences to zero in on Michael, who was a pint-sized scene stealer. The act was rechristened the Jackson 5, with Jackie, Tito, Jermaine, Michael and Marlon. Michael became the lead singer whose falsetto voice dripped with emotion and maturity beyond his tender years. Joe Jackson wanted precision performances from his kids, and their lives soon became a cycle of rehearsals and shows, with plentiful whippings in between. The chronic physical and verbal abuse made Michael fear his father and probably created the childlike shell that he would feel most comfortable in for the rest of his life.

After releasing a record locally in 1968, the Jackson 5 signed with Motown, the world's leading rhythm-and-blues label, helmed by Berry Gordy, where they got the exposure and nurturing they needed. Their first singles—"I Want You Back," "ABC," "The Love You Save," and "I'll

Be There"—topped the charts and moved the family to Hollywood, California, and into celebrity circles, where former Supremes singer, Diana Ross, took a special shine to young Michael. On her own TV specials and later on Jackson 5 shows, Ross and Michael would sing duets and exchange comedy quips, guaranteeing huge ratings, more lucrative recording sessions, and bigger international arenas for the Jackson 5. By the mid-1970s, Michael was releasing solo albums, and his crooning of the theme song of the movie *Ben* was so soulful, it was easy to forget that it was a love tune to a rat. In 1975, the Jackson 5 left Motown and signed with Epic Records, renaming themselves the Jacksons and switching in Randy to replace Jermaine, who had gone solo. But the family band was losing steam as Michael's independent career was soaring. In 1978, he and Diana Ross starred in *The Wiz*, an urban retelling of *The Wizard of Oz*, with Ross playing Dorothy and Jackson playing the Scarecrow. It was not a commercial success, but the music arranger was Quincy Jones, the legendary master of all musical forms, who saw in Michael someone who had not yet reached his potential. Jones produced Michael's 1979 album *Off the Wall*, with its monster hits "Don't Stop 'Til You Get Enough" and "Rock with You." Selling over twenty million albums, Michael swept the *American Music Awards* and *Billboard Year-End Awards* and snagged a Grammy. He would soon garner the highest royalty rate of any performing artist.

Also in 1979, Jackson broke his nose while working on a complex dance routine and underwent his first rhinoplasty, or cosmetic nose surgery. It left him with breathing difficulties, so he had another procedure performed by Beverly Hills plastic surgeon Dr. Steven Hoefflin. With Hoefflin's help, Michael began to redesign his appearance, morphing from an African American boy with a wide nose and full, curly hair, to a chiseled, lighter-skinned, more feminine-looking individual who wore his hair (or wig) straight, with tendrils curling down his face.[6] Michael's mother was never pleased about her son's repeated cosmetic surgeries. In an interview with Oprah Winfrey after the singer's death,

Katherine Jackson said she believed Michael was "addicted" to plastic surgery and that his nose kept getting smaller from repeated operations until it looked "like a toothpick." Mrs. Jackson even told one of Michael's doctors that if the star came in for another procedure, to just "pretend" to perform the surgery.[7]

More prestigious projects and awards followed, culminating in *Thriller*, in 1982, which became the bestselling album of all time, world-wide, and continues to sell—over 170 million copies to date. Chart-busting singles, including "Billie Jean," "Beat It," and "Wanna Be Starting Something," became the ultimate dance music soundtracks, crossing generations, cultures, and economic groups. The long-form video version of the title cut featured Jackson boogying with zombies and creepy creatures, with a voice-over by horror film king Vincent Price. When Michael's fellow Jehovah's Witnesses condemned the video, Jackson left the church, although some members of his family—including his mother—still practice the faith. In 1983, before an NBC television audience of forty-seven million, Michael reunited with his brothers and other seminal musical acts for the *Motown 25: Yesterday, Today, and Forever* special. Wearing a black sequin jacket and one rhinestone-studded glove, Michael performed his hit "Billie Jean," dazzling the world with a dance step he had been working on for three years: the "moonwalk." Jackson glided backward while appearing to move forward, an illusion of timing and delicacy that would become his signature move.[8]

On January 27, 1984, Michael, his brothers, and a full audience of excited fans, were at Los Angeles' Shrine Auditorium, filming an elaborate and expensive Pepsi commercial when a pyrotechnic mishap set Michael's hair on fire. Released footage of the accident shows Jackson blithely dancing, then a quick blast of light, out of which Michael is seen again, still dancing and apparently unaware that his hair is engulfed in flames. It takes more than twelve long seconds for crew members to realize the disaster, and even longer for the fire to be extinguished. The camera's last shot shows a tennis ball-sized, pink bald spot near the top of Michael's head. He was rushed to the hospital with second- and third-degree burns.[9] Not only would the alarming event leave a physical defect for the remainder of his life, but it set him on a path of prescription pill addiction from which he would never break free.

Also in the 1980s, Michael began manifesting symptoms of vitiligo, which caused white splotches to appear on various parts of his body. He used a skin lightener and pancake makeup to even out the color of his face, neck, and hands—and, if he had to appear sleeveless in a music video, his arms. He started a long association with dermatologist/cosmetic surgeon Dr. Arnold Klein, who would become one of Jackson's closest friends. Around this time, too, Jackson's onstage behavior became more peculiar. Many of his dance moves included grabbing his crotch and crying out, and some of his videos took on a darker, violent tone. But his voice, now covering several octaves, was strong and sensual—and his various exclamations, chirps, and other unique vocalizations made his sound utterly distinctive.[10]

Other defining events in Jackson's life included cowriting and performing in 1985's star-studded single and music video "We Are the World," which raised unprecedented funds for African famine relief; his acquisition of publishing rights—and attendant humongous income—of the majority of songs and compositions by the Beatles; collaboration with movie auteur Francis Ford Coppola on the seventeen-minute 3-D film *Captain Eo*, which has become a Disney theme park mainstay; his *Bad* album, with its hits "The Way You Make Me Feel" and "Man in the Mirror," and its seven-month-long world tour; and in 1988, his autobiography, *Moonwalk*, which was edited by Jacqueline Kennedy Onassis and became an instant bestseller. In it, Jackson discusses the abuse he suffered as a child, as well as his changing appearance, which he attributed to weight loss, vegetarianism, a different hairstyle, and lighting.

In 1988, Jackson opened Neverland Ranch, a 2,770-acre, $17 million property that was both his home and personal theme park.[11] Nestled near Santa Barbara, California, in the rural community of Santa Ynez, it boasted a Ferris wheel and rides; movie theater with full snack bar; his own security force and dozens of servants; a menagerie, including a chimp named Bubbles, whom he dressed in matching military outfits similar to his own; and odd memorabilia, such as the hyperbaric chamber, or glass coffin, in which he would sleep and be oxygenated to stave off aging, and, reportedly, the bones of Joseph (John) Merrick, also known as the Elephant Man. As Jackson's eccentricities became wilder, it was difficult to separate what he was actually doing from what his press agents said he was doing. But it's a fact that he provided the *National Enquirer* with a Polaroid snapshot of him in his hyperbaric chamber, with the condition that the magazine publish it and label it as "bizarre." When the image was deemed of insufficient quality to reprint, he posed inside the chamber for another, more usable, picture, and the photo ran with the "bizarre" headline. Later, Michael would become insulted when the tabloid nicknamed him "Wacko Jacko."[12]

Within fifteen years, Neverland would be valued at $100 million. Jackson used the facilities for countless charity events, often inviting underprivileged or sick children and their families to enjoy the property free of cost. Around this time, Jackson acquired the appellation the "King of Pop," which he liked so much he insisted it be used as part of any formal introduction of him. Even his friend Elizabeth Taylor used the term when she presented him with the *Soul Train* Heritage Award in 1989. Jackson was especially fond of Taylor, a former child star turned world-renowned icon who understood the demands on his life in a way others could not.

The year 1991 brought the release of Michael's *Dangerous* album and its smashes "Black or White" and "Remember the Time." The ballad "Gone Too Soon" was composed by Larry Grossman and Buz Kohan, but it was Michael's plaintive rendering that made it a standard still heard at funeral services today; the song would be sung at Jackson's own memorial. The *Dangerous* world tour consisted of thirty-seven concerts before a total of 3.5 million fans over a period of fifteen months and ended with an HBO television special, the $20 million licensing fee of which has never been topped. While touring, Michael visited some of Africa's poorest countries, where he received an education on the scourge of HIV/AIDS. This awareness, along with his friendship with teenager Ryan White, who would soon die of AIDS, inspired Jackson to urge President Bill Clinton and other world leaders to increase research monies for the deadly disease.

In 1992, Jackson founded the Heal the World foundation and raised millions of dollars for children caught in war-torn countries. In 1993, the Super Bowl XXVII half-time show began with Jackson in glittery military regalia, clenching his hand and remaining motionless while the crowd cheered for a full ninety seconds. Then he broke into four of his biggest songs and earned the sporting event its highest-ever viewership.[13]

The same year, trouble hit Neverland. Sometimes—some would say too often—Jackson would invite pubescent kids, usually boys, upstairs to his personal bedroom, while relegating their parents or guardians to accommodations away from the main building. Michael and the kids would get into their pajamas, have the cook downstairs prepare whatever kind of meal or snack they craved, then watch classic comedy movies in Michael's bed or play fantasy games. Whatever happened in that room remained Michael's—and the kids'—secret. The hallway was rigged with an alarm that would let him know when a servant or unauthorized person was approaching. If parents protested, Michael would act hurt and assure them he could never harm a child. He offered them lavish shopping sprees at toy shops for the kids and jewelry stores for the moms that usually made any queasiness evaporate. That summer, Jackson was accused of child sexual abuse by a thirteen-year-old boy and his dentist father, who felt the singer had taken inappropriate liberties with the lad. The dentist demanded payment from Jackson, and when Michael refused, he contacted police. The teen's mother, who was divorced from the dentist, insisted nothing untoward had occurred.[14] The Neverland

Ranch was raided, and Jackson was forced to submit to a strip search. A Santa Barbara County grand jury was assembled to consider indicting the performer. On the advice of counsel, Jackson reached an out-of-court settlement with family members to the tune of at least $22 million, and he admitted no wrongdoing. With authorities no longer having cooperating witnesses, no further legal action could be taken. Still, the perception that Michael Jackson had bought the silence of a young victim increased public skepticism about his character.

During the investigation, Jackson turned to an old friend, Lisa Marie Presley, for emotional support. Lisa Marie was the only child of the late rock innovator Elvis Presley and actress Priscilla Presley, who had arranged for her to see the Jackson 5 when she was just seven years old. A divorced mother of two, ardent Scientologist, and an aspiring musician, Lisa Marie married Jackson when she was twenty-six, in May 1994. They epitomized rock-and-roll royalty: the King of Pop and the daughter of the King. They even had matching tourist sites: Michael's Neverland and Lisa Marie's Graceland—Elvis's Memphis, Tennessee, landmark, of which Lisa Marie was the sole heir.[15] As dual presenters on the September 1994 *MTV Video Music Awards*, Jackson surprised the audience and even his own wife by planting a huge kiss on Lisa Marie's lips, in hopes of quelling criticism that the marriage was a sham. Lisa Marie has stated repeatedly that she had a "normal" relationship with Jackson, but the couple divorced in January 1996.[16] In an October 21, 2010, interview with talk show host Oprah Winfrey, following Jackson's death, Presley said she was clueless about Michael's drug addiction until just before she filed for divorce. She described an occasion during which Michael was promoting his double album *HIStory*, when he was rushed to the hospital. While doctors blamed a viral infection, Presley felt she was reliving her father's 1977 drug-related death. "There were times when I would pick him up from a certain doctor's office and he would not be coherent," she said about Jackson. The duo might have weathered the storm had she agreed to get pregnant with his child, which he pressured her to do. "I did want to, but I just wanted to make sure," she explained. "I was looking into the future and thinking, 'I don't ever want to get into a custody battle with him.'" Lisa Marie's hesitation made Jackson look elsewhere, specifically at Debbie Rowe, who worked as a nurse in the office of dermatologist Dr. Arnold Klein. In October 1996, with the ink still wet on his divorce papers, Jackson announced that Rowe was pregnant with his child, an act Lisa Marie described as "retaliatory."[17]

On the *HIStory* world tour, which would last thirteen months, would gross $150 million, would hit fifty-eight cities, and would entertain 5.8 million fans, Jackson and Rowe had an impromptu wedding ceremony in Sydney, Australia. Michael Joseph Jackson Jr.—known as Prince, in honor of a surname on Katherine Jackson's side of the family—was born on February 13, 1997. A year later, on April 3, 1998, Rowe gave birth to Paris-Michael Katherine Jackson. The couple divorced in 1999, with Jackson getting full custody of the children and observers wondering what kind of payoff Debbie got to bear kids, then walk away from them.[18] Although there was one photo taken of the foursome while the children were still babies, Debbie had almost no contact with Prince or Paris since that photo was taken. She was forbidden to tell them that she was their mother, and the kids always referred to her as "Miss Debbie." After Jackson's death, his mother reintegrated Debbie into the lives of her two youngsters, although there are no details as to how close their connection might be now.[19]

Michael's career slowed down while he was waiting until 2001 to release the album *Invincible*, which, according to him, got little push from the record label with whom he was feuding. Because of this, he refused to tour the world or make many videos. The nastiness continued when Michael accused Tommy Mottola, head of Sony Music Entertainment, of being a racist. It was not the first time Jackson had stepped into those muddy waters; "They Don't Care about Us," a tune from *HIStory*, included anti-Semitic lyrics, causing the Anti-Defamation League and other groups to protest. Jackson eventually released a version of the song without the offending passages, but the controversy made people wonder what level of hostility Jackson carried within him—a hostility that seemed to conflict with his public promotion of global peace and tolerance. (It should be noted that Debbie Rowe is Jewish.)

In September, Jackson performed sold-out concerts at Madison Square Garden to celebrate his thirtieth year in show business. Other performers for the momentous two-night affair included Whitney Houston, *NSYNC, Destiny's Child, Mya, Luther Vandross, Monica, and Slash. The next day, the 9/11 attack on America took place, with the Twin Towers falling in Manhattan. Jackson quickly organized a benefit concert with an all-star lineup in Washington, DC, for September 21. In November, a two-hour CBS television special aired: *Michael Jackson: 30th Anniversary Celebration: The Solo Years.*

On February 21, 2002, Michael's third child—Prince Michael Jackson II, nicknamed "Blanket"—was born to an undisclosed surrogate mother.[20] Very little footage of the children was released due to Michael's concerns for their security; when they could be seen in public, they were wearing scarves or masks to hide their faces. In November, Michael greeted fans from the fourth-floor balcony of Hotel Adlon in Berlin, blowing kisses and holding up hand-lettered signs, one of which said "Burn All Tabloids." He brought each of the older children to the window and had them wave, although their faces were covered. But when Jackson held Blanket, wearing a turquoise onesie and face scarf, over the railing of the balcony, with nothing below him but a long drop, critics had a field day. Child advocates filed legal papers questioning Jackson's parenting skills and asking that the children be put into protective custody. Nothing came of these complaints, but Michael later apologized, saying it was a "terrible mistake."[21] Aside from that incident, Jackson seemed a devoted father, having the kids home-schooled at the Neverland Ranch when they weren't touring the globe with him, sometimes for extended stays outside the United States. He also exposed them to numerous artistic and cultural pursuits that come from being peripatetic and very wealthy.[22]

The question of whether Michael Jackson biologically fathered any of his children is debatable, and I don't have an answer. Even though Debbie Rowe is a blue-eyed blonde, and Paris has an unmistakable resemblance to her, and we don't know Blanket's birth mother's genetic makeup, there appears to be no trace of Michael's physicality in any of the kids. There are occasional genetic anomalies in life that result in a child having vastly lighter facial coloring and different features from a birth parent, but for that to happen three times out of three is unusual, to say the least. I know that several associates of Jackson spoke out after his death and said that Michael had asked them to contribute sperm to a fertility clinic for the purpose of fathering a child for him—a favor they were glad to do. More important, though, is that Michael surely loved those three children, however he came by them, and that should be the only basis for affirmatively declaring him their father. If one or more of the kids at some point were to request a DNA test to confirm paternity, that could be done easily and without the media finding out.[23]

In May 2002, Jackson granted permission to British newsman Martin Bashir and his ITV video crew to shoot a documentary called *Living with Michael Jackson*. The Hotel Adlon's "baby-dangling" footage was captured by Bashir's crew, as well as many tender encounters between Michael and his children, albeit with the kids' faces covered. The film aired worldwide in the spring of 2003 and portrayed Jackson as an unstable lunatic. The most contentious scene was one shot at Neverland, featuring Jackson holding the hand of a thirteen-year-old boy who had been invited with his mother to stay at the ranch after undergoing cancer treatment. The boy's mother was housed in another building, while the teen stayed in Jackson's room—and in his bed.[24] "Why can't you share your bed?" Jackson asked. "It's the most loving thing you can do, is to share your bed with someone."[25] In a later interview with Ed Bradley of

CBS's *60 Minutes*, Jackson defended the idea of sharing a bed with a child, saying that he was "not Jack the Ripper" and "not a pedophile." Then he backtracked a bit by saying he didn't actually sleep with the child—although there would have been nothing wrong with that if he had. Jackson said he slept on the floor and let the child have the bed.[26]

After the Bashir documentary aired, officials with the Santa Barbara County district attorney's office opened a criminal investigation, and in November 2003, Michael Jackson was arrested and charged with seven counts of child molestation and two counts of furnishing a minor with an intoxicating drink, all of which Jackson vociferously denied. Jackson didn't deny there were sleepovers, but he said nothing illegal occurred. *The People vs. Michael Jackson* trial began in Santa Maria, California, on January 31, 2005, making headline news nearly every day with lurid testimony, countercharges, and a circuslike environment that prevailed both inside and outside the courtroom. In June, the jury's verdict acquitted Jackson of all counts.[27] Two of the jurors would later tell a reporter they regretted voting not guilty. "People just wouldn't take their blinders off long enough to really look at all the evidence that was there," said Ray Hultman. And Eleanor Cook stated: "No doubt in my mind, whatsoever, that boy was molested, and I also think he enjoyed to some degree being Michael Jackson's toy." Thomas Mesereau, Jackson's lead defense attorney, called the comments "embarrassing and outrageous."[28]

Shaken by the ordeal, Michael took his kids and a few staffers and moved to Bahrain, as guests of Prince Abdullah, a music lover who had loaned money to the beleaguered pop star to pay his legal bills. Jackson recorded one of the prince's compositions to benefit disaster victims around the world, but it was never released. In May 2006, the Jackson party departed for Ireland. The prince would later sue Michael for recovery of the loaned funds, which Jackson argued was a gift; an out-of-court settlement was struck in 2008.[29] Neverland Ranch was closed in 2006, its employees laid off, and its zoo animals and theme park rides relocated. Today it is a rundown shadow of its former glory, its property unlikely to be developed due to community protesters who don't want the traffic in the area. The Jackson group returned to the states in December 2006 so that Michael could deliver a eulogy at the funeral of soul icon James Brown, one of Michael's original inspirations. Jackson's lawyers were trying to restructure his massive debts, which, at one point, threatened his income from the acquired song publishing business and his own catalog, as well as property he owned called the Hayvenhurst Estate, in Encino, California, where his mother and various relatives lived. Sony Music stepped in to help reorganize his debts, and together they bought a portion of other artists' catalogs, including those of Lady Gaga, Eminem, Bob Dylan, Neil Diamond, the Jonas Brothers, and Shakira. During this time, Jackson recorded extensively with some of the industry's newest bright lights, from will.i.am of the Black Eyed Peas to RedOne and Akon, but he didn't release any of the recordings. While Michael averted financial doom through his new publishing deals, his no-holds-barred spending gave him little cash flow. One way to turn all his red ink into black would be to plan a series of live concerts. Even though he hadn't done a world tour since 1997, promoters knew the fans would still be at the ticket windows, money in hand. The plan was made for AEG to promote the London shows. Now all they needed was to whip Jackson back into shape, but first, Michael would need to pass a physical so he could be insured.[30] AEG hired a New York ear-nose-and-throat specialist, Dr. David Slavit, who conducted an exam of the performer and gave him a clean bill of health. But Michael wanted a doctor to travel with him, someone who would stay by his side through the tour and write prescriptions for the drugs that he'd need to keep going. Enter Dr. Conrad Murray, whom Jackson had first met in Las Vegas in 2008 when one of Michael's children had a cold.[31]

When Michael persuaded Conrad Murray to trade in his practices in Houston and Las Vegas for taking care of just one patient, it must have seemed like the answer to each other's prayers. Murray had enormous child support payments to make each month, having fathered seven children with several different women. Jackson offered him $150,000 per month, saying all he'd have to do is administer the drugs Michael needed to sleep and be on call if Michael required anything. Murray would travel to England and anywhere else, all expenses paid, and stand on the sidelines watching the world's greatest singer-dancer wow the crowds as a key member of Jackson's entourage. For his part, Jackson would get a doctor who knew his way around a drug-dependent celebrity. Murray had treated Adrienne Brown, who had fought a pain pill addiction and died in 1996 of heart disease complicated by PCP ingestion while at an unlicensed Los Angeles spa recuperating from liposuction. Murray had nothing to do with her death nor, presumably, with the 2006 congestive heart failure death of her husband, "Godfather of Soul" James Brown, who may have been Murray's patient too. As Brown's longtime producer and assistant, Jacque Hollander, told a reporter, "James Brown and Michael Jackson were inseparable and they used the same 'safe doctors'—doctors who would get them anything they wanted. If James Brown wanted drugs, he knew he could get them from these safe doctors in Dallas, Houston, Las Vegas, and Los Angeles."[32]

Born in February 1953 on the island country of Grenada but raised in his mother's homeland of Trinidad, Conrad Murray still has a lilting Caribbean accent. He immigrated to Houston, Texas, in the late 1970s to be near his father, the late Dr. Rawle Andrews, who had a practice there.[33]

In 1994, Andrews had his medical privileges restricted for five years by the Texas Medical Board for prescribing drugs that were "nontherapeutic." Murray, in 1985, while attending Meharry Medical College in Nashville, Tennessee, was arrested for "fraudulent breach of trust" after Patricia Mitchell, his then-girlfriend and mother of his daughter, filed a complaint against him, the charges of which are not listed in the court records. He was released on a $2,000 bond, and the case was soon dismissed. This took place during his four-year marriage to Zufan Tesfai, a pharmacist now living in New Jersey. They split up in 1988, the year before he graduated from medical school. He had at least one other marriage, but many other girlfriends.[34] Murray met Nicole Alvarez, the mother of his youngest son, in 2005, when she worked as a stripper at a club he frequented.[35] He was a fellow in cardiology at the University of Arizona at Tucson when he was arrested in 1994 for domestic violence against one of his "baby mamas," Janice Adams; he was later acquitted.[36] Despite a checkered personal life, Conrad Murray has his defenders, including patients who praised him to reporters after Jackson died. Also, in May 2010, a woman who had passed out for half an hour on a flight between Houston and Phoenix awoke to find an IV in her arm and hearing Murray's soothing words, "You probably know me, I was Michael Jackson's doctor." The woman, who was later treated in the hospital and released, told reporters she was "incredibly grateful" to Dr. Murray.[37]

One ironic note: Murray, who scored the big paying gig with Michael Jackson for enough money to feed and clothe his children for a long while, never received as much as a penny from the performer. Jackson arranged for the funds to come directly from AEG, and even though Murray had been working for six weeks, his first check had not arrived.[38] Murray has threatened a lawsuit against AEG for nonpayment, citing a binding contract. His spokesperson said that Murray will not be making a creditor's claim against the Jackson estate.[39]

Michael Jackson's autopsy was performed on June 26 by Dr. Christopher Rogers, the LACCO's chief of forensic medicine, and his supervisor, Dr. Lakshmanan Sathyavagiswaran, the chief medical examiner-coroner. Los Angeles police detective Scott Smith of the robbery and homicide division witnessed the procedure. The coroner's report was not publicly released until after the toxicology results were in, which, in that very busy office, generally takes up to eight weeks. But due to the unprecedented media interest, a preliminary finding was released on August 27 by the chief of operations/chief public information officer, Craig

Harvey. The most significant element was the change in the manner of death—from accident/natural to homicide.

Michael Joseph Jackson, also known as Coroner Case #2009-04415, died of acute propofol intoxication, with a contributing condition of benzodiazepine effect. The two primary drugs that killed him were propofol and the sedative lorazepam. But there were other pharmaceuticals detected in his system: the sedatives midazolam and diazepam, the anesthetic lidocaine, and ephedrine, which is both a decongestant and an appetite suppressant. According to the official fifty-one-page autopsy report, Jackson was five-foot-nine and weighed one hundred and thirty-six pounds. There was much evidence of the attempted resuscitation, from the endotracheal tube in his mouth, to the intravascular catheters in his left jugular vein and both femoral vessels, to the intra-aortic balloon pump in his femoral artery. Numerous puncture wounds covered both arms, his left knee, and his right ankle. His chest showed several irregular abrasions and bruises, and his sternum was fractured at the third rib. His right fourth and fifth ribs were also fractured, as were his left third, fourth, and fifth ribs.[40] This is not an uncommon phenomenon; broken ribs are often the result of vigorous chest compressions.[41]

Jackson's body was riddled with scars and discolorations. Behind both ears were ¾-inch scars that were likely from a facelift or eyebrow lift. Scars at the base of his nose measuring ⅗ of an inch at the right nostril and ⅝ of an inch at the left were from rhinoplasty, and there was a bandage on the tip of his nose.[42] There is no way to determine from the autopsy report how many rhinoplasties Jackson underwent, although he admitted to two. He also said he had a dimple surgically created in his chin, but the LA coroner's report makes no mention of an artificial chin cleft. Photos show a cleft, however, so perhaps it was performed through his lower lip and didn't leave a mark that would show up in the X-rays that were taken at autopsy. It was suggested by some people that Jackson had had cheek implants, which would leave no visible scarring because the incisions are made either inside the lower eyelid or inside the mouth where the gums and lips meet. The coroner would have seen such a scar, and a foreign implant would have been noted in the X-rays, so this is something that can be dispelled.[43]

His left arm showed a ¼-inch scar on the front elbow and a ⅛-inch one to the right; these were likely sites for IVs. A 2-inch surgical scar was in the right lower quadrant of his abdomen, but since elsewhere in the report it was indicated that his appendix was intact, I can only surmise that this was from an inguinal, or groin, hernia procedure. A 2⅛-inch semicircular scar was on his right knee, with smaller scars near it; the origin of these marks is unexplained in the report. Also of unknown origin were an irregular scar of about 4 inches in diameter on his right shoulder; two downsloping scars on each side of the base of his neck, measuring 3 inches on the right and 3¼ inches on the left; a ⅞-inch scar at the base of his right thumb, and a ⅛-inch scar on the left. A ⅝-inch scar was near his navel in the area where the gallbladder might be removed by laparoscopic surgery, but since Jackson's gallbladder was intact, the source of that scar is unknown. Michael suffered from vitiligo on his chest, abdomen, face, and arms, which left splotches lacking in pigment; he always claimed that he used the topical skin bleaches to even out his coloration, not to try to appear more Caucasian than African American. But on the front of his right shin is a 5-by-2½-inch area of hyperpigmentation, a markedly darker splotch that he apparently didn't try to lighten. Jackson also had tattoos for cosmetic purposes: darkening both eyebrows and around both eyelids, pink inking on his lips, and dark inking on his scalp to cover the baldness from the 1984 mishap during the Pepsi commercial when his hair caught on fire. Typically he wore a wig or hair weave to even out his hairstyle, and the autopsy report indicated that beneath his hairpiece was a scalp with mottled pigmentation. The rest of the external examination showed the irises of his eyes to be brown with no jaundice and his teeth to be in good repair.

The post-mortem report noted that Jackson had not suffered from heart disease, a fact borne out by his internal examination and subsequent microscopic slide analyses made of sections of his right and left ventricles (cardiac chambers), interventricular septum (the area between the chambers), and aorta (the body's largest artery). All these sections showed normal myocardial structure without significant inflammation or atherosclerosis. His heart, brain, liver, gallbladder, kidneys, pancreas, spleen, bladder, and thyroid gland were all unremarkable. Jackson's genitalia were those of an adult male; his penis appeared to be uncircumcised. There was a tiny polyp of the sigmoid, or pelvic, colon, and a similarly small mass near his adrenal gland, but neither would have presented a health risk or pain. His gastrointestinal system showed no portions of tablets or capsules. The biggest physical indicator of a traumatic event was from Michael's congested lungs, each of which weighed about a thousand grams—about three times too heavy for someone of his size and weight.[44] Such wet, congested lungs would signify a lingering death, perhaps one that took hours.

A more diligent doctor sitting at Jackson's bedside would have noticed Jackson's downward spiral. His breathing would have become stertorous, or given to a raspy, gurgling sound that is an unmistakable indicator of respiratory failure. As his lungs collected fluid, his heartbeats would have become irregular, until there was a total depression of all his organs. I can't imagine how any competent physician could not have seen this warning sign, particularly a doctor whose main practice was cardiology. This oversight describes why investigators have taken issue with Murray's standard of care in his treatment of Michael Jackson and it raises other questions. For example, if Jackson, in a comalike state due to the propofol, was wearing an oxygen mask and the oxygen tank was hissing, would Murray have been able to visually or audibly discern any evidence of respiratory distress? And did paramedics or anyone else rushing into the room witness Jackson wearing an oxygen mask?

The information gathered at Jackson's autopsy was buoyed by experts whom the medical examiner asked for specific consultations. The Los

Angeles office has a high degree of excellence, but there's no question Jackson's postmortem got extra attention. Perhaps the LA crew knew that with such a high-profile case, the eyes of the world would be upon them, and so they wanted to make sure every *i* was dotted and every *t* was crossed.[45] Major portions of Jackson's lungs were embedded in paraffin and processed at the University of Southern California's Keck School of Medicine and its Pulmonary Pathology Department, where the deputized consultant, Russell P. Sherwin, MD, studied the tissue and reported that there was "a depletion of structural and functional reserves of the lung"—a diminished amount of lung capacity. He noted that this was a result of "widespread respiratory bronchiolitis and chronic lung inflammation, in association with fibrocollagenous scars and organizing/recanalizing thromboemboli of small arteries." In plain English, the doctor was identifying that Jackson had had a previous lung injury that left scar tissue and caused small blood clots in the vessels, but the passageways had begun healing and reopening. Sherwin summed up with the following: "The above lung injury with reserve loss is not considered to be a direct or contributing cause of death. However, such an individual would be especially susceptible to adverse health effects."[46] Jackson's pre-existing bronchial condition might have been asthma. We know he had oxygen on hand for some reason, and his records should have clarified what treatment, if any, he got for the condition and whether he ever used a nebulizer, or sprayer, with a bronchodilating drug like albuterol. Murray should have had access to those records and known about any such condition before medicating his patient.[47]

There was a consult by Cathy Law, DDS, a forensic odontologist, who studied post-mortem X-rays of Jackson's teeth and skull to see if there might be a dental component to his cause of death. This study was done to eliminate the presence of abscesses or infectious processes that might have caused Jackson pain, and thereby caused him to take drugs to alleviate it. But while the dentist found routine restorative work and root canal therapy, there was no gross pathology seen on the X-rays. A neuropathology consult with deputy medical examiner John Andrews, MD, analyzed specimens of Jackson's brain and cranial dura mater, the fibrous membrane layer beneath the skull. His findings showed mild cerebral vascular congestion—minimal engorgement of the blood vessels—and mild diffuse brain swelling, which is characteristic of the changes that occur as someone is dying from a drug overdose. Neither of these findings would indicate chronic disease or any painful condition. Andrews noted mild basal ganglia mineralization, or calcium deposits, on the midbrain, but he deemed it "an incidental finding unrelated to the cause or matter of death." Donald Boger, MD, conducted a whole-body radiographic, or X-ray, survey but could find no chronic trauma or natural disease. He noted some mild degenerative osteoarthritis of Jackson's fingers and lower thoracic spine, and mild calcified arterial atherosclerosis of both legs—but nothing abnormal for an individual of fifty years. Parakrama T. Chandrasoma, MD, the chief of surgical pathology of the USC Keck School, reviewed the slides and overall autopsy information, and confirmed the findings of Drs. Rogers and Sathyavagiswaran.

The most critical consultation came from anesthesiologist Selma Calmes, MD. Her two-page report reflected upon the coroner's investigators' findings of propofol vials at Jackson's residence and explained what the drug is and how it should have been used. Propofol, she wrote, has been in clinical practice since 1989 as an intravenous anesthetic for surgeries and in ICUs for sedating critically ill patients, but it is used only when the patient is intubated and ventilated to ensure his or her airway remains open. She also noted that the drug is sometimes used in pain clinic settings to relieve acute migraine headaches. It produces a rapid onset of sedation and/or unconsciousness and is usually predictable when administered properly. In its favor is a quick return of consciousness with little post-anesthesia "hangover" effect, which can include nausea and vomiting. She cautioned that respiratory and cardiovascular depression can occur if the introduction of the propofol is too large a dose administered into a vein in too short a time. The potential for trouble is accentuated if other sedatives, such as benzodiazepines, are present. Calmes wrote that she had never before heard of propofol being used for insomnia relief, and stated: "The only reports of its use in homes are cases of fatal abuse (first reported in 1992), suicide, murder, and accident."[48]

Propofol is painful upon injection, so lidocaine is usually given, either before the injection or mixed into the amount to be infused. In a surgical setting, a trained anesthesiologist should be present for the entire procedure, and equipment should be used for continuous monitoring, including a pulse oximeter, which clips onto the patient's finger to measure oxygen saturation in arterial blood, an electrocardiogram (EKG), which uses electrodes and a computer screen to measure the patient's heartbeat, an automatically inflatable blood pressure cuff, and a carbon dioxide (CO_2) monitor to maintain the patient's proper blood pH balance and to document that the patient is breathing and has an open airway. If the pulse oximeter or CO_2 levels fall, alarms will sound, indicating that prompt attention is needed. Oxygen should be near the patient at all times, and skilled nurses should be onsite during the patient's recovery.[49] In Jackson's case, Calmes wanted to know whether trained medical personnel were present to continuously observe the patient while the drug was administered. She wrote that there was no evidence of a pump for control of an IV infusion and that no monitors were found at the scene, although a blood pressure cuff and pulse oximeter were recovered from a closet in the next room. The oxygen tank was near the bed, but the bag with a clear plastic mask was not attached. Multiple vials of propofol were found, with small amounts of the drug—all of which should have been discarded within six hours after opening to avoid bacterial growth. Calmes's report addressed the question of whether Jackson might have been able to administer the propofol to himself via the IV catheter in his left leg, below the knee. This would have been a nearly impossible feat, due to the positioning of the items in relation to where he laid in the bed, as well as to the short-acting quality of the drug, which would have required a continuous infusion to have been effective. In reviewing the toxicology report, Calmes found that the levels of propofol Jackson had in his system were similar to those found during general anesthesia for major intra–abdominal surgery—but such a patient would be hospitalized, intubated, and ventilated. She also found that the lorazepam, "a long-acting benzodiazepine, was present at a pharmacologically significant level and would have accentuated the respiratory and cardiovascular depression from [the] propofol."[50]

When I first heard that propofol was a factor in Jackson's death, I was puzzled: Why would that be administered to him at the hospital if he'd been dead on arrival? Then I heard it was used in his home, with his cardiologist in attendance, and it still didn't make sense. Was he so wealthy and famous that he had a surgical arena in his home because he didn't want to have some procedure done at a medical center? And, if so, what was the procedure, and how many doctors and nurses were present? I knew that propofol was considered a very decent anesthesia for surgeries or colonoscopies or endoscopies, but I had never heard of it used privately—and never as a sleep aid. As you can imagine, information was released in bits and pieces, so it was several days before it became clear that Dr. Murray was a one-man show and that the propofol had reportedly been used as a sleeping aid for Jackson. To say I was stunned doesn't go nearly far enough. More revelations about Murray would soon follow.

Following Jackson's LACCO autopsy, the coroner issued a statement that the official cause and manner of death would not be announced until the toxicology results and various lab tests were completed. This did not sit well with the Jackson family, who believed Michael died as a result of foul play and wanted proof. They hired an independent California forensic pathologist who conducted a second autopsy. I perform second autopsies regularly, and when done immediately after the primary postmortem, they're useful as a way to learn the basics of what happened without having to wait for police officials to reveal everything. A private toxicology lab is likely to expedite testing and attain results more quickly than an overburdened county lab, where the work is generally done in the order in which it's logged in and the results can take weeks to come back. Second postmortems are sometimes ordered if family members distrust the authorities or want a medical examiner to talk with them at greater length or in more detail than a county official might be willing to do. A second procedure will take fresh samples of tissues and fluids and send them to a private lab, perhaps fast-tracking them for a quicker response. But there's always going to be some kind of wait. A death investigation is a methodical process of creating a chain of evidence that can be admissible in court. It isn't complete until all the reports from the labs, police, witnesses, other doctors, and so forth, can be reviewed as a whole. I told numerous media outlets that I doubted very much that Michael Jackson's second physical examination would reveal anything that would be of news to the Los Angeles coroner. The answers to Michael's death would be in the reports, not from fresh looks at the body. The Jacksons were told the same thing by Vidal Herrera, the owner of 1-800-AUTOPSY, a private firm that purportedly declined a Jackson family request to conduct a third postmortem on Michael.[51]

At the hospital after Jackson was pronounced dead, coroner's investigator Elissa Fleak collected his bodily fluids for toxicology testing. She, or someone, labeled the tubes with the name "Trauma, Gershwin." I suppose that was for security reasons, although I think the legendary last name of two earlier musical geniuses, George and Ira, would itself attract undue attention. Still, she amassed a complete collection of femoral and heart blood, blood taken at the hospital, syringes, needles, IV bags, and urine from the jar in Jackson's house. When the performer was wheeled into that trauma room, the doctors could tell he'd had a catastrophic drug reaction and were fastidious about getting plenty of blood samples for the lab to assess. The next day, during autopsy, more samples were taken for testing, including urine, vitreous (the liquid of an eyeball), liver, and stomach contents. Weeks later, the results came back. When Michael died, there was propofol in his heart blood, hospital blood, femoral blood, vitreous, liver, gastric contents, urine, and the urine from the jar in his house. Lidocaine was also present in all the locations, except for the vitreous. Diazepam (Valium) was found only in the heart and hospital bloods, and nordiazepam, its metabolite, or what it breaks down into, was present only in the heart blood. Lorazepam (Ativan) was in both the heart and femoral blood, and minute amounts of midazolam (Versed) were in the heart blood, urine, and jar of urine. Ephedrine was present only in the two urine samples. Propofol and lidocaine were detected in white fluid from a 10cc syringe barrel with plunger, and propofol, lidocaine, and flumazenil (Anexate) were in a white-tinged syringe and yellow IV tubing. No drugs were detected in clear fluid from another IV tube, attached to an IV bag, or in clear fluid in another IV bag.[52]

In the days that followed, it was imperative that LAPD detectives lock Conrad Murray into a statement. He was interviewed by Orlando Martinez of the robbery and homicide division. Murray told the detective that he had been a practicing cardiologist for about twenty years, in Las Vegas, Nevada, and Houston, Texas. Murray claimed he had administered several drugs to the pop star in the early morning hours of June 25 and had found that Jackson had stopped breathing around eleven in the morning. Murray said he tried CPR, then accompanied the singer to UCLA Medical Center. Martinez called Dr. Sathyavagiswaran of the Los Angeles County Coroner's Office and learned that Jackson's toxicology report indicated lethal levels of propofol in his blood. Murray purportedly told Martinez that he had administered 25 mg of propofol, along with lidocaine, to Jackson in those hours after midnight.[53]

Houston police narcotics division officer E. Glen Chance served search warrants to Murray's medical office and self-storage facility, and on July 22, he seized the following items: assorted documents from Acres Home Heart and Vascular Institute, United Health Care, and Twelve Oaks Medical Center; documents about incomplete charts and a suspension notice from Doctors Hospital; notices from the Internal Revenue Service; a Texas Department of Public Safety controlled-substance registration; a document from the public records office of the Texas comptroller; an amalgamated account receivable notice; seven CDs; a medical board certificate that expired August 31, 2008; an important contact list; correspondence to a Stacey Howe; and two Samsung computer hard drives.[54] It would seem that authorities wanted to study Murray's billing records, medication orders, transport receipts, and computerized files to determine whether the doctor should be charged with the criminal offense of manslaughter.[55]

Martinez filed a similar affidavit for a California search warrant and was looking for all the different names Michael Jackson had used for procuring a variety of drugs, including propofol. He also established what Murray had said to the paramedics who tried to revive Jackson—that he had given the singer lorazepam before he stopped breathing. Murray repeated this to UCLA's Dr. Richelle Cooper, saying he had given Michael two separate 2 mg doses during the night. When Cooper pronounced Jackson dead, Murray refused to sign the death certificate, then, amid the flurry of activity, Murray slipped away from the authorities and went incommunicado for more than a day. Detectives and coroners' reps who went to the mansion and investigated the area around the bed Jackson had been in when his health faded discovered pill bottles written to Jackson from Murray and other doctors. Murray got a defense attorney and met with police on June 27. Murray had worked for Jackson for only the past six weeks, he said, and the main thing he was treating him for was insomnia. He also said he feared that if he didn't give Jackson what the singer demanded, the whole concert tour would fall apart.

The affidavit stated that each night Murray would administer an IV drip containing 50 mg of propofol, diluted with lidocaine. Murray worried that his patient might be forming an addiction to propofol and tried to wean Jackson from the drug. On June 22, three days before Jackson's death, the doctor gave Michael 25 mg of propofol, with lorazepam and midazolam, but Jackson still couldn't sleep. The next night, Murray gave only lorazepam and midazolam, withholding the propofol, and Jackson slept fine. Just after 1:30 a.m. on the twenty-fifth, he tried to induce Jackson's sleep once again without the propofol, giving him instead a 10 mg tab of diazepam. A half-hour later, when Jackson still couldn't sleep, Murray injected him with 2 mg of diluted lorazepam, pushing it slowly into his IV. Another hour later, with Jackson still awake, Murray slowly introduced 2 mg of midazolam into the IV, and when 5 a.m. hit and Michael was still awake, Murray slowly pushed into the IV another 2 mg of diluted midazolam. Murray assured the officers that he stayed at Jackson's bedside continuously and had a pulse oximeter connected to Jackson's finger. Still awake at 10:40 a.m., Michael insisted upon and got his propofol—25 mg, diluted with lidocaine, via the IV drip. At last, Michael slept soundly, with Murray monitoring him.

Approximately ten minutes later, Murray said he went to the bathroom to relieve himself and was out of the room for "two minutes maximum." When he came back, he found his patient was no longer breathing. Murray began attempting CPR on the star and also administered 2 mg of flumazenil to counter the effects of the sedative, while using his personal cell phone to call Jackson's assistant, Michael Amir Williams Muhammad. He told Muhammad there was an emergency and to send security guards. When no one responded, Murray stopped his compressions on Jackson, ran into the hall, then downstairs to the kitchen. He shouted at the cook, Kai Chase, to send Michael's older son, Prince Michael, upstairs. Prince and security man Alberto Alvarez rushed to Murray and saw the doctor performing one-handed chest compressions on Jackson. Alvarez used the doctor's cell phone to call for help.[56] Amazingly, when the 911 operator asked the location of the person being given CPR, Alvarez said, "He's on the bed." The operator responded, "Let's get him on the floor," and Alvarez repeated the comment to Murray.[57] Any cardiologist, or anyone trained in basic lifesaving techniques, should know that chest compressions must be done with two hands, with the patient on a hard surface. A bed is not an acceptable spot, no matter how firm the mattress might seem.[58] With Jackson now on the floor, Murray continued conducting CPR until the ambulance arrived, then he joined paramedics in the vehicle that went to the hospital. Murray claimed he helped notify family members, then left the hospital for a while because he did not know that he "was needed." He also said he left his medical bag at Jackson's home.[59]

Some of these matters would be expanded on during a preliminary court hearing in January 2011. Alvarez testified that while waiting for paramedics to arrive, Murray ordered him to collect medical vials and an IV bag with a milk-like substance and put them into other bags. Murray, who seemed flustered and was sweating profusely, at one point reportedly asked the gathering of staffers if anyone in the room knew CPR, which caused the observers to look at each other in shock. Alvarez described Murray as being hunched over Jackson and administering mouth-to-mouth resuscitation. On his second breath, Murray allegedly came up and said in his Caribbean patois, "You know, this is the first time I give mouth to mouth, but I have to do it, he's my friend." Alvarez also told the court that he did not see any heart or blood pressure monitors in the room, but he watched as Murray affixed the pulse oximeter to Jackson's finger right before paramedics entered the home.[60] Had the doctor been properly monitoring his patient with the alarm device from the beginning, the emergency might not have occurred. And, as we would learn from other testimony, Murray kept no written account of his prescription history with Michael, which is unconscionable.[61]

Martinez's Los Angeles affidavit stated that Murray was not the first doctor to use propofol on Jackson. The singer was very familiar with the white emulsion and referred to it as "milk" and described the lidocaine that took away its sting as "anti-burn." Murray complained that although he repeatedly asked Jackson what other physicians were treating him and for what maladies and with what medications, Jackson would not disclose the information. He would only say that Drs. Arnold Klein and Allan Metzger, both in the Los Angeles area, gave him the drug, but it was not working. Murray also cited two unnamed doctors in Germany who had furnished the musician with propofol, according to the affidavit. Once, when Murray asked about injection marks on Jackson's hands and feet, Jackson said that "Dr. Cherilyn Lee" had been giving him a "cocktail" to help him, something Murray interpreted to mean a propofol mix, the document stated. Murray also recounted that in the spring of 2009, Jackson had called him in Las Vegas and asked him to phone an anesthesiologist, Dr. David Adams, to get Michael a propofol prescription. Murray did so and met with Jackson and Adams at the office of an unnamed cosmetologist, where Jackson got the sedation he desired. Around this time, Jackson requested Murray to be his personal physician for the upcoming London concerts.

Martinez did some investigation, which seemed to contradict Murray's account of his actions immediately prior to discovering that Jackson was not breathing. According to the affidavit, Murray's initial statement to police was that he found Jackson unresponsive at just before 11 a.m. and began vigorous CPR, but his cell phone records showed the doctor to be on the phone with three separate numbers on calls that added up to forty-seven minutes between 11:18 a.m. and 12:05 p.m. Murray had not mentioned these calls to police.

Using a search warrant, Martinez obtained Murray's doctor bag and supplies. Recovered were "multiple bottles/vials" of propofol, lidocaine, lorazepam, midazolam, and flumazenil—none of the items were labeled with the name of any patient. Martinez also contacted Drug Enforcement Administration (DEA) agent Spencer Shelton, who searched their computerized database with records of all prescription narcotic traffic. Shelton explained that each propofol bottle has a lot number on its label, making it easy to link back to whatever surgical center or hospital requested it. But Conrad Murray's name, medical license number, and/or DEA number were not listed as having ordered, purchased, or received any propofol. Yet, at Jackson's house, Martinez witnessed approximately eight bottles of the drug, along with numerous other prescription drugs.

A Jackson family attorney contacted Martinez and gave him the name of Beverly Hills anesthesiologist Dr. Randy Rosen, who had been treating the superstar. The family also offered pseudonyms that Michael's various doctors had used to write him prescriptions: Jack London, Mike Jackson, Mick Jackson, Frank Tyson, and Mic Jackson; they also said Michael had used the names of his family members and staffers. Martinez's affidavit described how he began interviewing individuals and determined that Jackson's closest colleagues were Michael Amir Williams Muhammad; Jimmy Nicholas; Blanca Nicholas; Roselyn Muhammad; Jackson's oldest child, Prince; Faheem Muhammad; and Kai Chase. Detectives received a phone call from an anonymous female who said she knew of aliases Jackson would use when he visited Dr. Klein: Omar Arnold, Fernand Diaz, Peter Madonie, and Josephine Baker—and cops recovered a prescription at Jackson's residence written by Klein to Omar Arnold, as detailed in Martinez's report.

LACCO investigator Fleak subpoenaed Jackson's medical records from Dr. Murray; Dr. Klein; Dr. Metzger; Dr. Adams; Las Vegas dentist Mark Tadrissi, whom Adams said stored his files; and Dr. Slavit, who had examined Jackson for the concert promoter, AEG. Murray's office supplied records dating back to January 2006 and stated that Jackson used the aliases of Omar Arnold, Paul Farance, and Paul Farnce. Klein's office furnished records dating back to March 2009, which he indicated were for Jackson's "recent treatment," and stated the performer used the alias of Omar Arnold. Tadrissi's records indicated Jackson used the aliases of Bryan Singleton and Mike Jackson, and that, per Jackson's request, Dr. Adams had administered a "conscious sedation" during a dental treatment. At the time Martinez wrote his warrant, Dr. Metzger had not yet complied. Detectives also interviewed Grace Rwaramba, the Jackson children's nanny. She stated that Dr. Klein was Michael's current physician, and that the last doctor to treat him was Beverly Hills cosmetic surgeon Larry Koplin.[62] Rwaramba, who had worked for Jackson for more than a decade, told a reporter that she witnessed his hopeless addiction to medicine. "I had to pump his stomach many times. He always mixed so much of it," the Rwandan native said, adding: "There was one period that it was so bad that I didn't let the children see him." Rwaramba said she reached out to Jackson's mother and a sister to stage a drug intervention, but Michael found out and accused her of betrayal. "He didn't want to listen."[63]

Also subpoenaed was Cherilyn Lee, who was not a doctor—as was written on one of the recovered prescription labels—but a Los Angeles nurse practitioner, who was able to prescribe medications and obtain controlled substances. She first met Jackson in January 2009 when she was asked to come to his home when his three children—Prince, Paris, and Blanket—suffered from colds. She conducted routine exams on the children, then spoke with Jackson, who complained of having low energy. She returned the next day to perform a full blood screening on him, the results of which showed a normal-to-low blood sugar level. She put the star on a diet of healthy food and protein drinks. On Easter Sunday, a distressed Jackson told her he couldn't sleep and mentioned needing propofol. Lee had never heard of the drug, but Jackson assured her his doctor—whom he didn't name—told him it was safe. Lee researched the drug and told him propofol was for anesthesiologists' surgical use and therefore unsafe for him, but Jackson insisted he wanted it. According to Lee, Jackson stated that he would pay her or any doctor she could find "whatever they wanted" to prescribe it. She refused and never saw Jackson again. On Father's Day, Lee received a call from

Faheem Muhammad, Jackson's personal bodyguard, saying that the performer was sick. Lee could hear Michael in the background saying, "One side of my body is hot and the other side is cold." Muhammad asked what that could mean, and Lee guessed that it could be a central nervous system problem and that Jackson should be taken at once to a hospital.[64]

Human hair grows about a half-inch per month, so a forensic toxicologist will ask that hairs be extracted from the body—living or dead—and brought to the lab for "segmental analysis." When drugs travel through a person's bloodstream and dissipate, their last stops are the urine and then the hair. Traces of the drug or drugs will molecularly bond with each hair strand, and, as the hair grows, the person's drug history becomes a measureable timeline. The scientist carefully lays out the hair, dissects it into horizontal half-inch pieces, and tests for the full spectrum of drugs—legal and illegal. A six-inch hair would offer a year's worth of drug ingestion data. The longer the hair, the more information, with the most recently taken drugs closer to the root. For example, "Person X's" six-inch hair would produce a computer printout of her past year of drug ingestion, chronicling the specific drugs, when they were taken, and for roughly how long.[65] This kind of testing is also valuable in heavy-metal poisoning cases, as I detailed in my 2003 book *Mortal Evidence*, about the 1991 murder of Robert Curley of Wilkes-Barre, Pennsylvania, by his wife Joann. At a 1996 preliminary hearing, I testified for the prosecution and described the segmental drug analysis of the victim's hair to prove that Mrs. Curley used thallium, a drug once used as rat poison, to kill her husband. In reaction to my testimony, Joann Curley confessed to the crime, the purpose of which was collecting life insurance money. She was convicted of third-degree homicide and was sentenced to state prison for a period of ten to twenty years. In 2009, for the third time, she was denied parole.[66]

At the request of LACCO's chief of laboratories Joseph Muto, on August 6, 2009, senior criminalist Jaime Lintemoot, chief of operations Craig Harvey, and forensic technician II Jose Hernandez visited Forest

Lawn Memorial Park in Glendale, where Michael Jackson's remains were stored and waiting to be buried. The group's mission was to collect hair samples from the decedent for potential toxicology tests.[67] At this point, Michael Jackson had had two official autopsies and had also been handled by the mortuary staff, but it was hoped that there would remain a few strands of hair that could be collected. The coroner's office wanted the samples to do its own hair analysis, if need be, on behalf of the district attorney's office, and to provide any opposing counsel with the material to conduct their own tests. There had been reports that Michael's father, Joe Jackson, and his attorney, Brian Oxman, were eager to find out just how long Michael had been taking drugs.[68]

Forest Lawn personnel escorted the coroner's team to a cubicle while Jackson's body was brought over from another part of the building. The group was soon joined by Forest Lawn personnel Darryl Drabing and Scott Drolet, and by La Toya Jackson and her male companion. Lying in a yellow casket with blue lining, Jackson was wrapped in white towels and sheets with only his hands and the top of his head exposed. A wig with long dark hair covered the top of Jackson's head. Beneath the wig, Michael's hair was dark and curly and about one and a half inches long at the temples. With her gloved hands, Lintemoot plucked hairs, as Hernandez took photos. Michael's short strands would provide only about three months' worth of answers. The propofol that killed him wouldn't have had a chance to get into his hair, but if he had been taking that drug for weeks or more, it would be measurable—and all the benzodiazepines and other pharmaceuticals he'd been taking would show up, too. Harvey, who had been observing the hair collection, lifted Jackson's hand to take a palm print to be able to exclude him from any other palm prints the criminalists might have encountered. The hair samples were packaged in aluminum and paper bindles, or packets, and, along with the print, were brought back to the Forensic Center.[69]

As the legal case developed, LAPD detectives learned from the chief medical examiner that preliminary toxicology results pointed to propofol as the cause of death. Investigators compared the statements the responding paramedics and UCLA trauma staffers had given to Murray's statements on June 25 at the residence and hospital. All agreed that Murray had disclosed that he had given lorazepam to Jackson in the hours before his death, but the UCLA team had also been told that Murray had given flumazenil to counter the lorazepam's effects. He had not mentioned propofol.

Believing that Jackson's death was a felony, authorities wanted to learn whether Murray had assistance with his procurement of propofol. They felt they needed more than just medical records of his doctors but also sign-in sheets; appointment calendars; correspondence; and billing, transportation, and delivery receipts from the doctors and pharmacies. Investigators were also troubled by Klein's refusal to give over his older records for Jackson. They needed to figure out whether the death was due to the actions of a single doctor in a single night or to grossly negligent treatment of several doctors over an extended period of time. Also complicating matters was the fact that Murray's and Adams's offices and residences were out of state and were not covered by the Los Angeles court's jurisdiction. Citing the California Business and Professions and Health and Safety Codes, physicians are required to maintain adequate and accurate records of their patients from the moment they first see the patient, and hospitals must keep medical records for seven years after a patient's discharge. Most doctors will adhere to the seven-year rule, although some will keep the files indefinitely. It's also common for doctors to keep patient files at their homes or in their vehicles, and Jackson investigators wanted to make certain they got all the files, from wherever they were stored. Until they had the full panoply of documents to create a medical timeline, they couldn't determine each doctor's knowledge of Jackson's drug-seeking behavior.

Because Detective Martinez considered that, at some time in the future, a defense attorney might suggest that the search warrant materials were subject to doctor-patient privilege, he wrote in his affidavit that, due to the nature of the crime, the privilege would not apply. Still, he requested that a special master be assigned to accompany the searching officers and to ensure the protection of the documents, the cost of which should be incurred by the court. There was also a provision for minimizing inconvenience to any of the medical offices that needed to remain open while having their computer files and digital devices searched—a search that might include making a copy of any pertinent information onsite, if possible, while avoiding copying files of other patients. At the same time, there was the recognition that hidden, encrypted, or deleted data might be encountered, which can happen in high-profile cases, and might require special handling. A crafty individual might use misleading file names and extensions or passwords to conceal information, including "booby traps" that could destroy or alter data if a qualified forensic computer expert were not employed for the search. The affidavit demonstrated the breadth and sophistication of modern technology and its nexus with law enforcement needs. Finally, the affidavit asked the court to seal the contents of the results of the searches until presented in a courtroom to preserve the integrity of the investigation.[70]

While the search warrant returns remained a secret, the filing of the affidavits became big news, and I appeared on numerous television and radio programs to discuss various aspects of the case. The TV morning news programs and evening crime shows asked for my opinion in the form of quick sound bites one can only offer on panels that are typically overbooked. But on radio, specifically in Los Angeles, I was afforded longer interviews for richer discussion. I spoke on various AM stations, including KABC, where my co-author, Dawna Kaufmann, has hosted talk shows; KFI; KFWB News; and KLAA, where Kathryn Milofsky and Jackson family attorney Brian Oxman co-hosted a program called *Insight*. The media requests continue whenever something new hits the press about this tragic case. After Jackson's autopsy report and toxicology results were made public, and Dr. Conrad Murray was arrested for manslaughter, the question became whether Murray should have been charged with a higher degree of homicide. I believed then, and still do now, that he should have been. Murray didn't set out to kill Michael Jackson, but as a licensed professional, his actions were reckless and negligent, and he should have recognized the potential for calamity.

Oxman, who had handled La Toya Jackson's divorce and other family business, became the representative for Joe Jackson, Michael's father. When no one but Conrad Murray was charged in Michael's death, Oxman and his client publicly stated that Murray was a fall guy for other doctors who seemed to have gotten a free pass from the prosecution.[71] But that didn't stop Joe Jackson from filing a $500,000,000 wrongful death lawsuit against Murray for the loss of Michael. Joe chose the half-billion-dollar figure because, as he rather nonsensically told a reporter, "The more you go, the less you get . . . so I went high."[72]

In early July 2009, Jackson's will was entered into probate, putting his $500 million estate into a family trust and naming his seventy-nine-year-old mother Katherine and his three children as beneficiaries. Joe Jackson was excluded. Katherine was appointed the children's guardian, with singer and actress Diana Ross named successor, should anything happen to Mrs. Jackson. Jackson's lawyer, John Branca, and family friend John McClain, a music executive, were named co-executors of the estate.[73]

In the days after Michael's death, plans focused on his memorial. It would require a Los Angeles venue large enough to accommodate thousands of attendees, many of whom wanted to speak or perform his music, and it would have to be televised to the world. The ceremony was held on July 7 at the Staples Center, with some 19,500 people inside the facility and an estimated one billion watching on television. In the United States, Nielsen ratings reported that 31.1 million people watched, making it the third-most watched memorial ever—President

Ronald Reagan's 2004 burial had 35.1 million viewers, while Princess Diana's 1997 funeral drew an audience of 33.1 million Americans. Jackson was in a 14-karat-gold-plated, gold and black closed casket, placed center stage. Stevie Wonder, Mariah Carey, Lionel Richie, John Mayer, Jennifer Hudson, and Jermaine Jackson performed songs in tribute, with Usher singing "Gone Too Soon." Michael's brothers, wearing matching black suits and one sparkling glove each, told sweet stories about him. Queen Latifah read a poem by Maya Angelou, and Motown Records founder Berry Gordy, Smokey Robinson, and Brooke Shields gave eulogies. Sitting in the front row—their faces no longer covered—were Michael's beautiful children, Prince, Paris, and Blanket. The Reverend Al Sharpton received a standing ovation when he looked at the trio and said: "Wasn't nothing strange about your daddy. It was strange what your daddy had to deal with. But he dealt with it anyway."[74] The most touching moment occurred when young Paris, surrounded by her aunts and uncles, cried as she told the crowd, "Ever since I was born, Daddy has been the best father you could ever imagine.... I just wanted to say I love him . . . so much."[75]

Michael's body was returned to cold storage at Forest Lawn Memorial Park in Hollywood, while his family decided what to do next. Jackson's will made no provision for where he wanted to be buried. Jermaine Jackson wanted his brother's final resting place to be at the Neverland Ranch, but Katherine Jackson and others argued that the location was ruined for Michael after the 2005 trial and would be the last place he'd want to spend eternity. There was also a security concern; it would be much wiser to have the body placed in a controlled environment.[76] The decision was made to bury Michael at the Glendale branch of Forest Lawn, which, a few miles from the Hollywood park, offered a mausoleum that could be closed to the public. Among the deceased at the Glendale park are actors Errol Flynn, Clark Gable, and Humphrey Bogart. On September 3, in a private memorial attended by family members, coworkers from the *This Is It* project, Debbie Rowe, Lisa Marie

Presley, Elizabeth Taylor, and sundry celebrity friends, Jackson was entombed in a marble crypt. As with the televised memorial, Pastor Lucius Smith led the prayer service. This statement was issued after the ceremony: "The Jackson Family wishes to once again thank all of Michael's fans around the world for their generous outpouring of support during this terribly difficult time. Their expressions of love for Michael and his music have sustained the Jackson Family."[77]

Michael's children now live at the Hayvenhurst Estate with Katherine and other family members, and for the first time ever, Prince and Paris are in public school. All are reportedly thriving.[78]

Dr. Murray was arrested and, on February 8, 2010, charged with involuntary manslaughter in the death of Michael Jackson. The criminal complaint states that Murray "did unlawfully, and without malice, kill Michael Joseph Jackson . . . in the commission of an unlawful act, not a felony; and in the commission of a lawful act which might have produced death, in an unlawful manner, and without due caution and circumspection." Bail for Murray, who has pleaded innocent, was set at $75,000, and his passport was surrendered.

At the end of July 2010, after a long investigation into all the California doctors who treated Jackson, officials announced no charges would be filed against any of the physicians, except for Dr. Murray. One unspecified doctor was reported to the state medical board for using an alias to prescribe drugs to the star.[79] I believe the reason the other doctors caught a break has to do with a little-known 2006 change to the state's Intractable Pain Law. The revised law addresses the use of controlled drugs for pain treatment and allows that a patient who is dependent on pharmaceuticals for pain prevention cannot be considered an addict. This dangerous loophole must have been greeted with cheers by Hollywood's substance abusers and the doctors who treat them. It's the reason several criminal counts were dropped by prosecutors in the state action against Anna Nicole Smith's doctors and lawyer for overmedicating her. In Jackson's case, while his other doctors won't be prosecuted, their prescribing histories for Michael may be brought up in court by Murray's defense.

I predict that a hotly debated issue at Murray's trial will be whether Jackson might have been able to self-administer the propofol, perhaps while the doctor was distracted on his cell phone. The defense might argue that the dosage Murray admitted giving his patient—25 mg— would have afforded only three to five minutes of sleep, and if Jackson awoke and didn't see Murray, he might have poured the propofol into his IV bag or even gulped it down. But I doubt that will be enough to win an acquittal since the many empty vials recovered would suggest the dosage was far greater than what Murray claimed. This angle also doesn't factor in the inanity of mixing the propofol with the other prescription medications, the lack of proper monitoring, the sloppy record keeping, and the inconsistencies of Murray's stories to so many people who will be testifying against him.[80]

The California Medical Board filed documents with the court, stating that Murray showed "utter disregard for the care and well-being of the persons entrusted to his care," and in January 2011, Los Angeles Superior Court judge Michael Pastor suspended the doctor's medical license in California and required him to notify the medical boards in Nevada and Texas, in case they also wished to also revoke his ability to practice medicine.[81]

On January 25, 2011, Dr. Murray appeared before Judge Pastor and pleaded not guilty to the charge of involuntary manslaughter in the death of Michael Jackson. Murray declared himself "an innocent man" and requested a speedy trial—which Pastor set for March 28. If convicted, he faces a maximum of four years in prison. Murray's attorney, Ed Chernoff, told the court that the doctor's income-earning ability has been diminished by the loss of his California medical license and the possible loss of his licenses in Nevada and Texas. Chernoff stated that seeing patients was keeping Murray alive, both financially and emotionally, and that they both prayed the medical boards in the other two states would wait for the outcome of the California trial before taking any action against him.[82] Days later, Pastor announced that he would allow the trial to be televised.[83]

And on February 3, ABC correspondent Ashleigh Banfield revealed on *Good Morning America* the identity of one of the people with whom Dr. Murray was on the phone when Michael Jackson went into cardiac arrest. Banfield traveled to Houston to interview a young woman named Sade Anding, who was a waitress in a steakhouse that Murray frequented. Anding confided that the doctor wooed her, telling her she was beautiful and lavishing her with about $2,000 in gifts, including cash tips, a dress, spa treatment, and a cell phone. She said he told her he was divorced with two children, not the seven she later learned he actually had. When Banfield informed her that Murray was still married, Anding was thunderstruck. He had boasted of his new job with Jackson, Anding said, and even offered to fly her to California so she could meet the performer and his children. She didn't know the specifics of his medical treatment of Jackson and had never heard about Jackson's problems with sleep or drugs. When Murray called her on June 25, 2009, they had not spoken in a while, and Anding said she began to chatter away before she realized Murray was not listening. She said it seemed as if he had put his cell phone in a pocket because the sound became diffused and she heard coughing and mumbling on his end. She hung up, called him back, and texted him, but he didn't reply. She sensed something was wrong, and soon after she learned of Michael's death. "I felt like it was my fault," Anding cried. "I really felt like if he wouldn't have called me, maybe all that stuff that happened wouldn't have happened." Days later, detectives contacted her, and when she called to tell Murray, he expressed dismay that they were involving her. From then on, he refused to discuss anything out of fear that their phones were tapped. Although Anding told Banfield that she didn't think he was capable of harming Michael, she is prepared to testify in court about their relationship and the critical phone call. Banfield wrapped up her report with news that one of Murray's attorneys said it might be a year before his trial gets under way.[84]

Michael Jackson topped *Forbes* magazine's list of Top-Earning Dead Celebrities for 2010, with $275 million, more than any musicians dead or alive, and more than the top-earning bands, U2 and AC/DC, combined. Other honorees include Elvis Presley at $60 million; J. R. R. Tolkien (author of the *Lord of the Rings* trilogy), $50 million; Charles Schulz (creator of the *Peanuts* comics empire), $33 million; John Lennon, $17 million; Stieg Larsson (author of the Millennium trilogy, featuring the popular character Lisbeth Salander), $15 million; Theodor Geisel (Dr. Seuss), $11 million; Albert Einstein, $10 million; George Steinbrenner (former owner of the New York Yankees), $8 million; and songwriter Richard Rodgers, $7 million. The results for 2011 will be disclosed in the fall of 2011, after this book has gone to press.[85]

Michael Jackson will continue to be missed by his fans and will make money for his estate from beyond the grave. A documentary combining footage from his rehearsals for the London shows, with behind-the-scenes interviews of those who worked with Jackson, was released theatrically, in both 3-D and IMAX versions, on October 28, 2009. Sony/Columbia's production of *Michael's Jackson's This Is It* quickly became the highest-grossing music concert film, earning more than $261 million worldwide, to date.[86] And there's been a steady stream of music to delight Jackson fans, from new albums to remastered classics. Michael Jackson may have "Gone Too Soon," but certainly, his legacy lives on.[87]

AFTERWORD

Ⅰf there is one thing we hope you have gleaned from the cases in this book, it is that forensic science is not black and white. It's not even lovely shades of gray. Forensic science is a glorious rainbow of color and light, with new hues constantly being discovered on a regular basis.

In the olden days, death investigators depended on fingerprints and blood typing to target and identify suspects in criminal matters. That was certainly a step up from eyewitness accounts, the predominant method of the past, which were wholly unreliable in practicality. The need for more precise training evolved, expanding to ballistic testing; dental and X-ray comparisons; shoe and tire impressions; handwriting analysis; and microscopic inspection of trace evidence, such as hair and fibers. Eventually our federal government established a computerized database to store samples of various forensic tools, allowing a detective in any community to tap into the national bank of research to quickly seek matches or information.

The mid-1980s saw a significant upgrade for crime solvers with DNA testing, in which the nucleic acid in cellular structures is analyzed to reveal genetic patterns from human semen, vaginal secretions, sweat, tears, saliva, and skin cells. By obtaining a noninvasive swab from the inside of a person's mouth, authorities can compare it to a known sample from a crime scene or a victim to find similar markers. Now a mainstay for law enforcement, DNA testing has its own national database where an expert, using a few keystrokes, can scroll through millions of contributors to find a match, and new donations are constantly added to the system. When presented in court, and explained to a jury by a scientist with impeccable expertise, the results can link, or clear, a suspect in a homicide or major criminal matter. DNA can be used to send a defendant to death row, or to spring a wrongfully convicted inmate from prison.

The chapters we've recounted here have featured an array of exciting new features of forensic science:

- Cell phone technology, using global-positioning signals from cell towers to track the location and activities of an individual, as well as separate GPS tracking of vehicles;
- The ability to collect and separate distinct elements in air samples, including odors from food, gasoline, dirty diapers, dead animals, and human body decomposition;
- Inspection of a hair shaft for signs of possible post-mortem banding and toxicological segmental hair analysis to determine a time frame for a person's drug ingestion;
- Analysis of the qualities of duct tape and plastic bags to determine when and where they were manufactured and sold, and comparing them to items a suspect or associate might have had access to;
- Re-creations of crime scenes to assess the plausibility of a suspect's story, or to show the position of a body when discovered;
- The effect of nature on a corpse, from temperature and meteorological conditions, to insect and animal activity, and soil and foliage samples;
- Computer forensics, from determining the author and the time and date of an e-mail or text message, to copying and preserving the content of a hard drive, without falling into a booby trap that will delete critical data, and;

- The importance of tissue sample reviews using a high-powered microscope to find or eliminate pre-existing disease as a contributing factor to someone's demise, among other techniques.

As this book goes to press, two of our seven cases have not yet been tried before a jury, but you now have a strong indication of what kind of evidence and testimony will be presented in court.

Beyond these cases, other crime-fighting systems are in use or on their way to gaining acceptance in our nation's courtrooms, including facial-recognition and age-advancement software, satellite imagery that can reproduce photos as small as a license plate number, marking gunpowder and explosive materials, linguistic analysis to measure patterns of speech or writing, voice and sound enhancement, identifying DNA in animals and plants, and calibrating the pressure one uses when applying pen to paper to determine authorship of a questioned document. These methods nicely complement the legwork that detectives do in gathering human intelligence and the intriguing behavioral analysis from the FBI's esteemed profiling unit. And there is always the dramatic push-pull between police, prosecutors, defense attorneys, and the media.

These cutting-edge breakthroughs are valuable not only to law enforcement but also to film and television scriptwriters, who turn the thrilling actual scenarios into fantastic cinematic projects. Whether it's real life, or reel life, there's a never-ending quest to use science as a means of telling stories.

We can only imagine what the future of forensic science will be. But it's gratifying to know that there will be a steady stream of interested students scaling new heights of intelligence and excellence.

Cyril H. Wecht, MD, JD
and Dawna Kaufmann

NOTES

CHAPTER ONE: CASEY ANTHONY

1. Orange County Sheriff's Office (OCSO) Investigative Report, Case Number 07-074777, in re: Defendant Casey Marie Anthony.

2. ABC timeline, http://abcnews.go.com/TheLaw/story?id=6448060.

3. Amy L. Edwards, Sarah Lundy, and Bianca Prieto, "Caylee Wasn't a Child Who Was Wanted," *Orlando Sentinel*, August 26, 2008.

4. ABC timeline.

5. http://www.youtube.com/watch?v_sd5PIeefc4g.

6. OCSO report.

7. http://transcripts.cnn.com/TRANSCRIPTS/11105/26/ng.01 .html.

8. OCSO report.

9. http://transcripts.cnn.com/TRANSCRIPTS/0809/16/ng.01 .html.

10. http://transcripts.cnn.com/TRANSCRIPTS/0809/11/ng.01 .html.

11. OCSO report.

12. ABC timeline.

13. OCSO report.

14. http://spoiledmom-mommyconfessions.blogspot.com/2011/07/ casey-anthony-photos-of-release-from.html.

15. OCSO report.

16. Notes of Cyril H. Wecht, MD, JD, re: Caylee Marie Anthony.

17. OCSO report.

18. Wecht notes.

19. OCSO report.

20. Wecht notes.

21. OCSO report.

22. http://www.foxnews.com/story/0,2933,411622,00.html.

23. ABC timeline.

24. http://www.leonardpadilla.net/LeonardPadilla.com/Leonard_Padilla.html.

25. http://transcripts.cnn.com/TRANSCRIPTS/0902/10/ng.01.html.

26. http://transcripts.cnn.com/TRANSCRIPTS/0809/17/ng.01.html.

27. OCSO report.

28. http://transcripts.cnn.com/TRANSCRIPTS/0808/28/ng.01.html.

29. Wecht notes.

30. http://www.trutv.com/library/crime/criminal_mind/forensics/texas_equusearch/1.html.

31. http://www.wftv.com/pdf/22918226/detail.html.

32. http://transcripts.cnn.com/TRANSCRIPTS/1009/21/ijvm.01.html.

33. http://transcripts.cnn.com/TRANSCRIPTS/1107/12/ijvm.01.html.

34. http://transcripts.cnn.com/TRANSCRIPTS/1009/21/ijvm.01.html.

35. http://crime.about.com/b/2008/09/16/casey-anthony-back-in-jail-again.htm.

36. OCSO report.

37. Wecht notes.

38. http://www.orlandosentinel.com/news/local/caylee-anthony/-orl-caylee-anthony-autopsy-2,0,3085300.htmlpage.

39. http://transcripts.cnn.com/TRANSCRIPTS/0809/05/ng.01.html.

40. OCSO report.

41. http://transcripts.cnn.com/TRANSCRIPTS/0809/16/ng.01 .html.

42. Wecht notes.

43. "Casey Calls 911 When Protestors Get Violent," WFTV 9 News, September 17, 2008.

44. OCSO report.

45. WFTV 9 News, September 17, 2008.

46. http://transcripts.cnn.com/TRANSCRIPTS/0809/19/ng.01 .html.

47. Wecht notes.

48. http://www.orlandosentinel.com/news/local/caylee-anthony/orl -casey-anthony-jose-baez-050309,0,1572952,full.story.

49. http://www.baezlawfirm.com/.

50. http://www.wesh.com/news/17030505/detail.html.

51. ABC timeline.

52. Wecht notes.

53. ABC timeline.

54. http://www.msnbc.msn.com/id/28159418/ns/dateline_nbc-crime _reports.

55. http://transcripts.cnn.com/TRANSCRIPTS/0810/21/ng.01 .html.

56. Wecht notes.

57. ABC timeline.

58. http://www.examiner.com/crime-in-national/casey-anthony -jailhouse-video-remains-sealed.

59. Robin Roberts, *Good Morning America*, ABC, January 13, 2009.

60. "Deputy Submits Letter of Resignation in Casey Case," WFTV, May 18, 2009.

61. Wecht notes.

62. ABC timeline.

63. http://transcripts.cnn.com/TRANSCRIPTS/0812/18/ng.01 .html.

64. Wecht notes.

65. Nikki Pierce, WDBO 1540 AM, January 5, 2009.

66. http://www.associatedcontent.com/article/1335656/casey _anthonys_one_tree_hill_internet.html.

67. Drew Petrimoulx, WDBO 1540 AM, January 21, 2009.

68. http://transcripts.cnn.com/TRANSCRIPTS/0901/21/ng.01 .html.

69. http://transcripts.cnn.com/TRANSCRIPTS/0901/23/ng.01 .html.

70. http://transcripts.cnn.com/TRANSCRIPTS/0904/22/ng.01 .html.

71. http://transcripts.cnn.com/TRANSCRIPTS/0902/10/ng.01 .html.

72. Wecht notes.

73. http://transcripts.cnn.com/TRANSCRIPTS/0903/17/ng.01 .html.

74. Wecht notes.

75. Sheelah Kohlhaktar, "The News Merchant," *Atlantic*, September 2010.

76. http://www.thedailybeast.com/blogs-and-stories/2011-05-24/ casey-anthony-bombshell-opening-arguments-accidents-incest-and-cover -ups/full/.

77. Wecht notes.

78. Kathi Belich, WFTV 9 News, March 10, 2009.

79. Wecht notes.

80. http://transcripts.cnn.com/TRANSCRIPTS/0904/01/ng.01 .html.

81. "Heart Sticker Convinces Childhood Pal That Mom Killed Caylee," *National Enquirer*, January 27, 2009.

82. ABC timeline.

83. Wecht notes.

84. Office of the Medical Examiner, District Nine, Orlando, Florida, Autopsy Report of Caylee Marie Anthony.

85. http://media.myfoxorlando.com/photogalleries/050109anthony casefbilabreports/1/lg/5581-5604_Page_16.htm.

86. Caylee Anthony autopsy report.

87. Bob Burns and Dawna Kaufmann, "No Escape for Caylee Mom," *Globe*, April 12, 2010.

88. http://transcripts.cnn.com/TRANSCRIPTS/0910/02/ng.01.html.

89. http://www.orlandosentinel.com/news/local/breakingnews/os-casey-anthony-documents-20091106,0,4673834.story.

90. Wecht notes.

91. http://www.wtsp.com/news/article/198927/19/Roy-Kronk-testifies-about-finding-Caylee-Anthonys-remains.

92. http://www.youtube.com/watch?v=was98d49IHo.

93. http://blogs.orlandosentinel.com/entertainment_tv_tvblog/?p=13737.

94. http://www.wftv.com/pdf/20533041/detail.html.

95. http://www.docstoc.com/docs/60652589/Casey-Anthony-Curtis-Jackson-letter-to-state-attorneys-office.

96. Mike Celizic, "Do Letters Show Casey Anthony Is [a] Psychopath?" MSNBC, April 15, 2010.

97. http://www.wesh.com/news/21661209/detail.html.

98. http://transcripts.cnn.com/TRANSCRIPTS/1009/14/ijvm.01.html.

99. *Geraldo at Large*, Fox News, September 4, 2010.

100. http://www.cfnews13.com/casey-anthony-timeline.

101. http://www.ninthcircuit.org/judges/chief_judge/index.shtml.

102. *Geraldo at Large*, Fox News, June 25, 2011.

103. Beth Karas, *In Session*, TruTV, June 22, 2011.

104. CFNews13 timeline.

105. http://www.deathpenaltyinfo.org/executions.

106. http://www.dc.state.fl.us/oth/deathrow/women.html#executed.

107. Wecht notes.

108. *48 Hours*, CBS News, April 16, 2011.

109. Wecht notes.

110. http://www.cfnews13.com/article/news/2011/may/247698/.

111. Jamal Thalhi, "Pinellas Jurors Who Heard Casey Anthony Trial Can Finally Come Home," *St. Petersburg Times*, July 6, 2011.

112. http://www.cfnews13.com/static/articles/images/news2011/casey-anthony-order-barring-release-of-juror-names.pdf.

113. http://www.wftv.com/caseyanthony/index.html.

114. Wecht notes.

115. http://www.thedailybeast.com/blogs-and-stories/2011-05-24/casey-anthony-bombshell-opening-arguments-accidents-incest-and-cover-ups/full/.

116. Wecht notes.

117. http://www.foxnews.com/on-air/on-the-record/transcript/casey-anthony039s-family-divided-and-torn-apart-caylee039s-murder-case.

118. http://transcripts.cnn.com/TRANSCRIPTS/1105/06/ijvm.01.html.

119. http://www.cfnews13.com/article/news/2011/may/251421/.

120. Wecht notes.

121. CFNews 13 witness list.

122. Wecht notes.

123. CFNews 13 witness list.

124. Wecht notes.

125. CFNews 13 witness list.

126. Wecht notes.

127. CFNews 13 witness list.

128. Lizette Alvarez, "Software Designer Reports Error in Anthony Trial, *New York Times*, July 18, 2011.

129. CFNews 13 witness list.

130. Wecht notes.

131. CFNews 13 witness list.

132. Wecht notes.

133. CFNews 13 witness list.

134. Wecht notes.

135. CFNews 13 witness list.

136. CFNews 13 timeline.

137. CFNews 13 witness list.

138. Wecht notes.

139. CFNews 13 witness list.

140. Wecht notes.

141. CFNews 13 witness list.

142. Wecht notes.

143. CFNews 13 witness list.

144. http://www.thedailybeast.com/articles/2011/07/01/casey -anthony-trial-why-casey-didn-t-testify.html.

145. Wecht notes.

146. CFNews 13 witness list.

147. Wecht notes.

148. CFNews 13 witness list.

149. Wecht notes.

150. CFNews 13 timeline.

151. CFNews 13 witness list.

152. Jacqui Goddard, "She Sacrificed Her Child," *Daily Mail* (London), July 4, 2011.

153. Dennis Murphy, *Dateline*, NBC, July 8, 2011.

154. Ashley Hayes, "Jurors to Begin Second Day of Deliberation in Casey Anthony Trial," CNN, July 5, 2011.

155. *Daily Mail*, July 4, 2011.

156. Wecht notes.

157. *Dateline,* July 8, 2011.

158. Wecht notes.

159. John Stevens, "The Verdict," *Daily Mail* (London), July 7, 2011.

160. Wecht notes.

161. CFNews 13 timeline.

162. http://blogs.orlandosentinel.com/entertainment_tv_tvblog/2011/ 07/casey-anthony-you-wont-see-her-in-playboy-hugh-hefner-says.html.

163. Wecht notes.

164. Bob Burns and Dawna Kaufmann, "Missing Evidence That Could Have Nailed Casey: Five Crucial Clues Jury Never Heard," *Globe*, August 1, 2011.

165. Wecht notes.

CHAPTER TWO: COLONEL PHILIP MICHAEL SHUE

1. Notes of Cyril H. Wecht, MD, JD, re: Colonel Philip Michael Shue.

2. http://www.colonelphilipmichaelshue.com.

3. Wecht notes.

4. http://www.cbs.com/primetime/48_hours/video/?pid=QOpO6Q Oc MrwuiYpi5fCs0MA0LhSepBWs&vs=homepage&play=true, March 26, 2009.

5. http://www.colonelphilipmichaelshue.com.

6. *48 Hours Mystery*, CBS News, March 26, 2009.

7. Dawna Kaufmann's interview with Tracy Shue.

8. http://www.kendallcountyattorney.com/Courts.html#peace.

9. Wecht notes.

10. Tracy Shue interview.

11. Wecht notes.

12. Bexar County Medical Examiner's Office: Autopsy Report of Colonel Philip Shue.

13. Tracy Shue interview.

14. Wecht notes.

15. Tracy Shue interview.

16. Bexar County Autopsy Report.

17. Wecht notes.

18. *48 Hours Mystery*.

19. Tracy Shue interview.

20. Wecht notes.

21. *48 Hours Mystery*.

22. http://www.colonelphilipmichaelshue.com.

23. Wecht notes.

24. Zeke MacCormack, "Duct-Taped Driver's Death Was Suicide," *San Antonio Express-News*, August 1, 2003.

25. Wecht notes.

26. Tracy Shue interview.

27. Wecht notes.

28. *48 Hours Mystery*.

29. Tracy Shue interview.

30. Wecht notes.

31. Dawna Kaufmann's interview with George Brown.

32. Tracy Shue interview.

33. *48 Hours Mystery*.

34. Wecht notes.

35. Anita Porterfield, "Philip Shue Case Reads Like a Novel," *Now Public*, June 5, 2008.

36. Tracy Shue interview.

37. Wecht notes.

38. *Now Public*.

39. Wecht notes.

40. Tracy Shue interview.

41. http://www.colonelphilipmichaelshue.com.

42. Tracy Shue interview.

43. Wecht notes.

44. Tracy Shue interview.

45. Wecht notes.

46. George Brown interview.

47. Tracy Shue interview.

48. Wecht notes.

49. Tracy Shue interview.

50. Wecht notes.

51. http://www.truthinjustice.org/sonia4.htm.

52. http://newscenter.nmsu.edu/expert/expert/?action=show&id=787.

53. http://www.truthinjustice.org/sonia4.htm.

54. Wecht notes.

55. *48 Hours Mystery*, October 24, 2009.

56. Wecht notes.

57. http://www.time.com/time/magazine/article/0,9171,969924,00.html.

58. Wecht notes.

CHAPTER THREE: BRIAN JONES

1. Geoffrey Giuliano, *Paint It Black: The Murder of Brian Jones* (London, England: Virgin Books, 1994), pp. 3–32.

2. Notes of Cyril H. Wecht, MD, JD, re: Brian Jones.

3. *The T.A.M.I. Show, Collector's Edition* DVD, Shout Factory LLC and Dick Clark Productions, 2009.

4. Giuliano, *Paint It Black*, pp. 32–37.

5. Ibid., pp. 45–58.

6. http://thehistoryofrockmusic.com/1960-s/police-raid-keith-richards-redlands-home-in-sussex-for-drugs/.

7. Giuliano, *Paint It Black*, pp. 60–65.

8. Ibid., pp. 66–84.

9. Ibid., pp. 85–106.

10. Ibid., pp. 107–151.

11. A. E. Hotchner, *Blown Away: The Rolling Stones and the Death of the Sixties* (New York: Simon & Schuster, 1990), pp. 298–301.

12. Wecht notes.

13. http://thehistoryofrockmusic.com/1960-s/brian-jones-of-the-rolling-stones-dies-in-his-swimming-pool/.

14. http://www.dailymail.co.uk/tvshowbiz/article-1090439/Has-riddle-Rolling-Stone-Brian-Joness-death-solved-last.html.

15. http://www.dailymail.co.uk/femail/article-1353783/Being-Brian-Joness-son-greatest-thing-happened-me.html.

16. Wecht notes.

17. http://www.youtube.com/user/Stoned65#p/a/40FE45A345ADC709/1/r8qaKtAu8HA.

18. http://samcutler.tumblr.com/page/2.

19. Wecht notes.

20. East Grinstead, Sussex County, Autopsy Report: Lewis Brian Jones.

21. Wecht notes.

22. East Grinstead Autopsy Report.

23. East Grinstead, Sussex County, Death Certificate: Lewis Brian Jones.

24. Wecht notes.

25. http://www.bbc.co.uk/pressoffice/pressreleases/stories/2006/11 _november/06/brian_jones.shtml.

26. Wecht notes.

27. Dawna Kaufmann's correspondence with the Sussex police department and the New Scotland Yard.

28. Giuliano, *Paint It Black*, p. 177.

29. Ibid., pp. 156–57.

30. http://www.youtube.com/watch?v=CCxRVYZJYfY&feature =related.

31. http://home.comcast.net/~cindystones1/.

32. http://www.rollingstones.com.

33. http://answers.yahoo.com/question/index?qid=20060616224728 AAuYbY6.

34. Giuliano, *Paint It Black*, p. 182.

CHAPTER FOUR: DREW PETERSON

1. Notes of Cyril H. Wecht, MD, JD, re: Kathleen Savio.

2. *Drew Peterson: Under Suspicion*, Biography Channel, December 20, 2010.

3. http://www.acandyrose.com/stacy_peterson_names.htm.

4. *Good Morning America*, ABC, October 5, 2009.

5. *Drew Peterson: Under Suspicion*.

6. Stacy Dittrich, *Murder behind the Badge* (Amherst, NY: Prometheus Books, 2010), pp. 21–30.

7. http://www.acandyrose.com/kathleen_savio_11142002letter.htm.

8. *Drew Peterson: Under Suspicion*.

9. *On the Record with Greta Van Susteren*, Fox News, November 12, 2007.

10. *Drew Peterson: Under Suspicion*.

11. http://www.patoneil.com/.

12. Wecht notes.

13. Official Will County Autopsy Report, by Bryan Mitchell, MD: Kathleen Savio.

14. Wecht notes.

15. Mitchell autopsy report.

16. Wecht notes.

17. Mitchell autopsy report.

18. Wecht notes.

19. Mitchell autopsy report.

20. Wecht notes.

21. Dittrich, *Murder behind the Badge*.

22. *Drew Peterson: Under Suspicion*.

23. *On the Record with Greta Van Susteren*, Fox News, December 11, 2007.

24. Dittrich, *Murder behind the Badge*.

25. http://www.acandyrose.com/stacy_peterson_recap3b.htm.

26. Dittrich, *Murder behind the Badge*.

27. http://www.acandyrose.com/stacy_peterson_recap3.htm.

28. *Geraldo at Large*, Fox News, November 11, 2007.

29. Wecht notes.

30. Dittrich, *Murder behind the Badge*.

31. Wecht notes.

32. Dittrich, *Murder behind the Badge*.

33. http://www.youtube.com/watch?v=ItwjPb23HIg.

34. http://today.msnbc.msn.com/id/22821093/ns/today-today_people/.

35. Erika Slife, "Drew Peterson's Former Fiancée, Christina Raines, Says It Was All a Publicity Stunt Cooked up by His Lawyer," *Chicago Tribune*, February 3, 2009.

36. RadarOnline, "Drew Peterson's Mug Shot; New Details of His Arrest," May 8, 2009.

37. *Drew Peterson: Under Suspicion*.

38. http://petersonstory.wordpress.com/2009/04/30/stacy-petersons-sister-confronts-drew-peterson-on-radio-show/.

39. http://www.willcosheriff.com/pages/cimis/details.asp?lname=peterson&CIMIS_NUMBER=20090003825#Visit.

40. "Peterson's Attorney Says He'll Watch Mock Trial," *Chicago Defender*, May 21, 2009.

41. Wecht notes.

42. Dan Rozek, "Court Limits Use of Hearsay Evidence in Drew Peterson Case," *Chicago Sun-Times*, July 26, 2011.

43. Stacy St. Clair, "Judge: Pathologist Can Testify in Peterson Murder Trial," *Chicago Tribune*, July 2, 2010.

44. http://www.crimefilenews.com/2009/06/watch-mock-trial-of-drew-peterson.html.

45. St. Clair, *Chicago Tribune*, July 2, 2010.

46. Wecht notes.

47. http://www.nypost.com/p/news/local/manhattan/victim_kin_slam_slay_injustice_7hzPALHXxTvrpXyf0g6bSM.

48. http://www.willcosheriff.com/pages/cimis/details.asp?lname=peterson&CIMIS_NUMBER=20090003825#Visit.

49. Wecht notes.

50. Brian Feldt, "Lifetime Movie Being Shot in Los Angeles," *Bolingbrook Patch*, July 12, 2011.

51. David Lohr, "Drew Peterson: Casey Anthony Verdict Pleasing," *Huffington Post*, July 11, 2011.

52. Stacy St. Clair and Steve Schmadeke, "Court Won't Allow Hearsay in Peterson Case," *Chicago Tribune*, July 27, 2011.

53. Wecht notes.

CHAPTER FIVE: GABRIELLE MIRANDA BECHEN

1. Notes of Cyril H. Wecht, MD, JD, re: Gabrielle Miranda Bechen.

2. Dawna Kaufmann's interviews with Mimi and Chris Bechen.

3. Michael A. Fuoco and Moustafa Ayad, "Ingrained in Rural Life, ATVs Used in Search for Girl, 12," *Pittsburgh Post-Gazette*, June 16, 2006.

4. Bechen interviews.

5. Wecht notes.

6. Bechen interviews.

7. Nate Guidry and Brian David, "Farmhand Charged in Death of Missing Girl," *Pittsburgh Post-Gazette*, June 19, 2006.

8. Richard Robbins, "Jury Could Sentence Greene Farmhand to Death," *Pittsburgh Tribune-Review*, May 9, 2008.

9. Milan Simonich, with Cindi Lash and Jim McKinnon, "Suspect in Girl's Death Lived on Fringes of Society," *Pittsburgh Post-Gazette*, June 20, 2006.

10. Dawna Kaufmann's interview with Jennifer Martin.

11. "Suspect in Girl's Death."

12. Martin interview.

13. Bechen interviews.

14. Milan Simonich, "Court Hears Confession in Killing of Girl, 12," *Pittsburgh Post-Gazette*, June 22, 2006.

15. Wecht notes.

16. Greene County Official Autopsy Report: Gabrielle Miranda Bechen.

17. Wecht notes.

18. Richard Robbins, "Parents of Slain Girl Hear Taped Confession," *Pittsburgh Tribune-Review*, May 6, 2008.

19. WTAE-TV4, "Farmhand Sentenced to Death," September 17, 2008.

20. Wecht notes.

21. Michael A. Fuoco, "Greene County Murder Trial Begins," *Pittsburgh Post-Gazette*, May 2, 2008.

22. Bechen interviews.

23. Wecht notes.

24. Cara Host, "DNA Ineffective in Murder Trial," *Observer-Reporter*, May 3, 2008.

25. Bechen interviews.

26. Richard Robbins, "Jury Could Sentence Greene Farmhand to Death," *Pittsburgh Post-Gazette*, May 9, 3008.

27. Martin interview.

28. Michael A. Fuoco, "Jury to Weigh Life or Death for Farmhand," *Pittsburgh Post-Gazette*, May 9, 2008.

29. http://www.cor.state.pa.us/portal/server.pt/community/death_penalty/17351.

30. Michael A. Fuoco, "Jury Takes One Hour to Decide Death for Farmhand," *Pittsburgh Post-Gazette*, May 10, 2008.

31. Wecht notes.

32. www.missingkids.com.

33. Bechen interviews.

34. http://gabrielle-bechen.memory-of.com/About.aspx.

CHAPTER SIX: CAROL ANNE GOTBAUM

1. Notes of Cyril H. Wecht, MD, JD, re: Carol Anne Gotbaum.

2. Cyril H. Wecht, MD, JD; Henry C. Lee, PhD; D. P. Van Blaricom; and Mel Tucker, *Investigation and Prevention of Officer-Involved Deaths* (Boca Raton, FL: CRC Press, 2011).

3. Wedding announcement, *New York Times*, June 11, 1995.

4. Wecht notes.

5. Wedding announcement.

6. Jen Chung, "Gotbaum's Family Grieves as Debate over Her Death Continues," *Gothamist*, October 6, 2007.

7. Dennis Wagner, Jahna Berry, and Casey Newton, "Police Recount Airport Death: Family Seeks Withheld Organs for 2nd Autopsy," *Arizona Republic*, October 4, 2007.

8. "Autopsy: Gotbaum Died from Asphyxia by Hanging," Associated Press, November 10, 2007.

9. Wagner, Berry, and Newton, "Police Recount Airport Death."

10. Leonardo Blair and Eric Lenkowitz, "Betsy In-Law Death: Dies under Arrest," *New York Post*, September 30, 2007.

11. Scott Wong, "Phoenix Settles for $250,000 in Gotbaum Airport Death," *Arizona Republic*, October 20, 2009.

12. http://www.youtube.com/watch?v=F-qdwltFgvU&feature=related.

13. Editorial, "They Played with Fire," *New York Daily News*, October 9, 2007.

14. http://www.youtube.com/watch?v=F-qdwltFgvU&feature=related.

15. Wecht notes.

16. Casey Newton and Jahna Berry with Connie Cone Sexton, "Security Cameras Seem to Support Police Account," *Arizona Republic*, October 4, 2007.

17. http://www.youtube.com/watch?v=IFkeg8BUj0c&feature=related.

18. Wecht notes.

19. Wong, "Phoenix Settles for $250,000 in Gotbaum Airport Death."

20. Wagner, Berry, and Newton, "Police Recount Airport Death."

21. Jahna Berry and Casey Newton, "A Desperate Call to Sky Harbor: Husband Warned Airport of Wife's Problems," *Arizona Republic*, October 5, 2007.

22. Maricopa County Autopsy Report: Carol Anne Gotbaum.

23. Wecht notes.

24. Wagner, Berry, and Newton, "Police Recount Airport Death."

25. Wecht notes.

26. Nikki Renner, "Handcuffed Man Dies in Police Custody," *Arizona Republic*, October 4, 2007.

27. Erin Einhorn, "Tears & Rage at Carol Anne Gotbaum's Funeral," *New York Daily News*, October 8, 2007.

28. Wecht notes.

29. David Schwartz and Cynthia R. Fagen, "Gotbaum Kin Sue Phoenix," *New York Post*, March 27, 2008.

30. Jahna Berry, "Gotbaum Family Files $8 Million Claim," *Arizona Republic*, March 26, 2008.

31. Wecht notes.

32. "Gotbaum Case against Phoenix Moved to Federal Court," *Arizona Republic*, May 21, 2008.

33. Andy Geller and David Schwartz, "Gotbaum Cops Off the Hook," *New York Post*, August 22, 2008.

34. Wong, "Phoenix Settles for $250,000 in Gotbaum Airport Death."

35. Wecht notes.

CHAPTER SEVEN: MICHAEL JACKSON

1. http://www.youtube.com/watch?v=c00CwFA5JNE.

2. Notes of Cyril H. Wecht, MD, JD, re: Michael Jackson.

3. Los Angeles County Coroner's Investigative Narrative.

4. Cyril H. Wecht, MD, JD, and Dawna Kaufmann, *A Question of Murder* (Amherst, NY: Prometheus Books), pp. 158–59.

5. http://www.rollingstone.com/music/artists/michael-jackson/news/artists/8865/65326/153001.

6. http://en.wikipedia.org/wiki/Michael_Jackson.

7. "Jackson's Mother Says Son Was Addicted to Surgery," Associated Press, November 8, 2010.

8. http://en.wikipedia.org/wiki/Michael_Jackson.

9. http://www.youtube.com/watch?v=d8Fop7eMjjE.

10. Wecht notes.

11. http://en.wikipedia.org/wiki/Michael_Jackson.

12. Dawna Kaufmann notes, re: Michael Jackson.

13. http://en.wikipedia.org/wiki/Michael_Jackson.

14. Kaufmann notes.

15. http://en.wikipedia.org/wiki/Michael_Jackson.

16. http://www.youtube.com/watch?v=I9E5YlbF7tw.

17. http://www.youtube.com/watch?v=Hw0nnYWvk4I&feature=related.

18. http://en.wikipedia.org/wiki/Michael_Jackson.

19. Lachlan Cartwright, "Jacko Kids to Learn Mom ID," *New York Post*, August 6, 2009.

20. http://en.wikipedia.org/wiki/Michael_Jackson.

21. http://www.youtube.com/watch?v=H2Gup1IFbto&NR=1.

22. http://en.wikipedia.org/wiki/Michael_Jackson.

23. Wecht notes.

24. http://en.wikipedia.org/wiki/Michael_Jackson.

25. Interview with ITV interviewer Martin Bashir, February 3, 2003.

26. http://www.youtube.com/watch?v=wQwY4ll1Kfc&feature=related.

27. http://news.bbc.co.uk/2/hi/entertainment/4216621.stm.

28. http://www.mtv.com/news/articles/1507174/two-jackson-jurors-regret-verdict.jhtml.

29. http://www.msnbc.msn.com/id/35259896/ns/dateline_nbc-news makers/.

30. http://en.wikipedia.org/wiki/Michael_Jackson.

31. Wecht notes.

32. Isabel Vincent and James Fanelli with Meredith Pierce and Tori Richards, "Doctor, 'I Feel Good!'" *New York Post*, August 2, 2009.

33. David Jones, "The Tawdry Truth about the Playboy 'Quack' Accused of Killing Jacko," *Daily Mail* (London), February 4, 2010.

34. *New York Post*, August 2, 2009.

35. *Daily Mail* (London), February 4, 2010.

36. *New York Post*, August 2, 2009.

37. TMZ.com, May 15, 2010.

38. Harriet Ryan with Kimi Yoshino and Ashley Powers, "Michael Jackson's Doctor Was Much Admired but Financially Strapped," *Los Angeles Times*, February 8, 2010.

39. TMZ.com, November 17, 2009.

40. Los Angeles County Coroner's Office (LACCO): Michael Jackson Autopsy Report.

41. Wecht notes.

42. LACCO Autopsy Report.

43. Wecht notes.

44. LACCO Autopsy Report.

45. Wecht notes.

46. LACCO Autopsy Report.

47. Wecht notes.

48. LACCO Autopsy Report.

49. Wecht notes.

50. LACCO Autopsy Report.

51. Wecht notes.

52. LACCO Autopsy Report.

53. Search Warrant Affidavit: Los Angeles, California.

54. Search Warrant Affidavit: Houston, Texas.

55. Wecht notes.

56. Search Warrant Affidavit: Los Angeles.

57. http://www.youtube.com/watch?v=iuzVZgfExjU.

58. Wecht notes.

59. Search Warrant Affidavit: Los Angeles.

60. Harriet Ryan and Victoria Kim, "Michael Jackson Hearing: Security

Guard Says Dr. Murray Told Him to Grab Evidence before Calling 911," *Los Angeles Times*, January 5, 2011.

61. Wecht notes.

62. Search Warrant Affidavit: Los Angeles.

63. Nancy Dillon, Larry McShane, and Rich Schapiro, "Nanny Says Michael Jackson's Stomach Had to Be Pumped," *New York Daily News*, June 27, 2009.

64. Search Warrant Affidavit: Los Angeles.

65. Wecht notes.

66. Cyril H. Wecht and Greg Saitz with Mark Curriden, *Mortal Evidence* (Amherst, NY: Prometheus Books), pp. 271–93.

67. Los Angeles County Coroner's Office (LACCO) Criminalist Report.

68. Wecht notes.

69. LACCO Criminalist Report.

70. Search Warrant Affidavit: Los Angeles.

71. Wecht notes.

72. TMZ.com, October 23, 2010.

73. "DEA Joins Michael Jackson Death Probe," Associated Press, July 2, 2009.

74. http://en.wikipedia.org/wiki/Michael_Jackson.

75. http://www.youtube.com/watch?v=ceU7shpTsxQ&feature=fvst.

76. Kaufmann notes.

77. Emily Sheridan, "Elizabeth Taylor Joins Jackson's Children for Final Goodbye at Funeral Service," *Daily Mail* (London), September 4, 2009.

78. Kaufmann notes.

79. TMZ.com, February 8, 2010.

80. Wecht notes.

81. TMZ.com, February 8, 2010.

82. Harriet Ryan, "Michael Jackson's Doctor, Conrad Murray, Pleads Not Guilty," *Los Angeles Times*, January 25, 2011.

83. TMZ.com, February 7, 2011.

84. http://abcnews.go.com/GMA/video/woman-says-she-heard -michael-jackson-die-on-phone-12830500.

85. http://www.forbes.com/2010/10/21/michael-jackson-elvis-presley -tolkien-business-entertainment-dead-celebs-10-intro.html.

86. http://www.boxofficemojo.com/movies/?id=michaeljacksonthisis it.htm.

87. Wecht notes.

INDEX